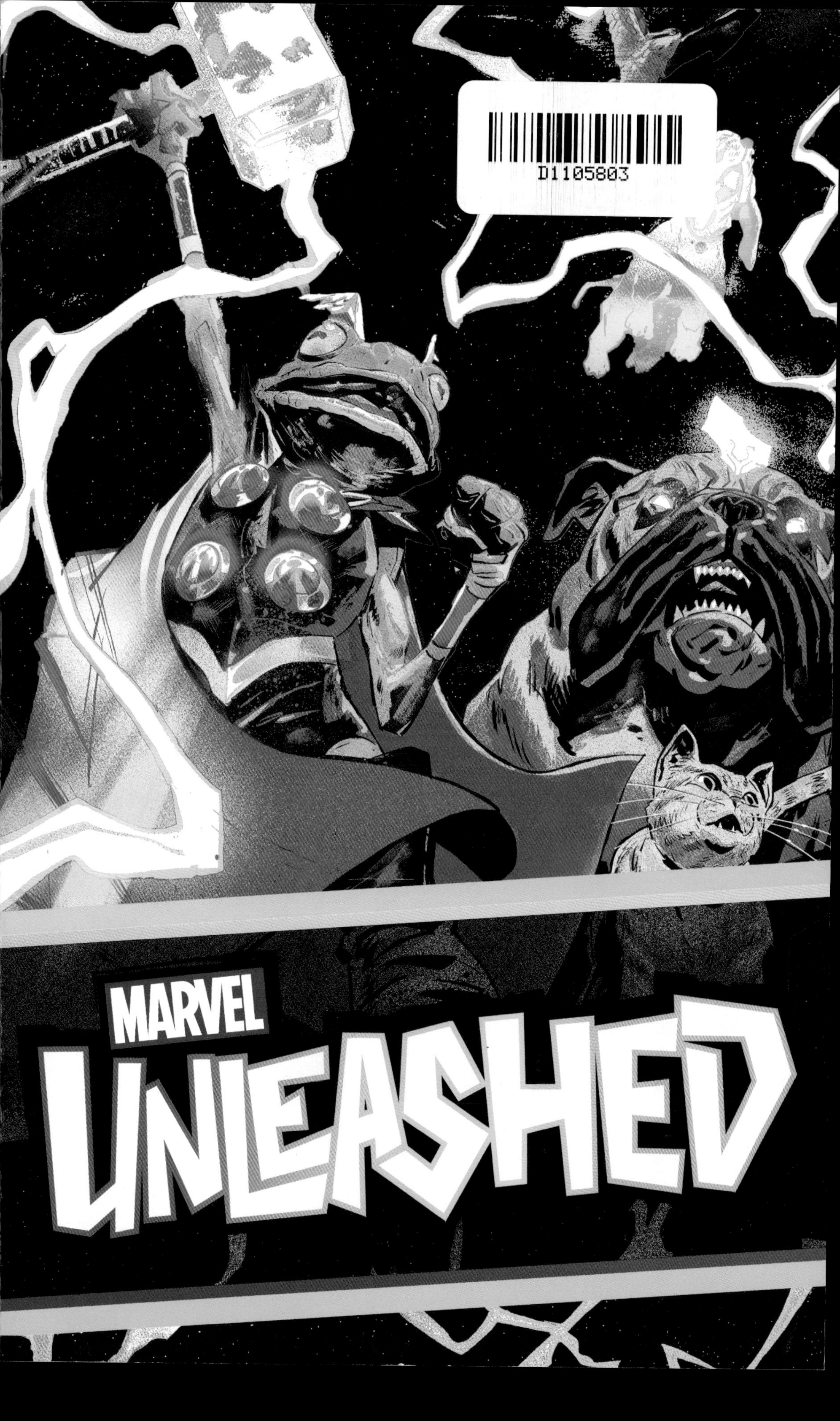
MARVEL
UNLEASHED

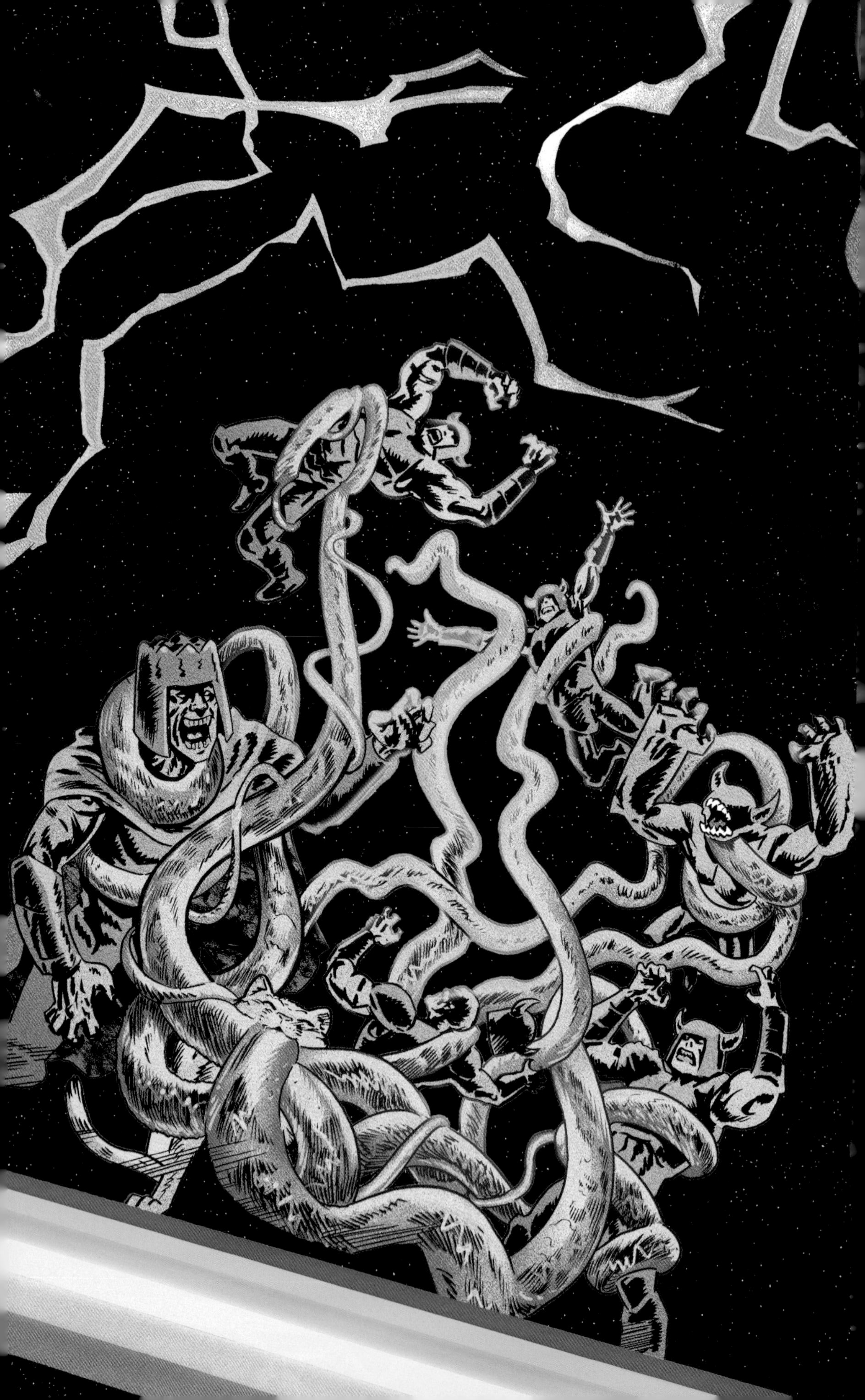

MARVEL UNLEASHED

WRITER KYLE STARKS

ARTISTS JESÚS HERVÁS (#1-2, #4) & JUAN GEDEON (#3)

COLOR ARTIST YEN NITRO

LETTERER VC's JOE CARAMAGNA

DANIEL KIRCHHOFFER
COLLECTION EDITOR

LISA MONTALBANG
ASSOCIATE MANAGER, TALENT RELATIONS

JENNIFER GRÜNWALD
DIRECTOR, PRODUCTION & SPECIAL PROJECTS

JEFF YOUNGQUIST
VP PRODUCTION & SPECIAL PROJECTS

STACIE ZUCKER
BOOK DESIGNER

ADAM DEL RE
MANAGER & SENIOR DESIGNER

JAY BOWEN
LEAD DESIGNER

DAVID GABRIEL
SVP PRINT, SALES & MARKETING

C.B. CEBULSKI
EDITOR IN CHIEF

COVER ART DAVID BALDEÓN & ISRAEL SILVA

ASSISTANT EDITOR KAITLYN LINDTVEDT

EDITOR ALANNA SMITH

MARVEL UNLEASHED. Contains material originally published in magazine form as MARVEL UNLEASHED (2023) #1-4. First printing 2023. ISBN 978-1-302-93112-4. Published by MARVEL WORLDWIDE, INC., a subsidiary of MARVEL ENTERTAINMENT, LLC. OFFICE OF PUBLICATION: 1290 Avenue of the Americas, New York, NY 10104. © 2023 MARVEL No similarity between any of the names, characters, persons, and/or institutions in this book with those of any living or dead person or institution is intended, and any such similarity which may exist is purely coincidental. **Printed in the U.S.A.** KEVIN FEIGE, Chief Creative Officer; DAN BUCKLEY, President, Marvel Entertainment; DAVID BOGART, Associate Publisher & SVP of Talent Affairs: TOM BREVOORT, VP, Executive Editor; NICK LOWE, Executive Editor, VP of Content, Digital Publishing; DAVID GABRIEL, VP of Print & Digital Publishing; SVEN LARSEN, VP of Licensed Publishing; MARK ANNUNZIATO, VP of Planning & Forecasting; JEFF YOUNGQUIST, VP of Production & Special Projects; ALEX MORALES, Director of Publishing Operations; DAN EDINGTON, Director of Editorial Operations; RICKEY PURDIN, Director of Talent Relations; JENNIFER GRÜNWALD; Director of Production & Special Projects; SUSAN CRESPI, Production Manager; STAN LEE, Chairman Emeritus. For information regarding advertising in Marvel Comics or on Marvel.com, please contact Vit DeBellis, Custom Solutions & Integrated Advertising Manager, at vdebellis@marvel.com. For Marvel subscription inquiries, please call 888-511-5480. **Manufactured between 11/24/2023 and 1/2/2024 by SEAWAY PRINTING, GREEN BAY, WI, USA.**

10 9 8 7 6 5 4 3 2 1

ONE

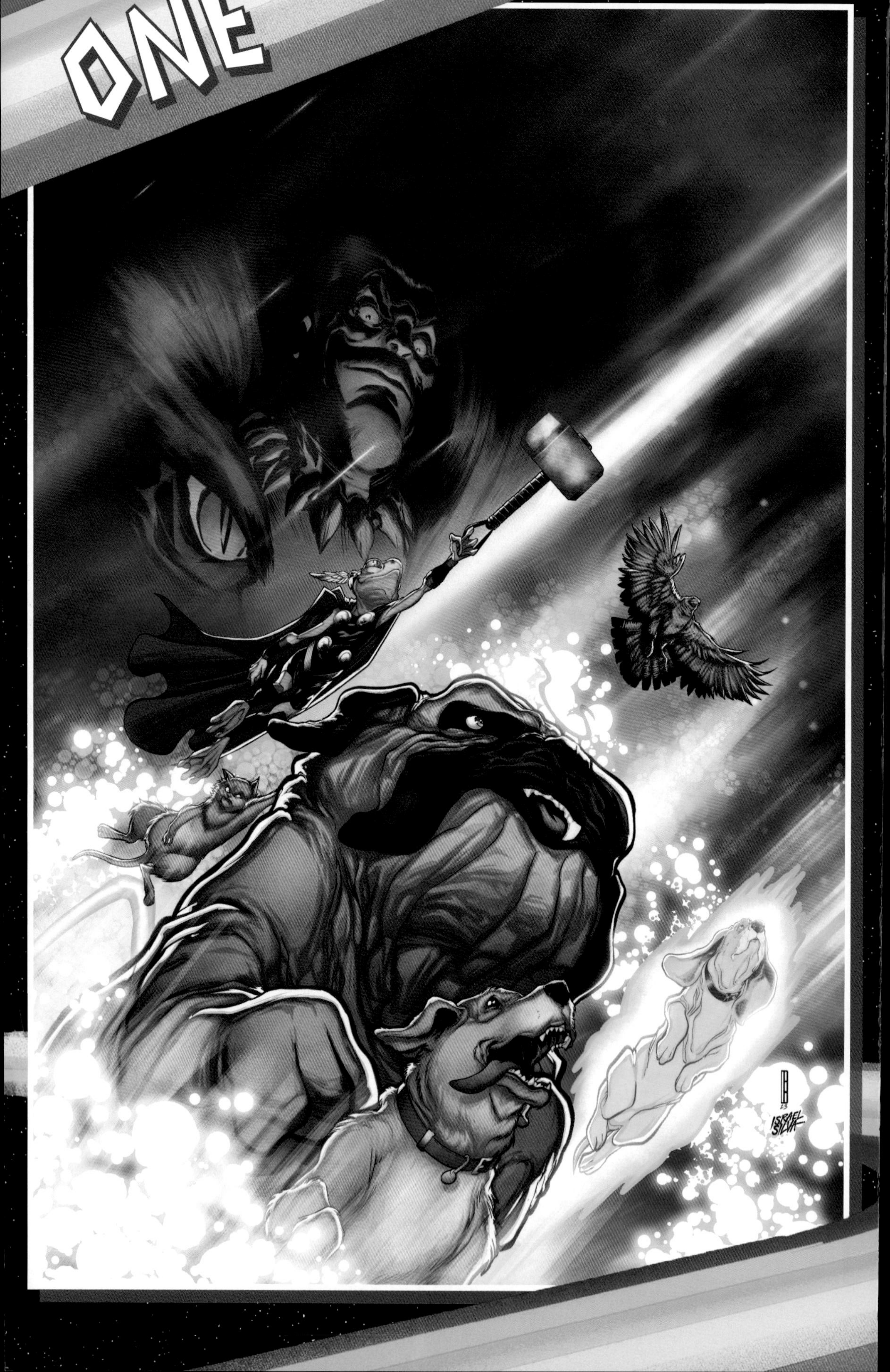
ISRAEL SILVA

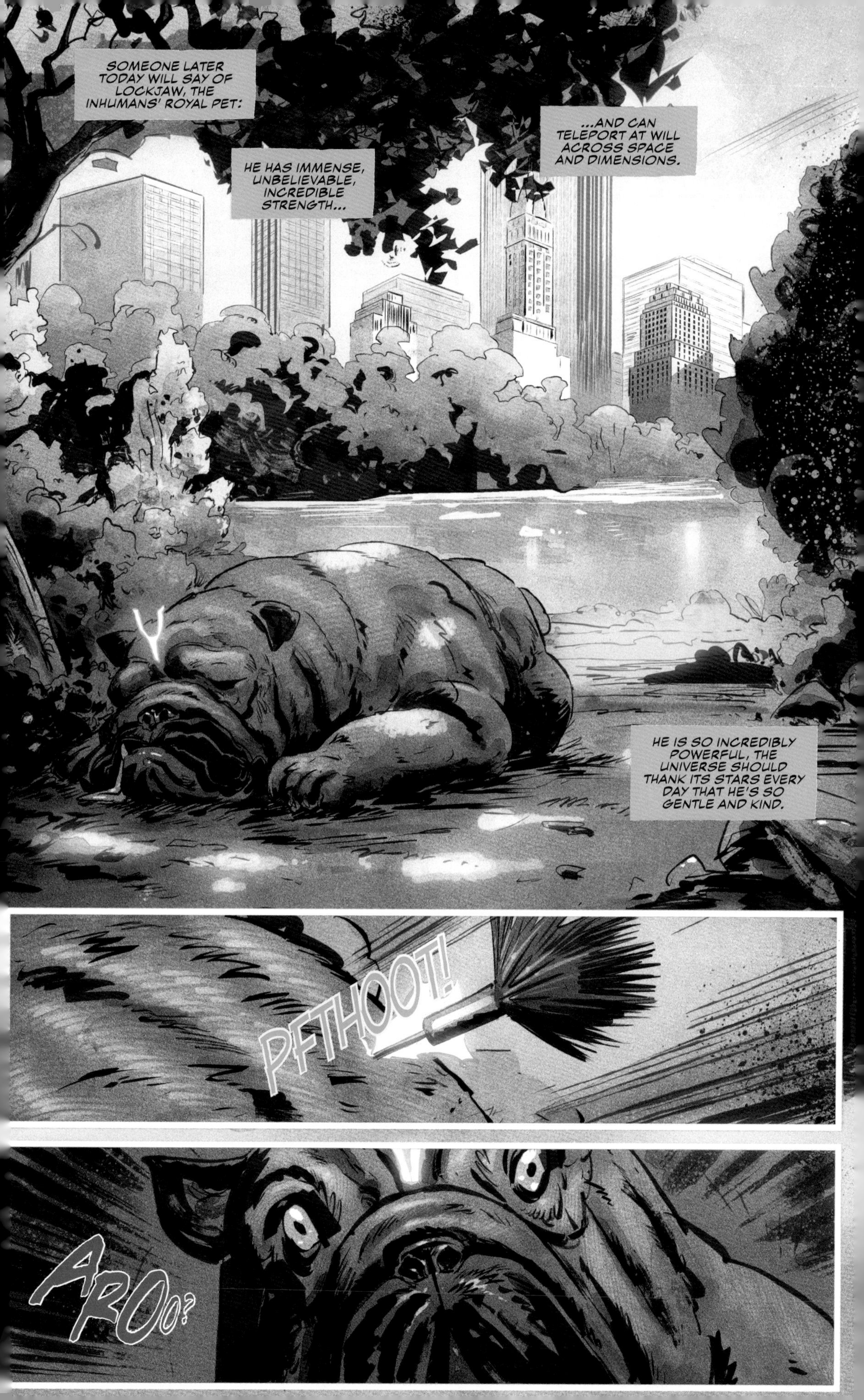
SOMEONE LATER TODAY WILL SAY OF LOCKJAW, THE INHUMANS' ROYAL PET:
HE HAS IMMENSE, UNBELIEVABLE, INCREDIBLE STRENGTH...
...AND CAN TELEPORT AT WILL ACROSS SPACE AND DIMENSIONS.
HE IS SO INCREDIBLY POWERFUL, THE UNIVERSE SHOULD THANK ITS STARS EVERY DAY THAT HE'S SO GENTLE AND KIND.
PFTHOOT!
AROOo?

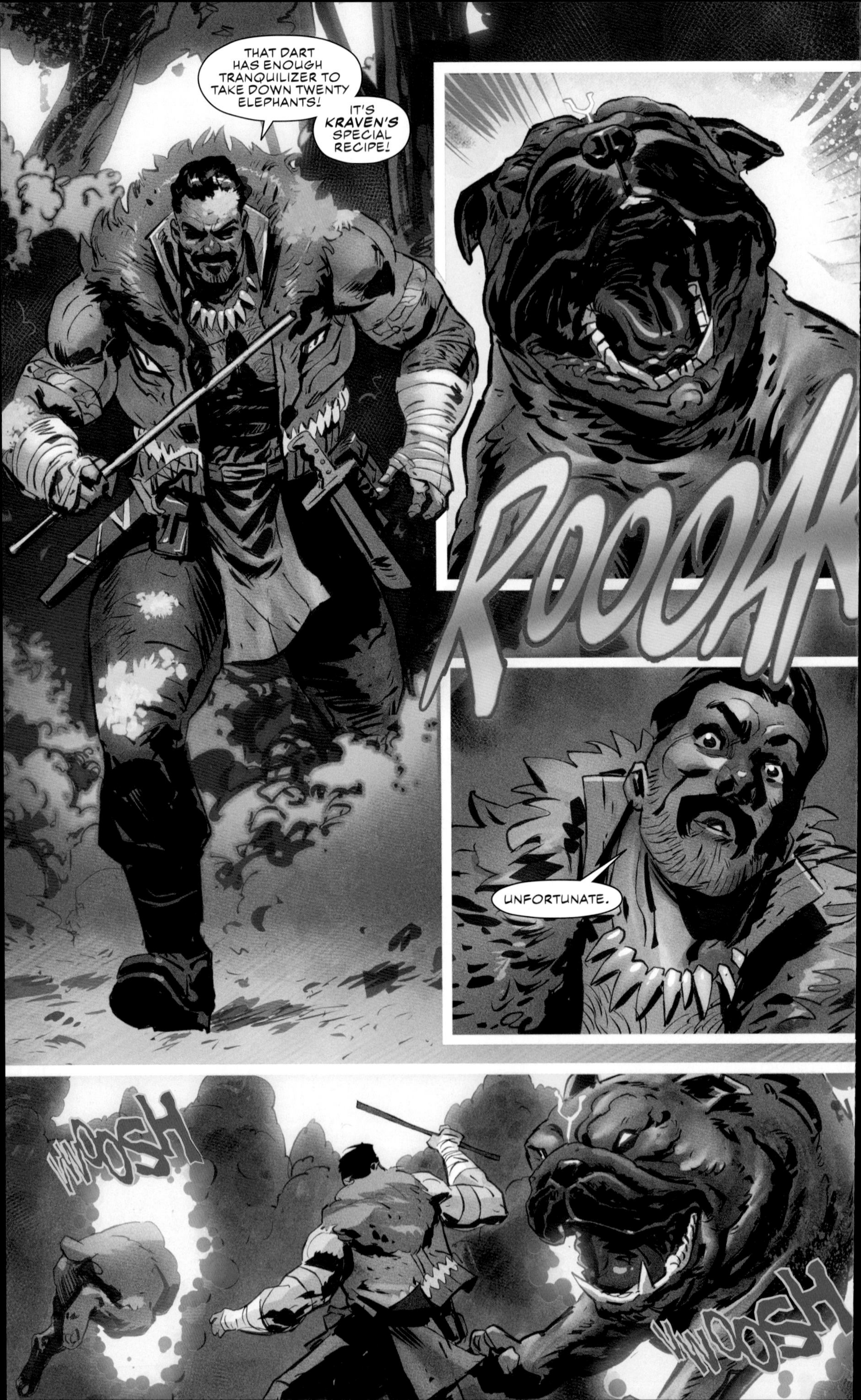
THAT DART HAS ENOUGH TRANQUILIZER TO TAKE DOWN TWENTY ELEPHANTS!
IT'S KRAVEN'S SPECIAL RECIPE!
ROOOAR
UNFORTUNATE.
WHOOSH
WHOOSH

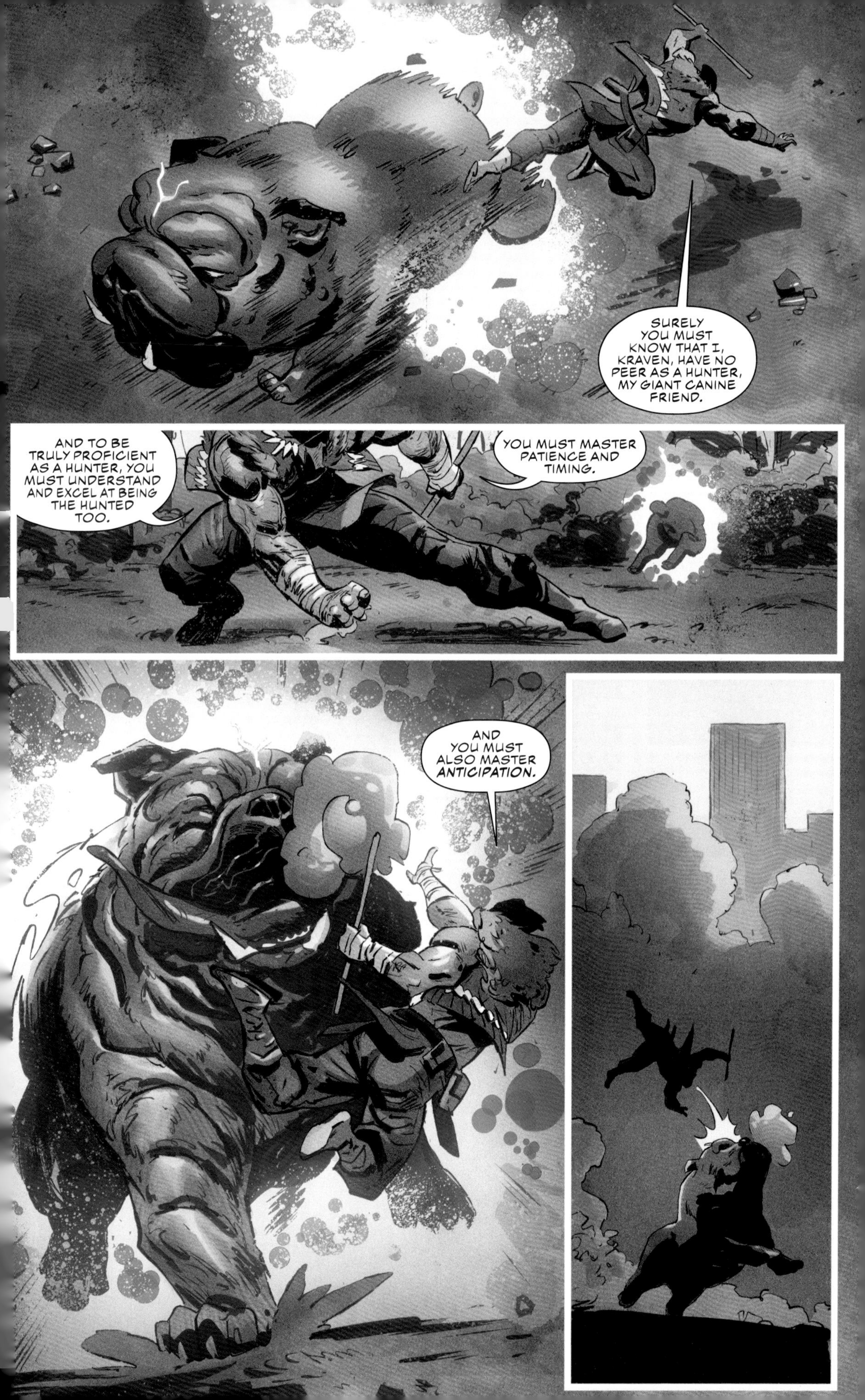
SURELY YOU MUST KNOW THAT I, KRAVEN, HAVE NO PEER AS A HUNTER, MY GIANT CANINE FRIEND.
AND TO BE TRULY PROFICIENT AS A HUNTER, YOU MUST UNDERSTAND AND EXCEL AT BEING THE HUNTED TOO.
YOU MUST MASTER PATIENCE AND TIMING.
AND YOU MUST ALSO MASTER ANTICIPATION.

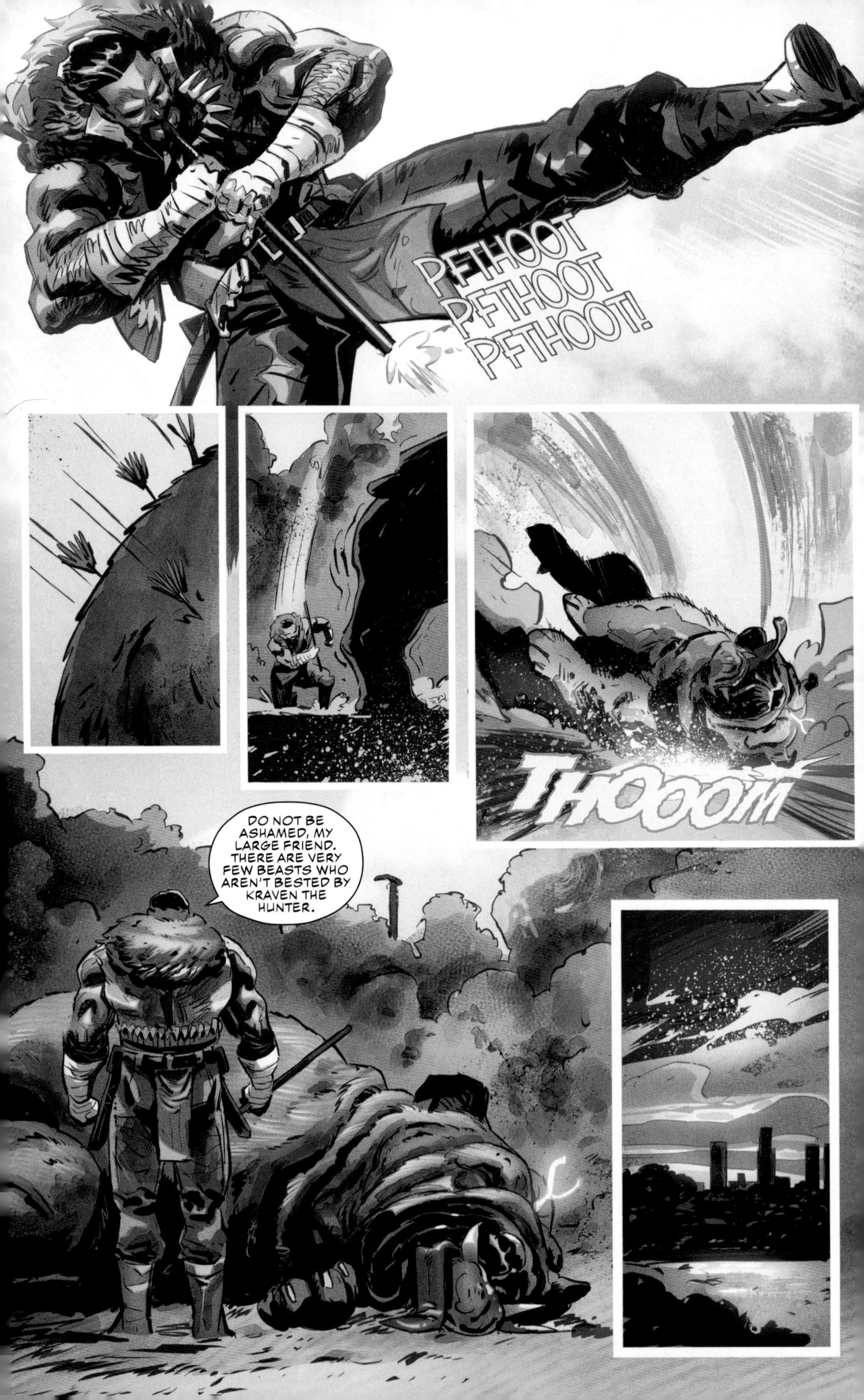
PFTHOOT
PFTHOOT
PFTHOOT!
THOOOM
DO NOT BE ASHAMED, MY LARGE FRIEND. THERE ARE VERY FEW BEASTS WHO AREN'T BESTED BY KRAVEN THE HUNTER.

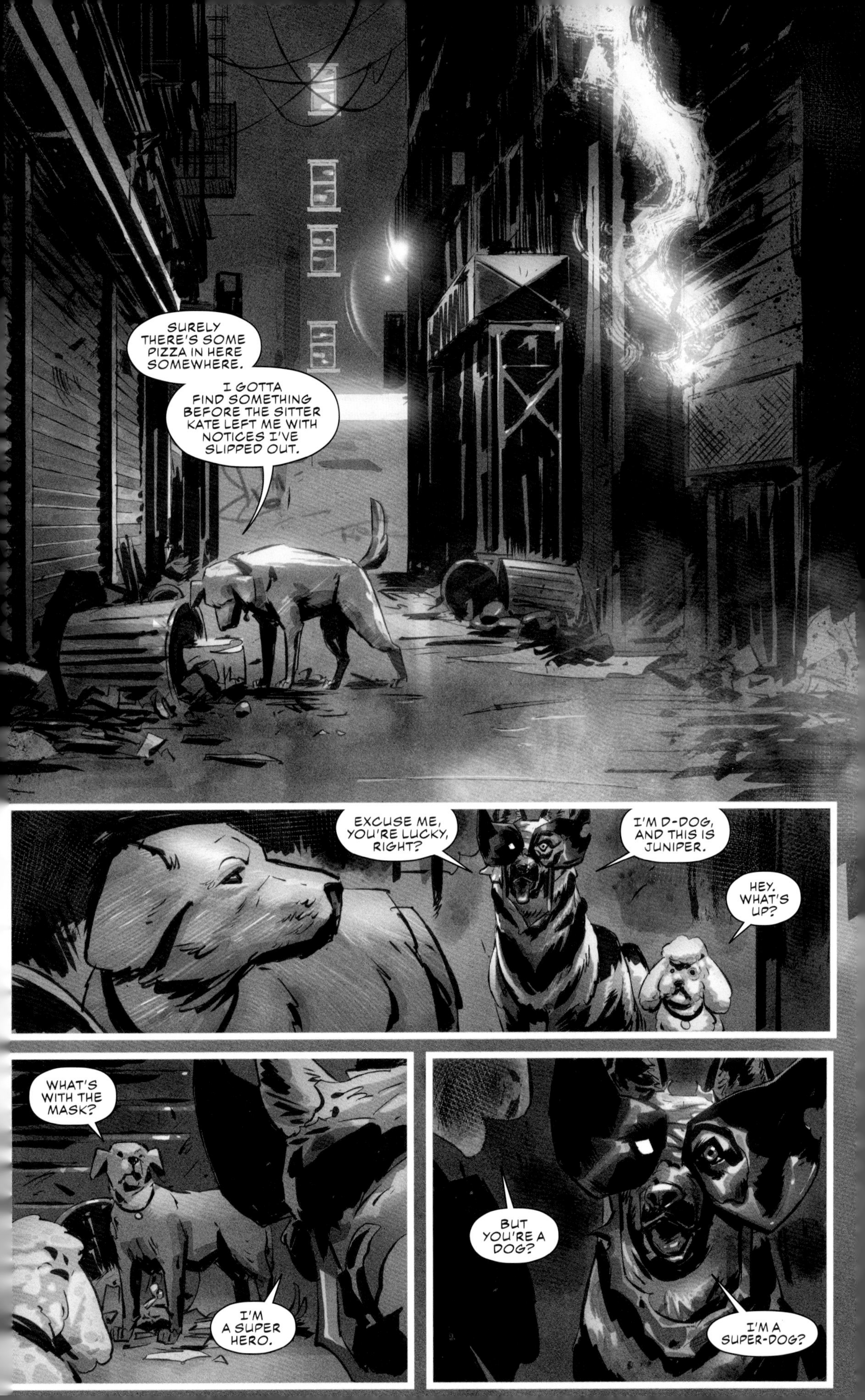
SURELY THERE'S SOME PIZZA IN HERE SOMEWHERE.
I GOTTA FIND SOMETHING BEFORE THE SITTER KATE LEFT ME WITH NOTICES I'VE SLIPPED OUT.
EXCUSE ME, YOU'RE LUCKY, RIGHT?
I'M D-DOG, AND THIS IS JUNIPER.
HEY. WHAT'S UP?
WHAT'S WITH THE MASK?
I'M A SUPER HERO.
BUT YOU'RE A DOG?
I'M A SUPER-DOG?

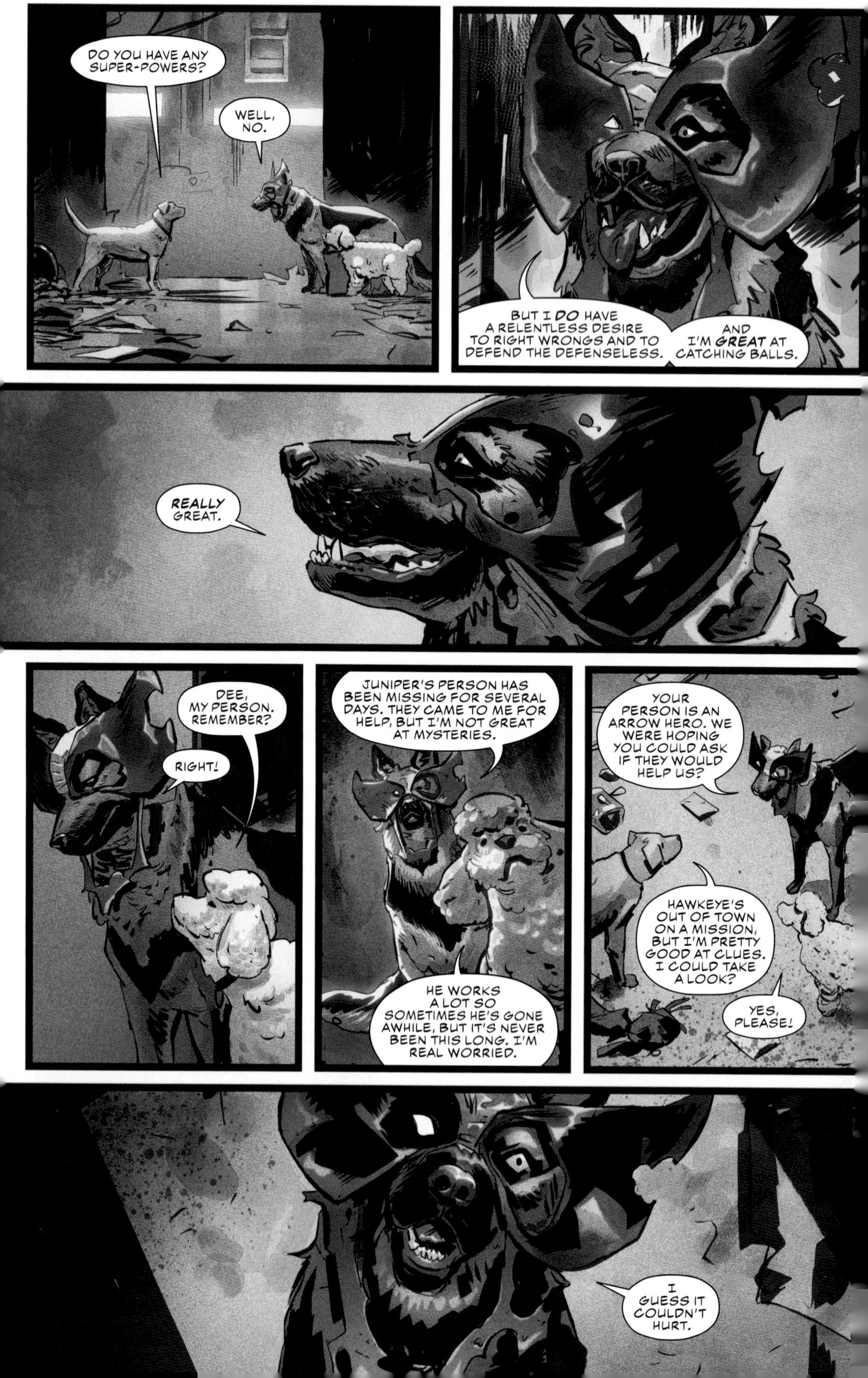
DO YOU HAVE ANY SUPER-POWERS?
WELL, NO.
BUT I DO HAVE A RELENTLESS DESIRE TO RIGHT WRONGS AND TO DEFEND THE DEFENSELESS.
AND I'M GREAT AT CATCHING BALLS.
REALLY GREAT.
DEE, MY PERSON. REMEMBER?
RIGHT!
JUNIPER'S PERSON HAS BEEN MISSING FOR SEVERAL DAYS. THEY CAME TO ME FOR HELP, BUT I'M NOT GREAT AT MYSTERIES.
HE WORKS A LOT SO SOMETIMES HE'S GONE AWHILE, BUT IT'S NEVER BEEN THIS LONG. I'M REAL WORRIED.
YOUR PERSON IS AN ARROW HERO. WE WERE HOPING YOU COULD ASK IF THEY WOULD HELP US?
HAWKEYE'S OUT OF TOWN ON A MISSION, BUT I'M PRETTY GOOD AT CLUES. I COULD TAKE A LOOK?
YES, PLEASE!
I GUESS IT COULDN'T HURT.

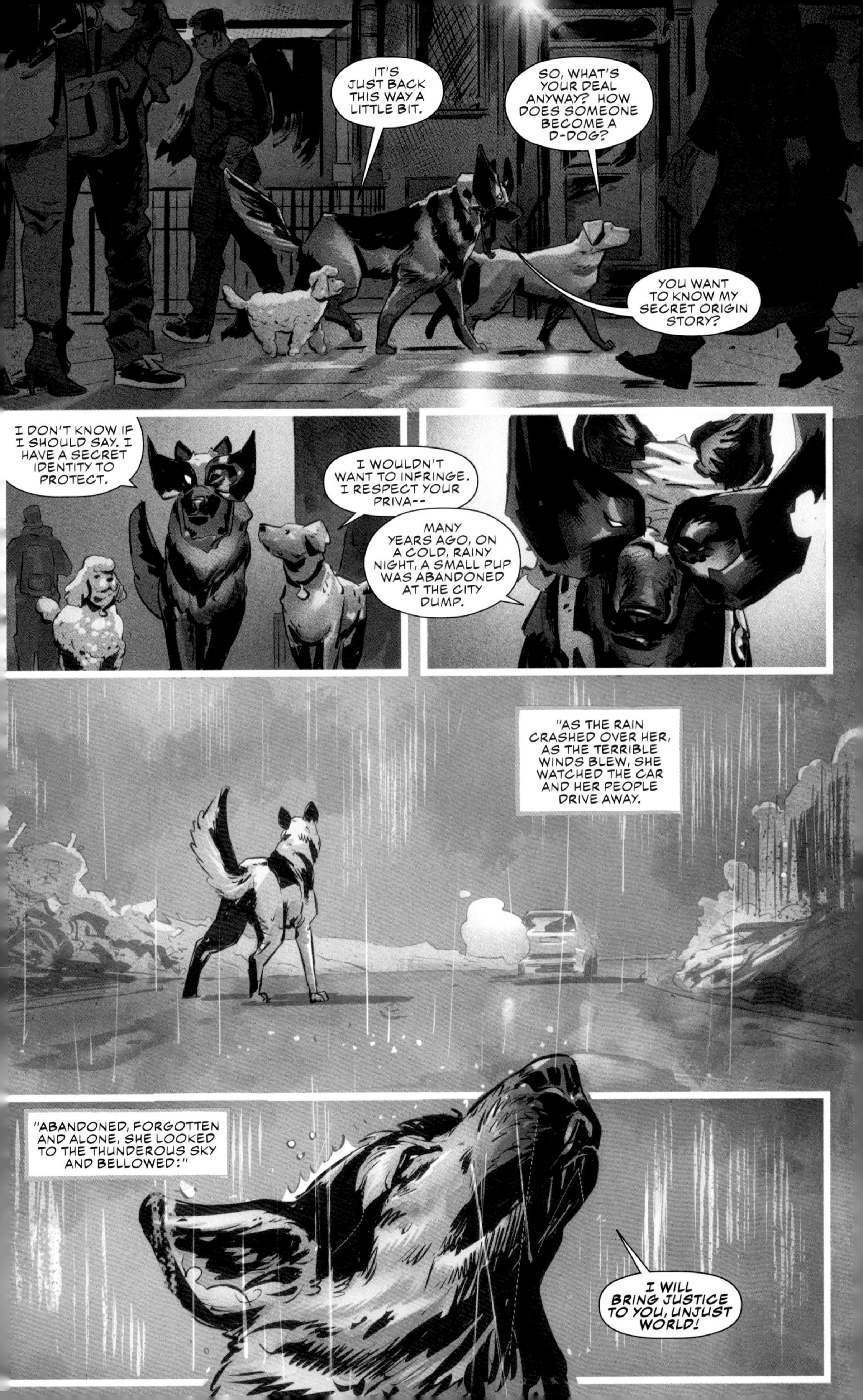
IT'S JUST BACK THIS WAY A LITTLE BIT.
SO, WHAT'S YOUR DEAL ANYWAY? HOW DOES SOMEONE BECOME A D-DOG?
YOU WANT TO KNOW MY SECRET ORIGIN STORY?
I DON'T KNOW IF I SHOULD SAY. I HAVE A SECRET IDENTITY TO PROTECT.
I WOULDN'T WANT TO INFRINGE. I RESPECT YOUR PRIVA--
MANY YEARS AGO, ON A COLD, RAINY NIGHT, A SMALL PUP WAS ABANDONED AT THE CITY DUMP.
"AS THE RAIN CRASHED OVER HER, AS THE TERRIBLE WINDS BLEW, SHE WATCHED THE CAR AND HER PEOPLE DRIVE AWAY.
"ABANDONED, FORGOTTEN AND ALONE, SHE LOOKED TO THE THUNDEROUS SKY AND BELLOWED:"
I WILL BRING JUSTICE TO YOU, UNJUST WORLD!

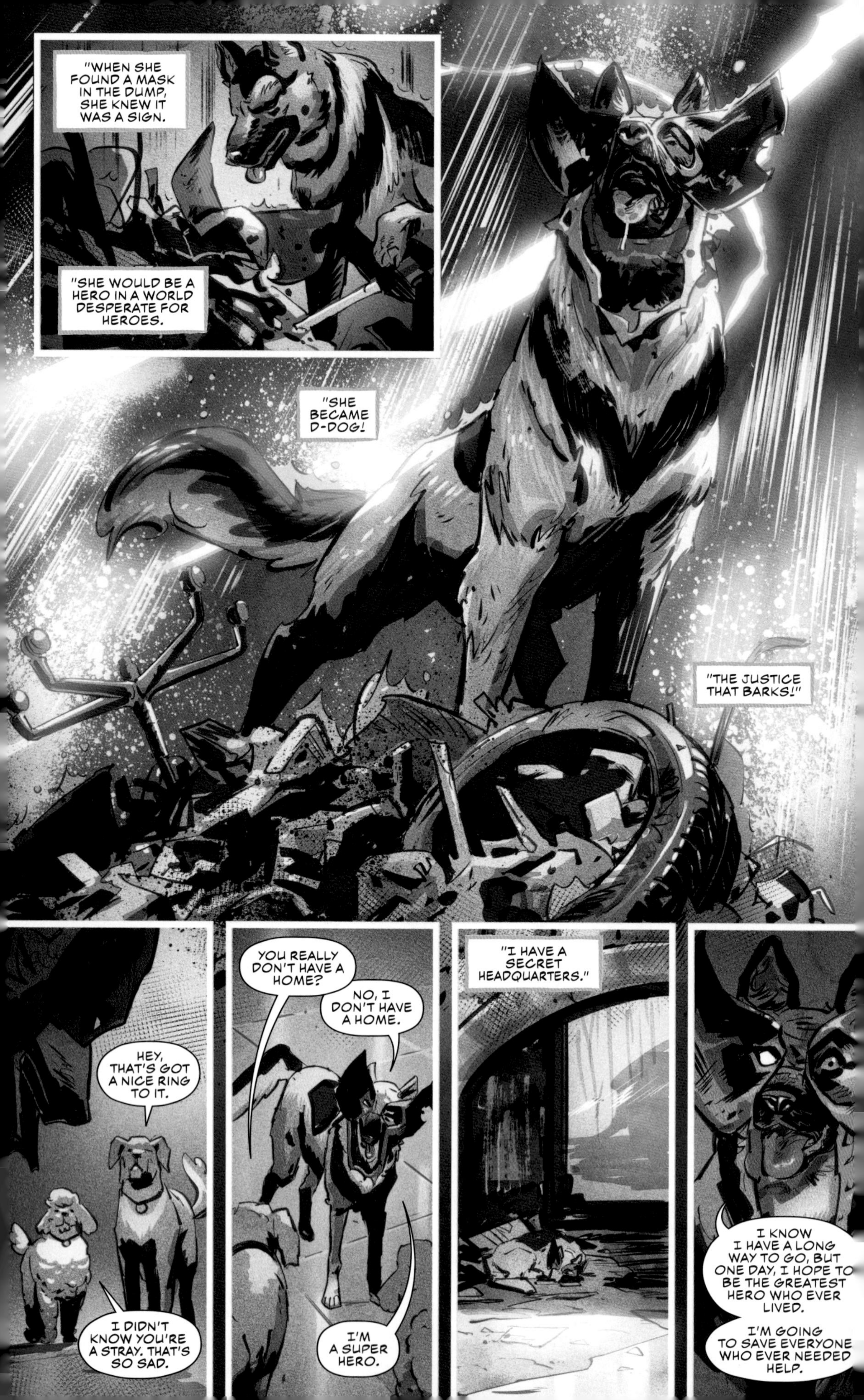
"WHEN SHE FOUND A MASK IN THE DUMP, SHE KNEW IT WAS A SIGN.
"SHE WOULD BE A HERO IN A WORLD DESPERATE FOR HEROES.
"SHE BECAME D-DOG!
"THE JUSTICE THAT BARKS!"
HEY, THAT'S GOT A NICE RING TO IT.
I DIDN'T KNOW YOU'RE A STRAY. THAT'S SO SAD.
YOU REALLY DON'T HAVE A HOME?
NO, I DON'T HAVE A HOME.
I'M A SUPER HERO.
"I HAVE A SECRET HEADQUARTERS."
I KNOW I HAVE A LONG WAY TO GO, BUT ONE DAY, I HOPE TO BE THE GREATEST HERO WHO EVER LIVED.
I'M GOING TO SAVE EVERYONE WHO EVER NEEDED HELP.

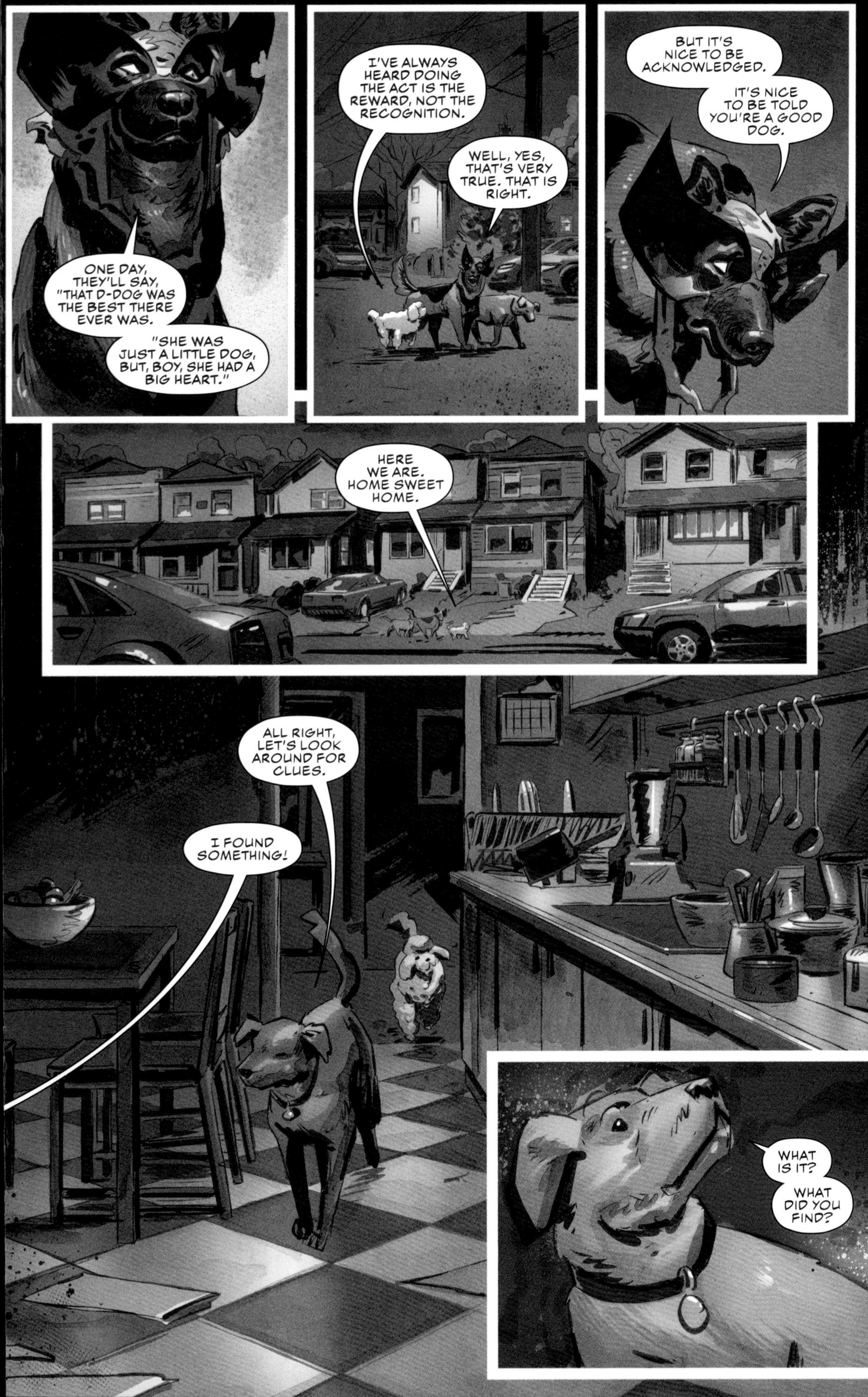
ONE DAY, THEY'LL SAY, "THAT D-DOG WAS THE BEST THERE EVER WAS.
"SHE WAS JUST A LITTLE DOG, BUT, BOY, SHE HAD A BIG HEART."
I'VE ALWAYS HEARD DOING THE ACT IS THE REWARD, NOT THE RECOGNITION.
WELL, YES, THAT'S VERY TRUE. THAT IS RIGHT.
BUT IT'S NICE TO BE ACKNOWLEDGED.
IT'S NICE TO BE TOLD YOU'RE A GOOD DOG.
HERE WE ARE. HOME SWEET HOME.
ALL RIGHT, LET'S LOOK AROUND FOR CLUES.
I FOUND SOMETHING!
WHAT IS IT?
WHAT DID YOU FIND?

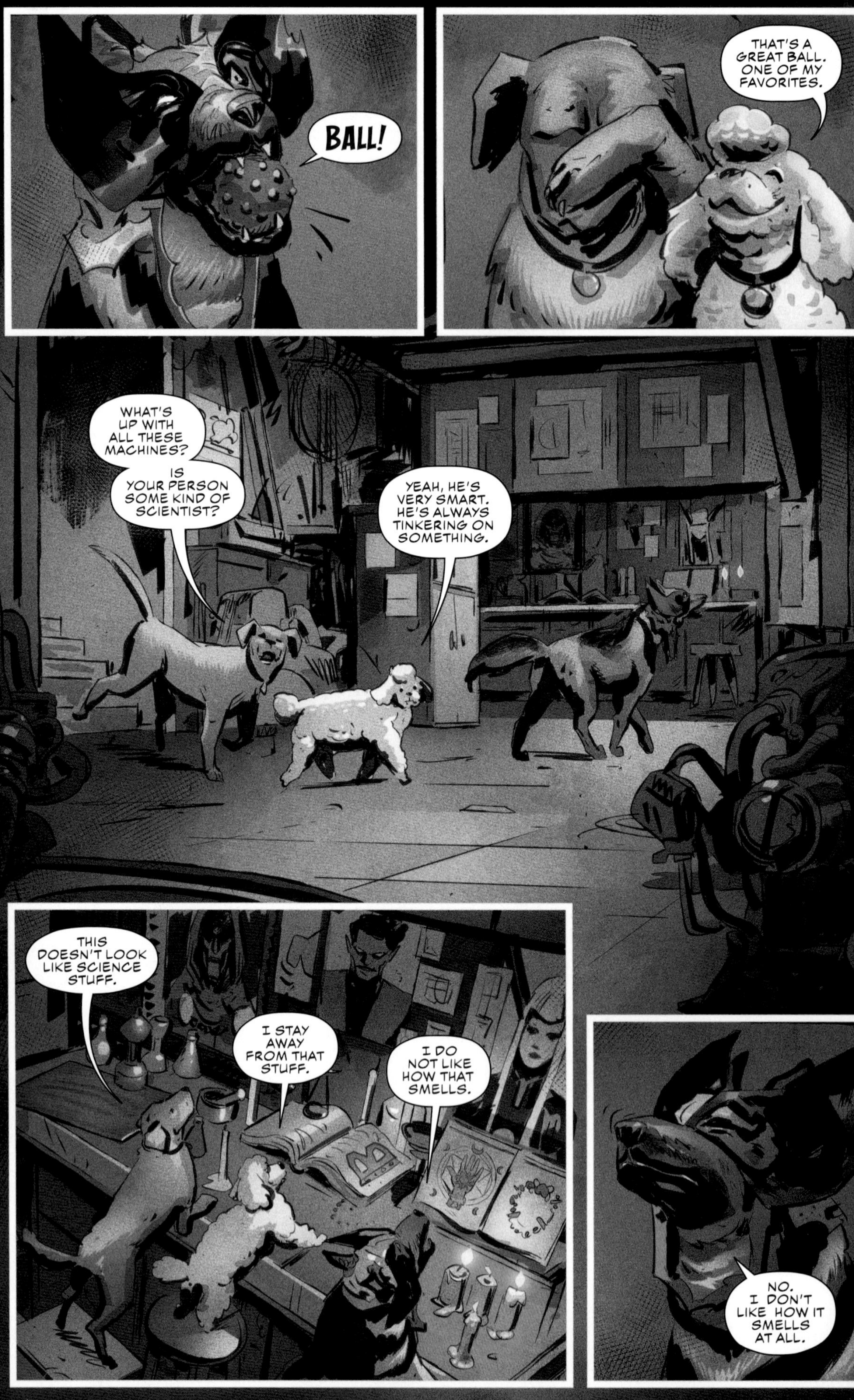
BALL!
THAT'S A GREAT BALL. ONE OF MY FAVORITES.
WHAT'S UP WITH ALL THESE MACHINES?
IS YOUR PERSON SOME KIND OF SCIENTIST?
YEAH, HE'S VERY SMART. HE'S ALWAYS TINKERING ON SOMETHING.
THIS DOESN'T LOOK LIKE SCIENCE STUFF.
I STAY AWAY FROM THAT STUFF.
I DO NOT LIKE HOW THAT SMELLS.
NO. I DON'T LIKE HOW IT SMELLS AT ALL.

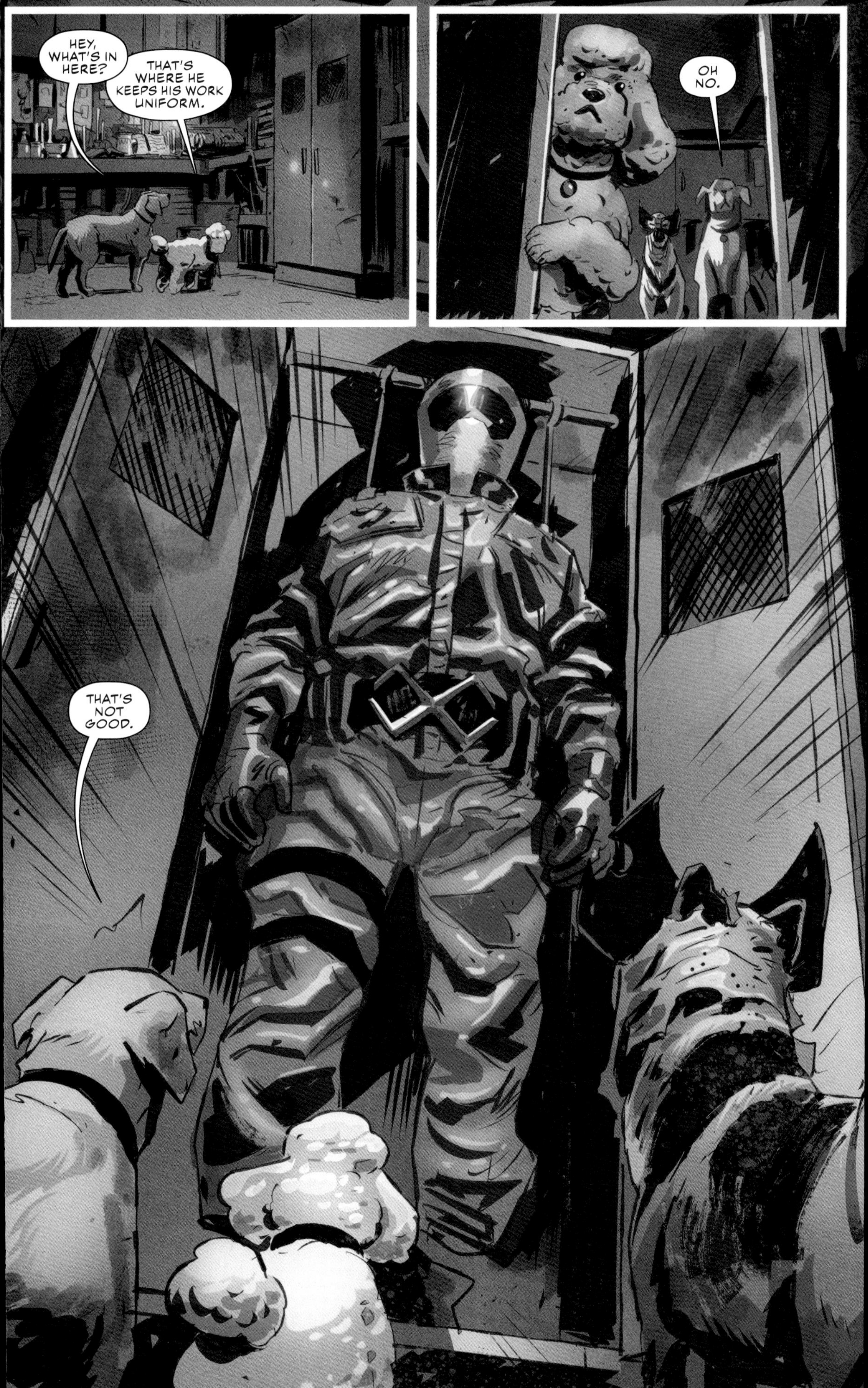
HEY, WHAT'S IN HERE?
THAT'S WHERE HE KEEPS HIS WORK UNIFORM.
OH NO.
THAT'S NOT GOOD.

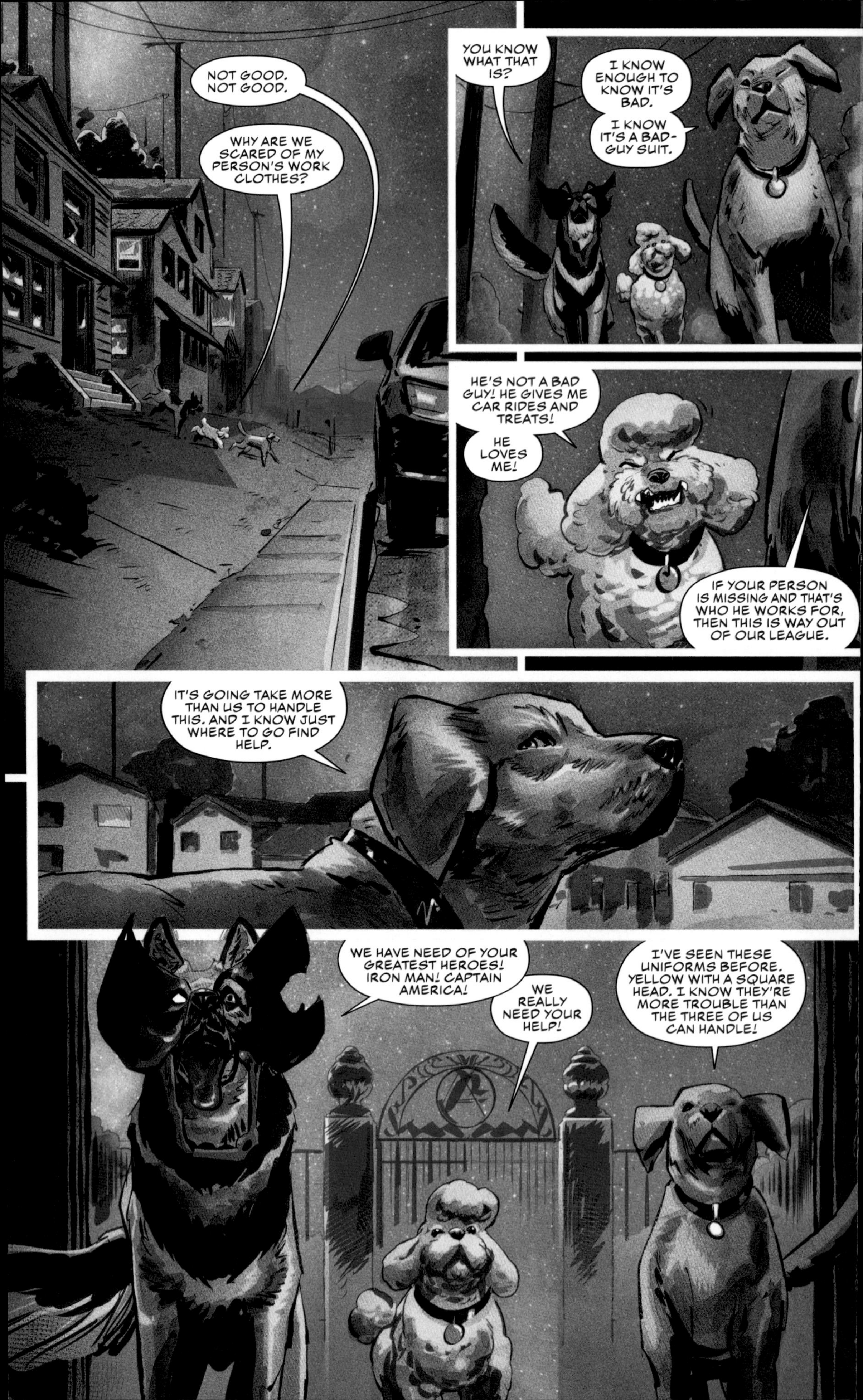
NOT GOOD. NOT GOOD.
WHY ARE WE SCARED OF MY PERSON'S WORK CLOTHES?
YOU KNOW WHAT THAT IS?
I KNOW ENOUGH TO KNOW IT'S BAD.
I KNOW IT'S A BAD-GUY SUIT.
HE'S NOT A BAD GUY! HE GIVES ME CAR RIDES AND TREATS!
HE LOVES ME!
IF YOUR PERSON IS MISSING AND THAT'S WHO HE WORKS FOR, THEN THIS IS WAY OUT OF OUR LEAGUE.
IT'S GOING TAKE MORE THAN US TO HANDLE THIS. AND I KNOW JUST WHERE TO GO FIND HELP.
WE HAVE NEED OF YOUR GREATEST HEROES! IRON MAN! CAPTAIN AMERICA!
WE REALLY NEED YOUR HELP!
I'VE SEEN THESE UNIFORMS BEFORE. YELLOW WITH A SQUARE HEAD. I KNOW THEY'RE MORE TROUBLE THAN THE THREE OF US CAN HANDLE!

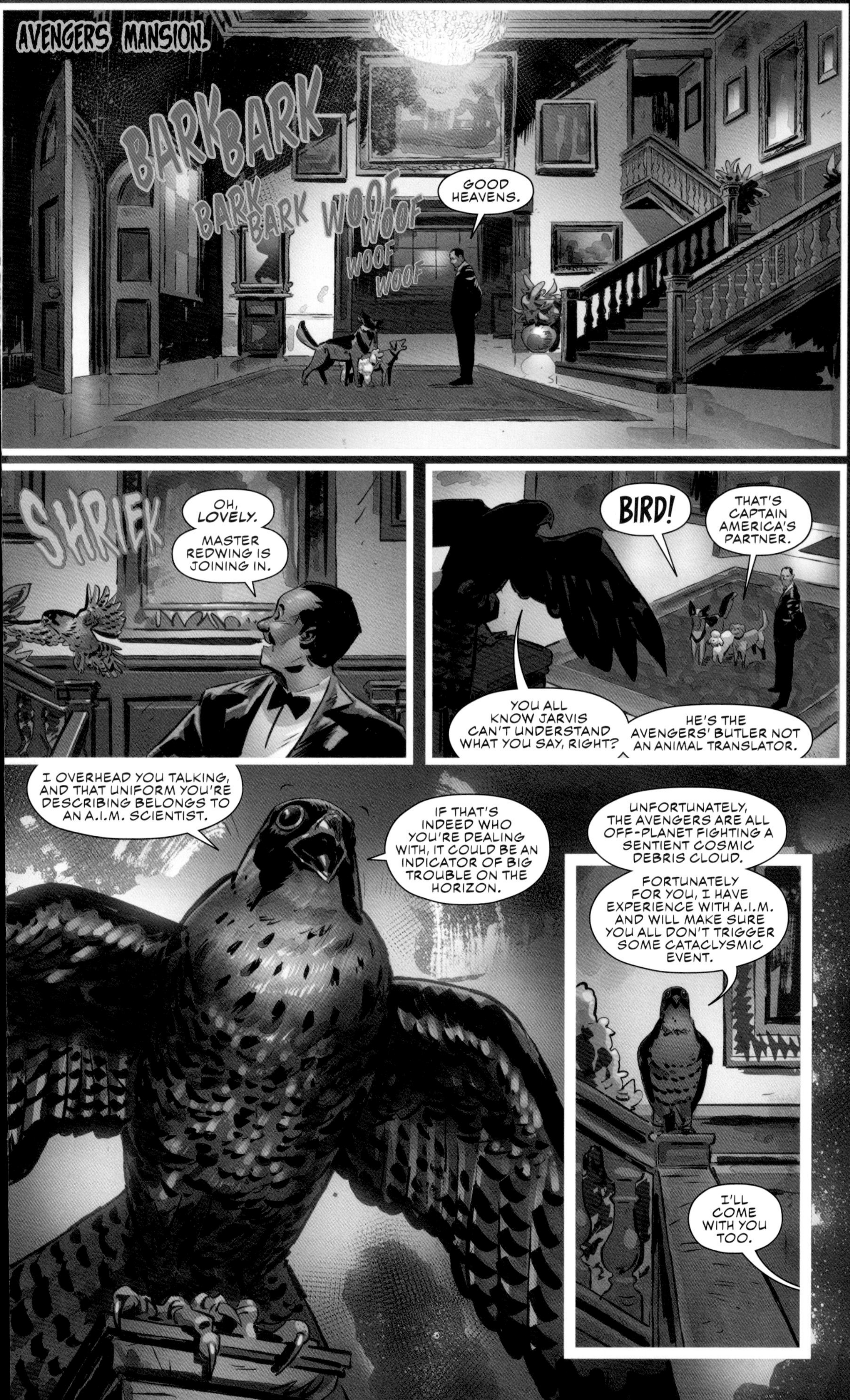
AVENGERS MANSION.
BARK BARK
BARK BARK WOOF WOOF WOOF WOOF
GOOD HEAVENS.
SHRIEK
OH, LOVELY.
MASTER REDWING IS JOINING IN.
BIRD!
THAT'S CAPTAIN AMERICA'S PARTNER.
YOU ALL KNOW JARVIS CAN'T UNDERSTAND WHAT YOU SAY, RIGHT?
HE'S THE AVENGERS' BUTLER NOT AN ANIMAL TRANSLATOR.
I OVERHEAD YOU TALKING, AND THAT UNIFORM YOU'RE DESCRIBING BELONGS TO AN A.I.M. SCIENTIST.
IF THAT'S INDEED WHO YOU'RE DEALING WITH, IT COULD BE AN INDICATOR OF BIG TROUBLE ON THE HORIZON.
UNFORTUNATELY, THE AVENGERS ARE ALL OFF-PLANET FIGHTING A SENTIENT COSMIC DEBRIS CLOUD.
FORTUNATELY FOR YOU, I HAVE EXPERIENCE WITH A.I.M. AND WILL MAKE SURE YOU ALL DON'T TRIGGER SOME CATACLYSMIC EVENT.
I'LL COME WITH YOU TOO.

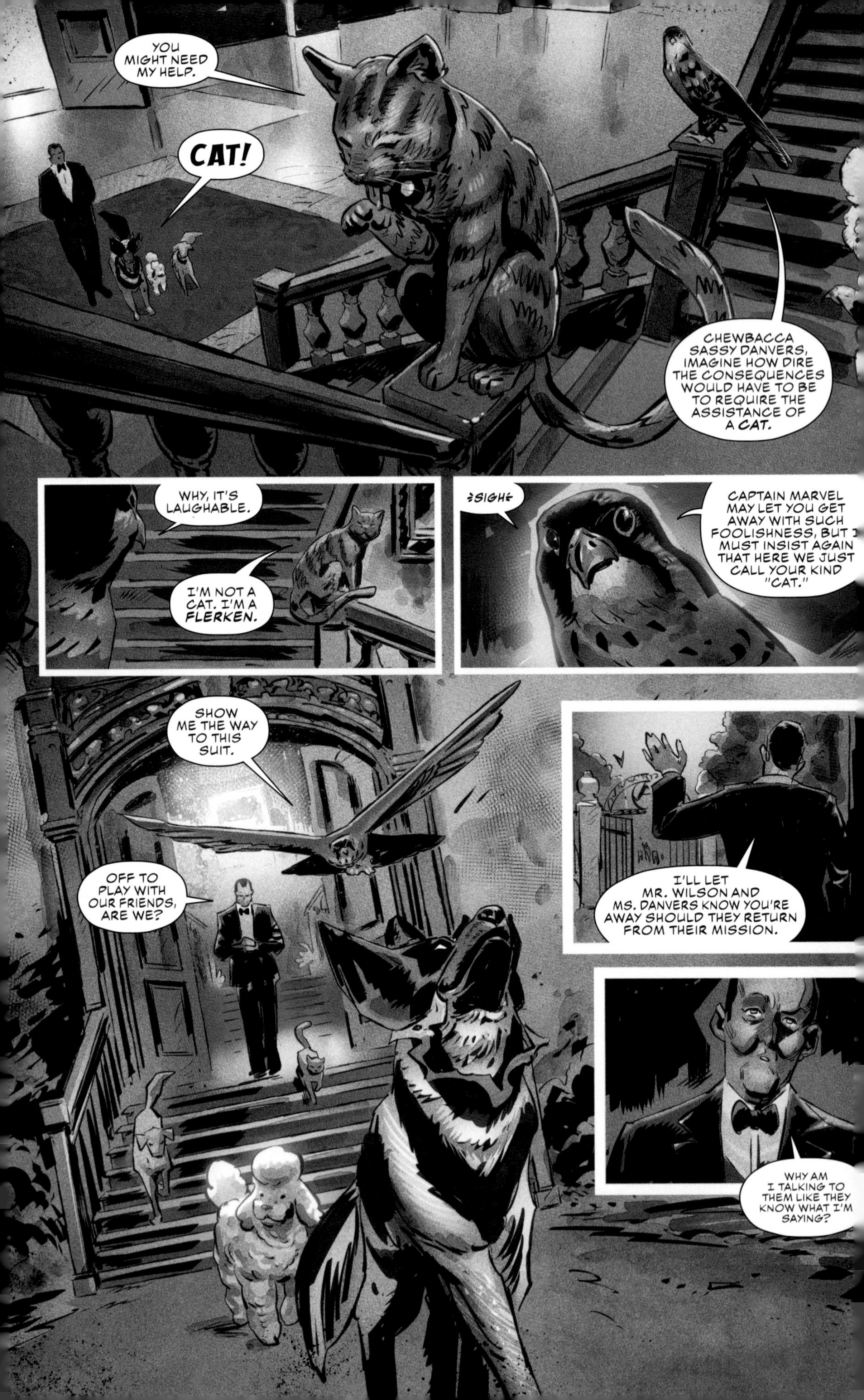
YOU MIGHT NEED MY HELP.
CAT!
CHEWBACCA SASSY DANVERS, IMAGINE HOW DIRE THE CONSEQUENCES WOULD HAVE TO BE TO REQUIRE THE ASSISTANCE OF A CAT.
WHY, IT'S LAUGHABLE.
I'M NOT A CAT. I'M A FLERKEN.
SIGH
CAPTAIN MARVEL MAY LET YOU GET AWAY WITH SUCH FOOLISHNESS, BUT I MUST INSIST AGAIN THAT HERE WE JUST CALL YOUR KIND "CAT."
SHOW ME THE WAY TO THIS SUIT.
OFF TO PLAY WITH OUR FRIENDS, ARE WE?
I'LL LET MR. WILSON AND MS. DANVERS KNOW YOU'RE AWAY SHOULD THEY RETURN FROM THEIR MISSION.
WHY AM I TALKING TO THEM LIKE THEY KNOW WHAT I'M SAYING?

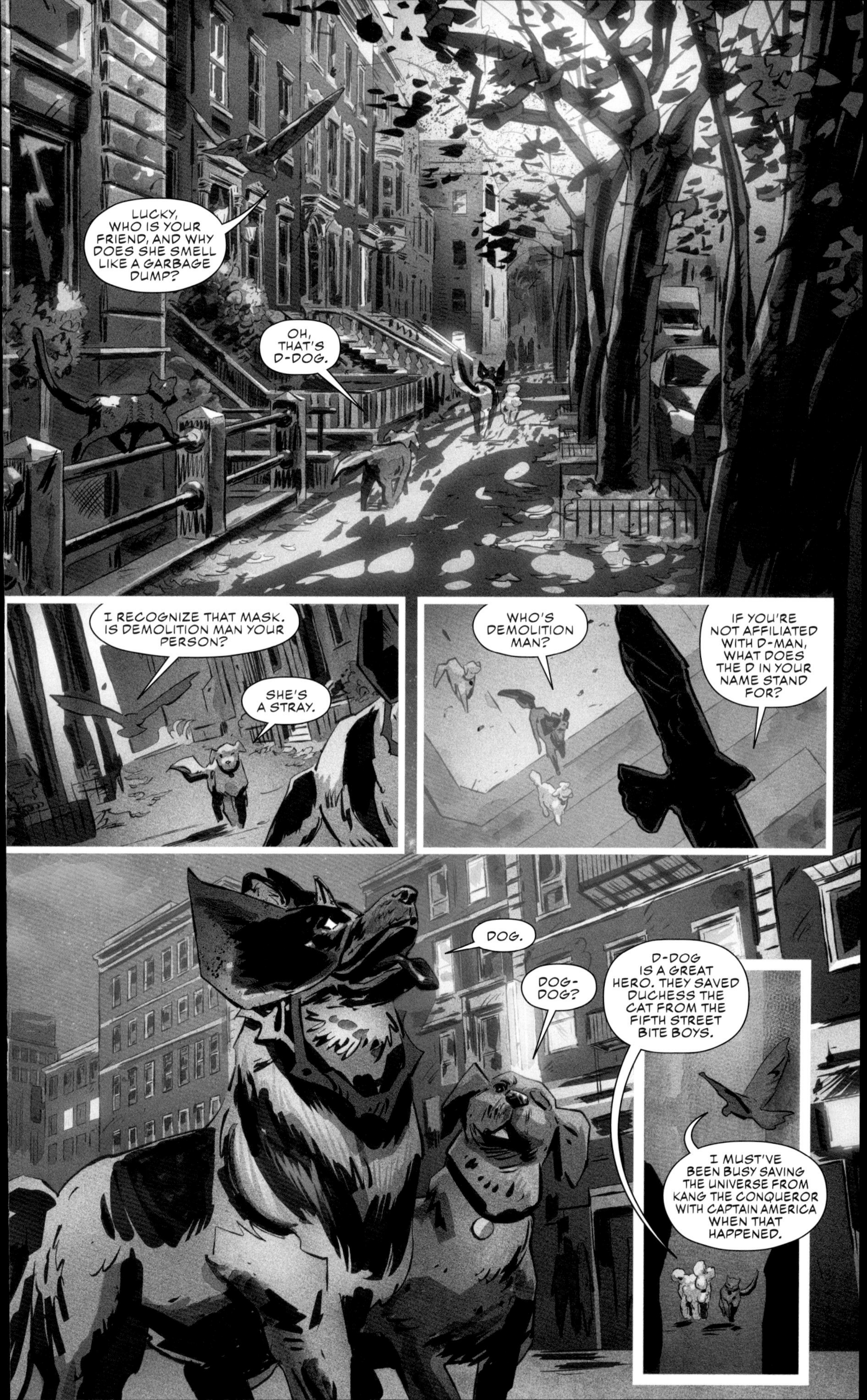
LUCKY, WHO IS YOUR FRIEND, AND WHY DOES SHE SMELL LIKE A GARBAGE DUMP?
OH, THAT'S D-DOG.
I RECOGNIZE THAT MASK. IS DEMOLITION MAN YOUR PERSON?
SHE'S A STRAY.
WHO'S DEMOLITION MAN?
IF YOU'RE NOT AFFILIATED WITH D-MAN, WHAT DOES THE D IN YOUR NAME STAND FOR?
DOG.
DOG-DOG?
D-DOG IS A GREAT HERO. THEY SAVED DUCHESS THE CAT FROM THE FIFTH STREET BITE BOYS.
I MUST'VE BEEN BUSY SAVING THE UNIVERSE FROM KANG THE CONQUEROR WITH CAPTAIN AMERICA WHEN THAT HAPPENED.

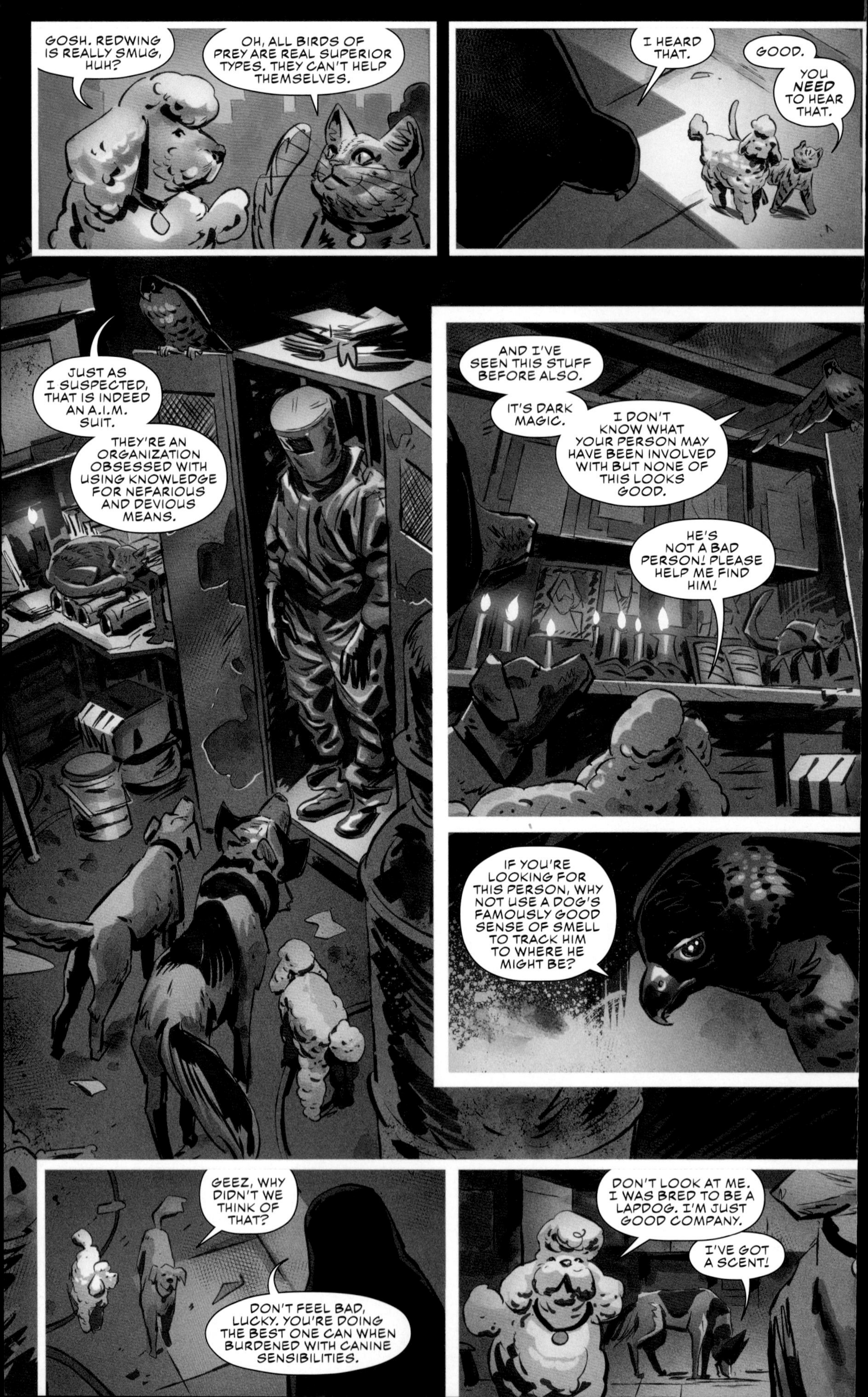
GOSH. REDWING IS REALLY SMUG, HUH?
OH, ALL BIRDS OF PREY ARE REAL SUPERIOR TYPES. THEY CAN'T HELP THEMSELVES.
I HEARD THAT.
GOOD.
YOU **NEED** TO HEAR THAT.
JUST AS I SUSPECTED, THAT IS INDEED AN A.I.M. SUIT.
THEY'RE AN ORGANIZATION OBSESSED WITH USING KNOWLEDGE FOR NEFARIOUS AND DEVIOUS MEANS.
AND I'VE SEEN THIS STUFF BEFORE ALSO.
IT'S DARK MAGIC.
I DON'T KNOW WHAT YOUR PERSON MAY HAVE BEEN INVOLVED WITH BUT NONE OF THIS LOOKS GOOD.
HE'S NOT A BAD PERSON! PLEASE HELP ME FIND HIM!
IF YOU'RE LOOKING FOR THIS PERSON, WHY NOT USE A DOG'S FAMOUSLY GOOD SENSE OF SMELL TO TRACK HIM TO WHERE HE MIGHT BE?
GEEZ, WHY DIDN'T WE THINK OF THAT?
DON'T FEEL BAD, LUCKY. YOU'RE DOING THE BEST ONE CAN WHEN BURDENED WITH CANINE SENSIBILITIES.
DON'T LOOK AT ME. I WAS BRED TO BE A LAPDOG. I'M JUST GOOD COMPANY.
I'VE GOT A SCENT!

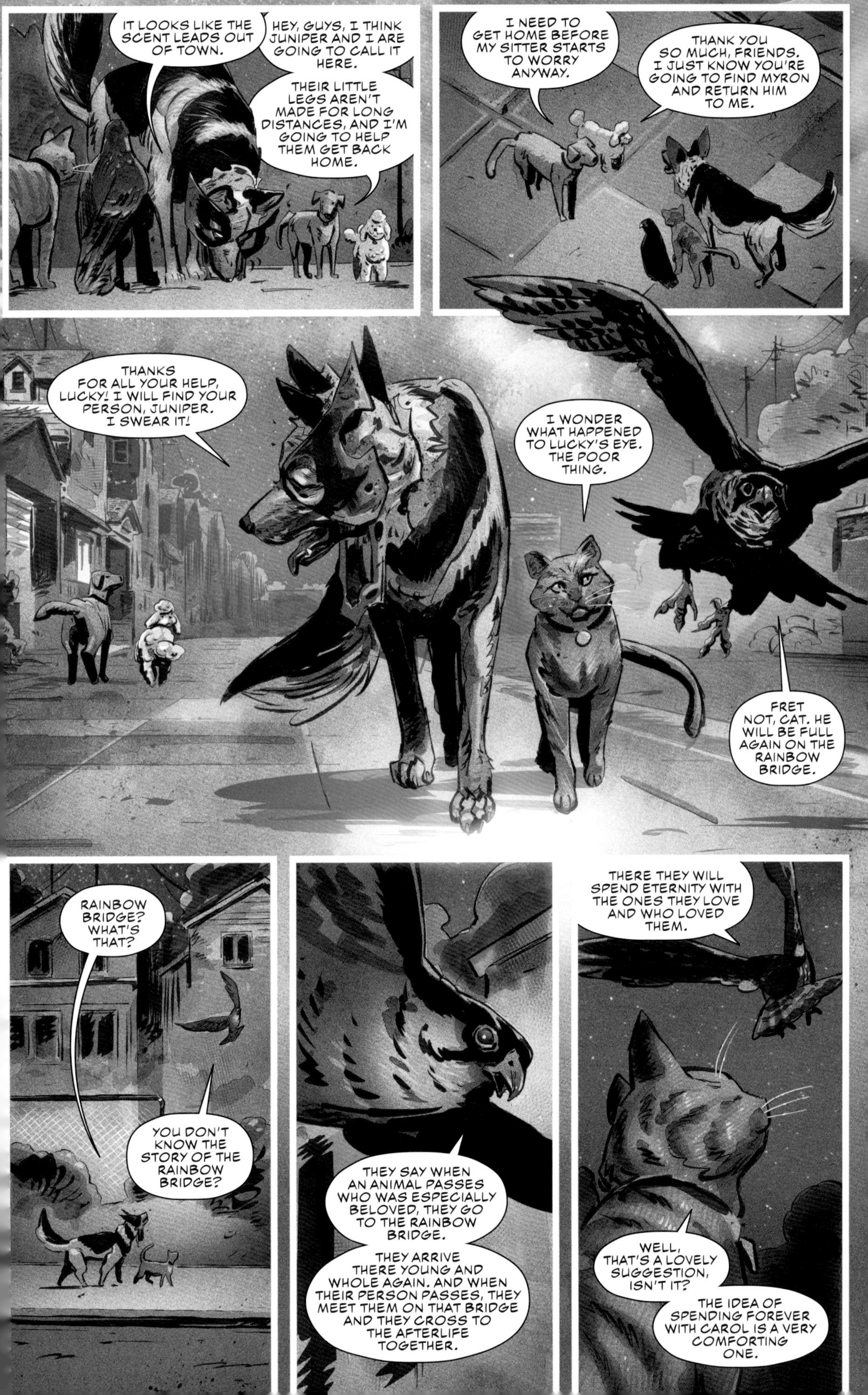
IT LOOKS LIKE THE SCENT LEADS OUT OF TOWN.
HEY, GUYS, I THINK JUNIPER AND I ARE GOING TO CALL IT HERE.
THEIR LITTLE LEGS AREN'T MADE FOR LONG DISTANCES, AND I'M GOING TO HELP THEM GET BACK HOME.
I NEED TO GET HOME BEFORE MY SITTER STARTS TO WORRY ANYWAY.
THANK YOU SO MUCH, FRIENDS. I JUST KNOW YOU'RE GOING TO FIND MYRON AND RETURN HIM TO ME.
THANKS FOR ALL YOUR HELP, LUCKY! I WILL FIND YOUR PERSON, JUNIPER. I SWEAR IT!
I WONDER WHAT HAPPENED TO LUCKY'S EYE. THE POOR THING.
FRET NOT, CAT. HE WILL BE FULL AGAIN ON THE RAINBOW BRIDGE.
RAINBOW BRIDGE? WHAT'S THAT?
YOU DON'T KNOW THE STORY OF THE RAINBOW BRIDGE?
THEY SAY WHEN AN ANIMAL PASSES WHO WAS ESPECIALLY BELOVED, THEY GO TO THE RAINBOW BRIDGE.
THEY ARRIVE THERE YOUNG AND WHOLE AGAIN. AND WHEN THEIR PERSON PASSES, THEY MEET THEM ON THAT BRIDGE AND THEY CROSS TO THE AFTERLIFE TOGETHER.
THERE THEY WILL SPEND ETERNITY WITH THE ONES THEY LOVE AND WHO LOVED THEM.
WELL, THAT'S A LOVELY SUGGESTION, ISN'T IT?
THE IDEA OF SPENDING FOREVER WITH CAROL IS A VERY COMFORTING ONE.

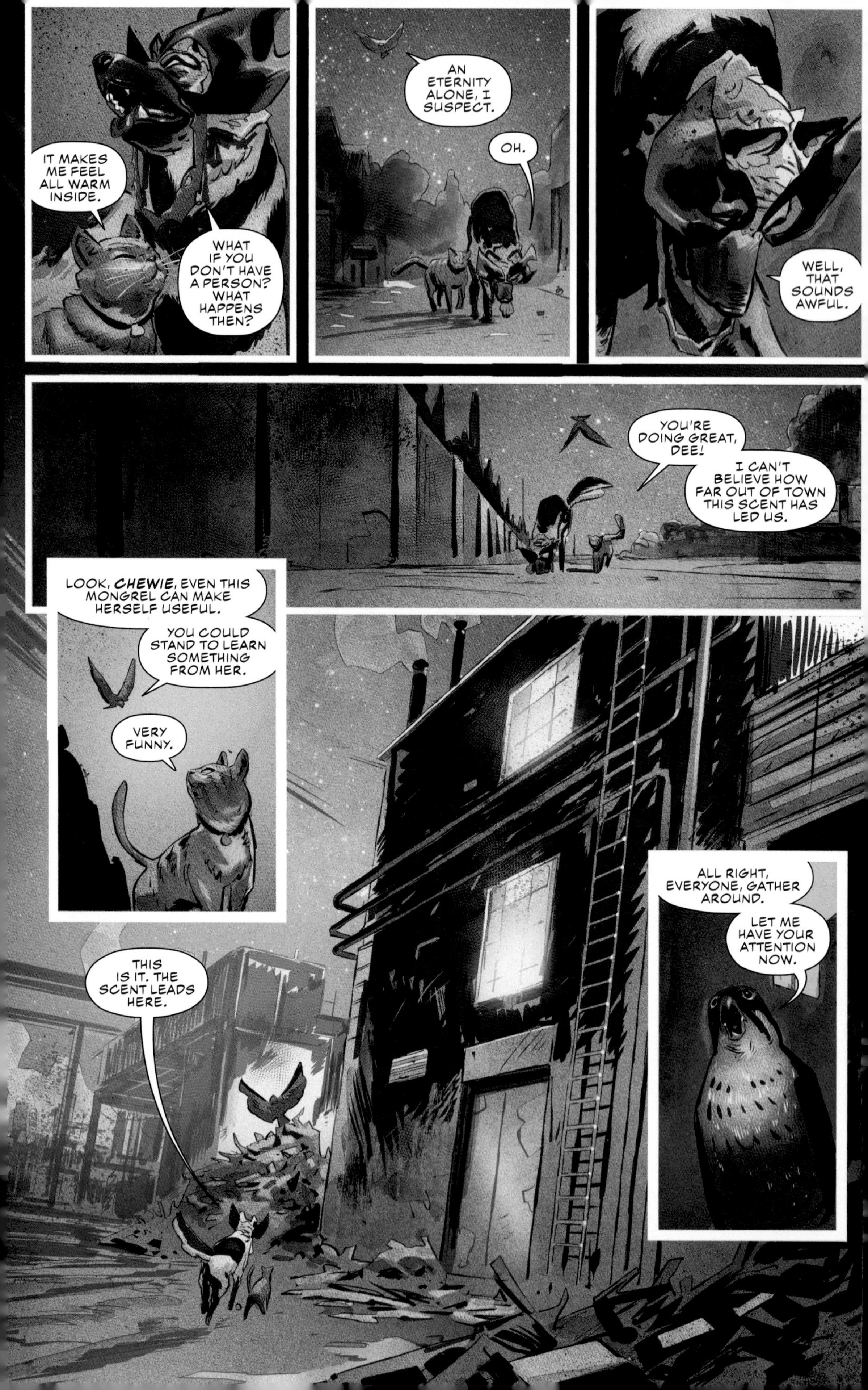
IT MAKES ME FEEL ALL WARM INSIDE.
WHAT IF YOU DON'T HAVE A PERSON? WHAT HAPPENS THEN?
AN ETERNITY ALONE, I SUSPECT.
OH.
WELL, THAT SOUNDS AWFUL.
YOU'RE DOING GREAT, DEE!
I CAN'T BELIEVE HOW FAR OUT OF TOWN THIS SCENT HAS LED US.
LOOK, CHEWIE, EVEN THIS MONGREL CAN MAKE HERSELF USEFUL.
YOU COULD STAND TO LEARN SOMETHING FROM HER.
VERY FUNNY.
THIS IS IT. THE SCENT LEADS HERE.
ALL RIGHT, EVERYONE, GATHER AROUND.
LET ME HAVE YOUR ATTENTION NOW.

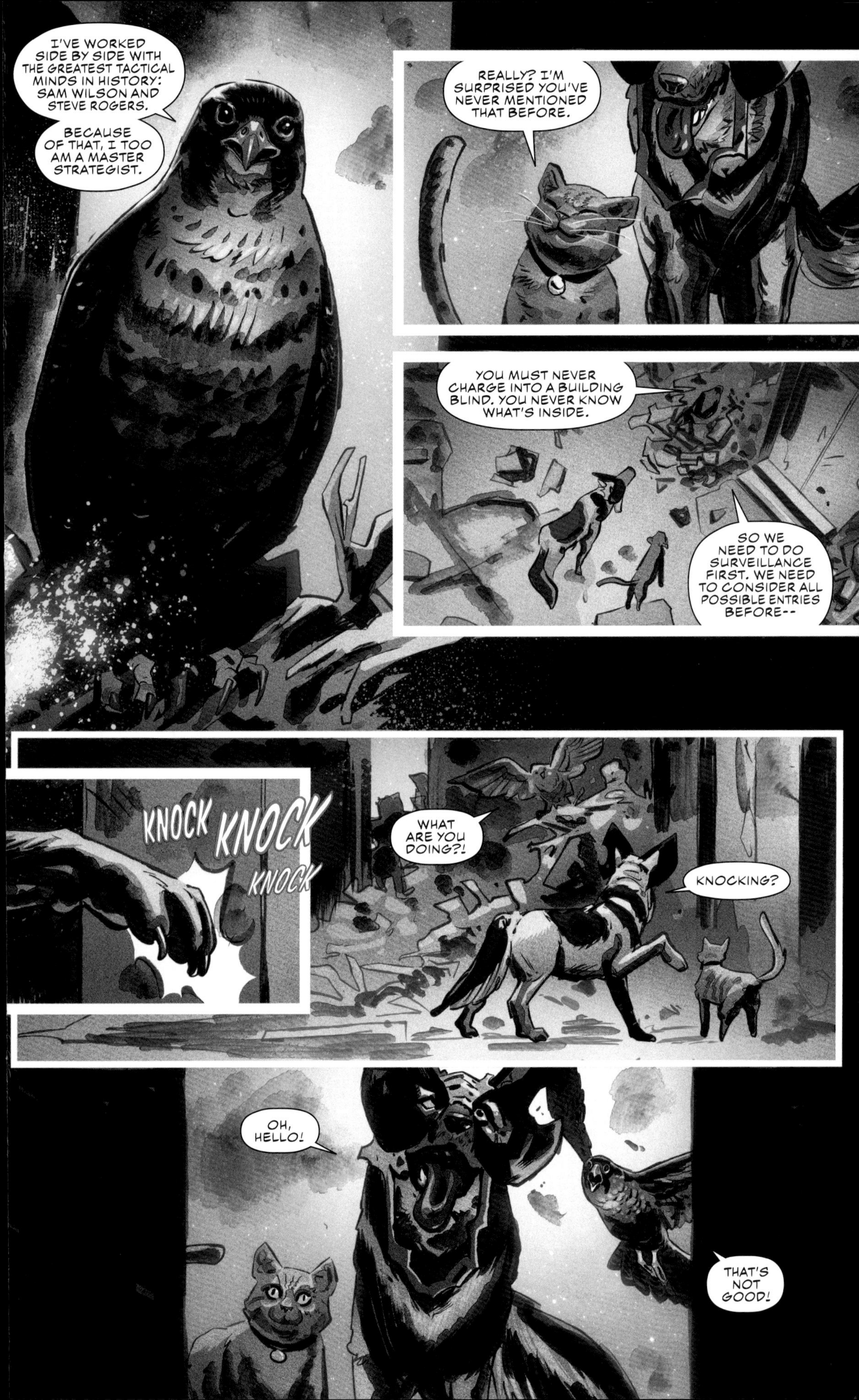
I'VE WORKED SIDE BY SIDE WITH THE GREATEST TACTICAL MINDS IN HISTORY: SAM WILSON AND STEVE ROGERS.
BECAUSE OF THAT, I TOO AM A MASTER STRATEGIST.
REALLY? I'M SURPRISED YOU'VE NEVER MENTIONED THAT BEFORE.
YOU MUST NEVER CHARGE INTO A BUILDING BLIND. YOU NEVER KNOW WHAT'S INSIDE.
SO WE NEED TO DO SURVEILLANCE FIRST. WE NEED TO CONSIDER ALL POSSIBLE ENTRIES BEFORE--
KNOCK KNOCK KNOCK
WHAT ARE YOU DOING?!
KNOCKING?
OH, HELLO!
THAT'S NOT GOOD!

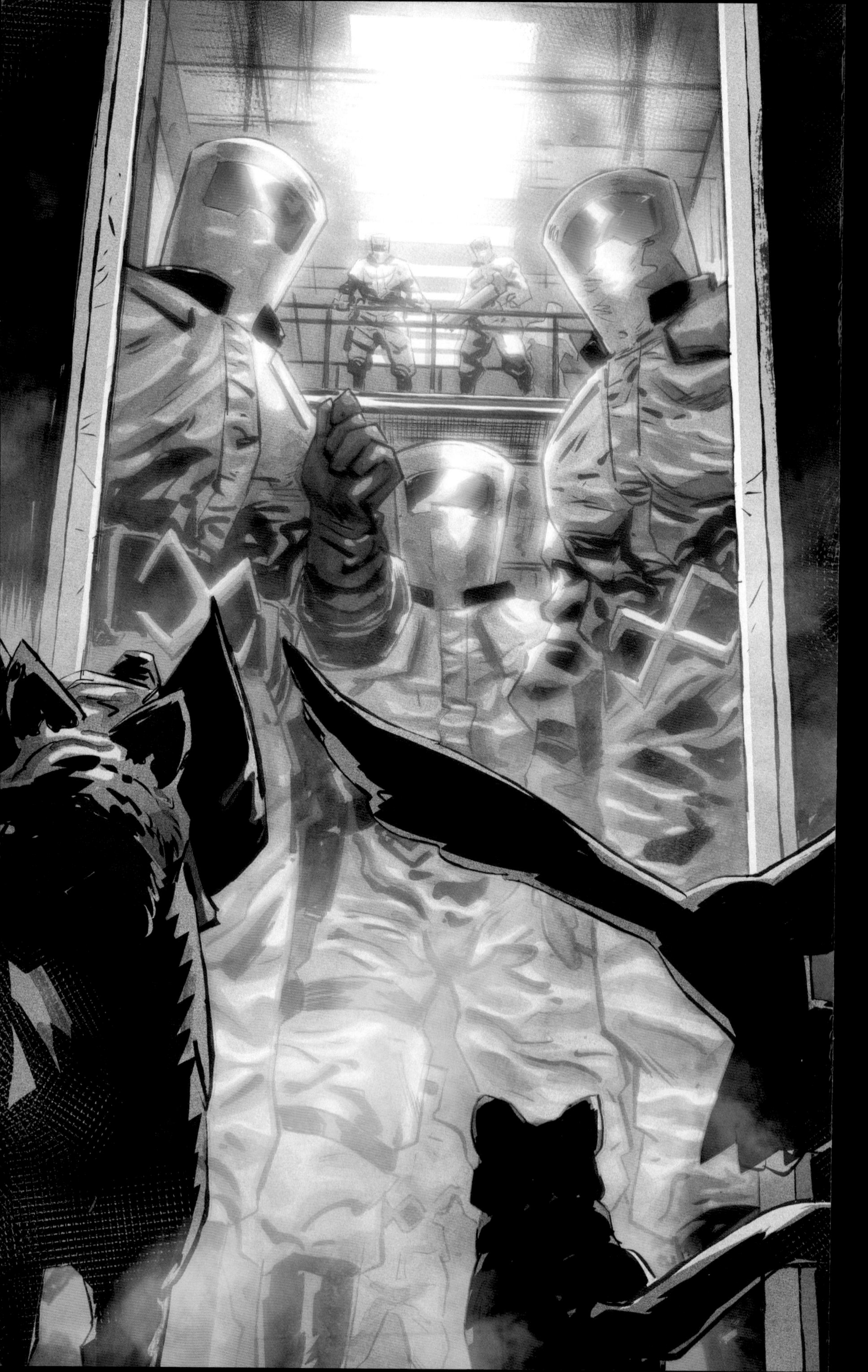

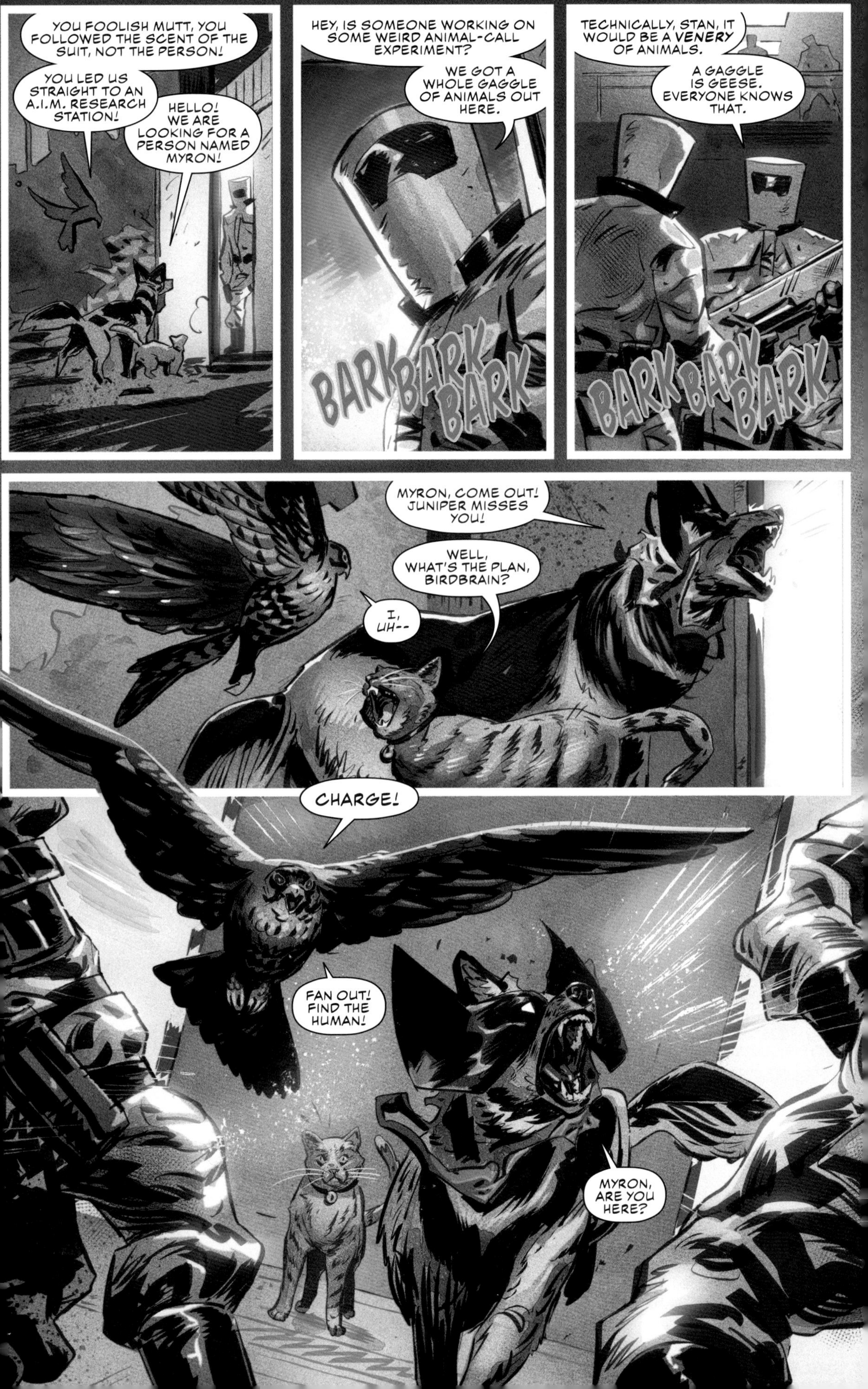
YOU FOOLISH MUTT, YOU FOLLOWED THE SCENT OF THE SUIT, NOT THE PERSON!
YOU LED US STRAIGHT TO AN A.I.M. RESEARCH STATION!
HELLO! WE ARE LOOKING FOR A PERSON NAMED MYRON!
HEY, IS SOMEONE WORKING ON SOME WEIRD ANIMAL-CALL EXPERIMENT?
WE GOT A WHOLE GAGGLE OF ANIMALS OUT HERE.
BARK BARK BARK
TECHNICALLY, STAN, IT WOULD BE A VENERY OF ANIMALS.
A GAGGLE IS GEESE. EVERYONE KNOWS THAT.
BARK BARK BARK
MYRON, COME OUT! JUNIPER MISSES YOU!
WELL, WHAT'S THE PLAN, BIRDBRAIN?
I, UH--
CHARGE!
FAN OUT! FIND THE HUMAN!
MYRON, ARE YOU HERE?

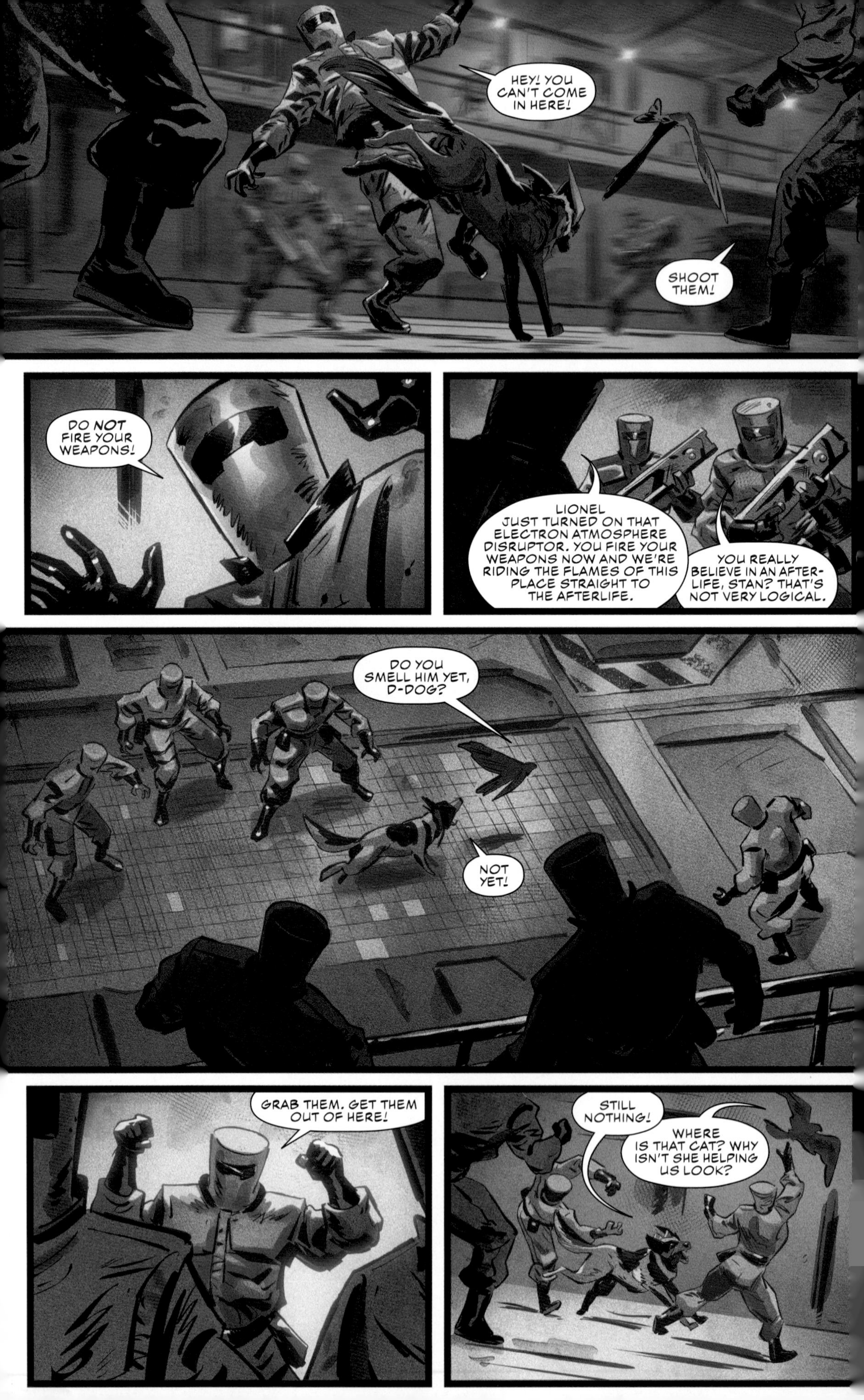
HEY! YOU CAN'T COME IN HERE!
SHOOT THEM!
DO NOT FIRE YOUR WEAPONS!
LIONEL JUST TURNED ON THAT ELECTRON ATMOSPHERE DISRUPTOR. YOU FIRE YOUR WEAPONS NOW AND WE'RE RIDING THE FLAMES OF THIS PLACE STRAIGHT TO THE AFTERLIFE.
YOU REALLY BELIEVE IN AN AFTER-LIFE, STAN? THAT'S NOT VERY LOGICAL.
DO YOU SMELL HIM YET, D-DOG?
NOT YET!
GRAB THEM. GET THEM OUT OF HERE!
STILL NOTHING!
WHERE IS THAT CAT? WHY ISN'T SHE HELPING US LOOK?

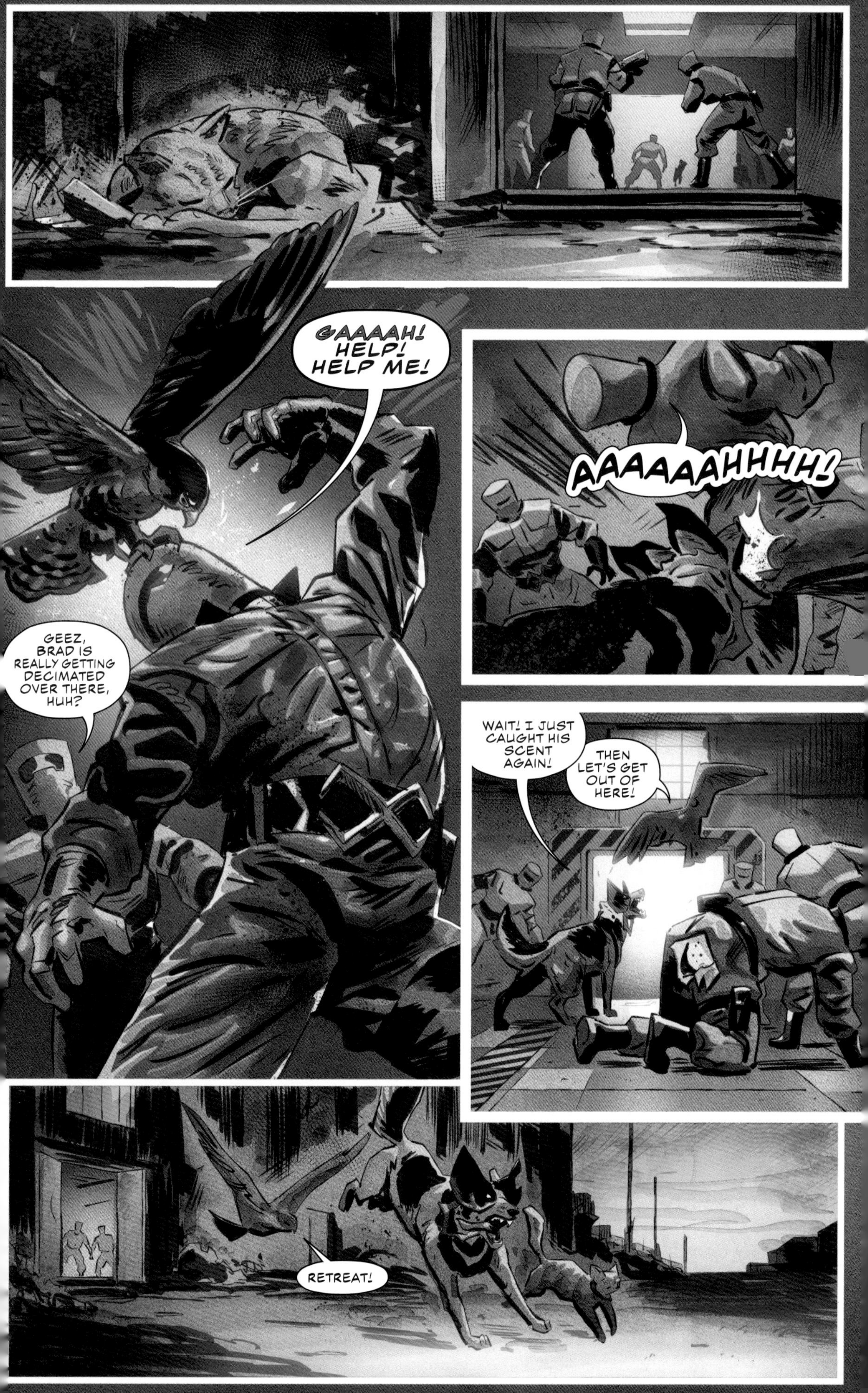
GAAAAH! HELP! HELP ME!
GEEZ, BRAD IS REALLY GETTING DECIMATED OVER THERE, HUH?
AAAAAAHHHH!
WAIT! I JUST CAUGHT HIS SCENT AGAIN!
THEN LET'S GET OUT OF HERE!
RETREAT!

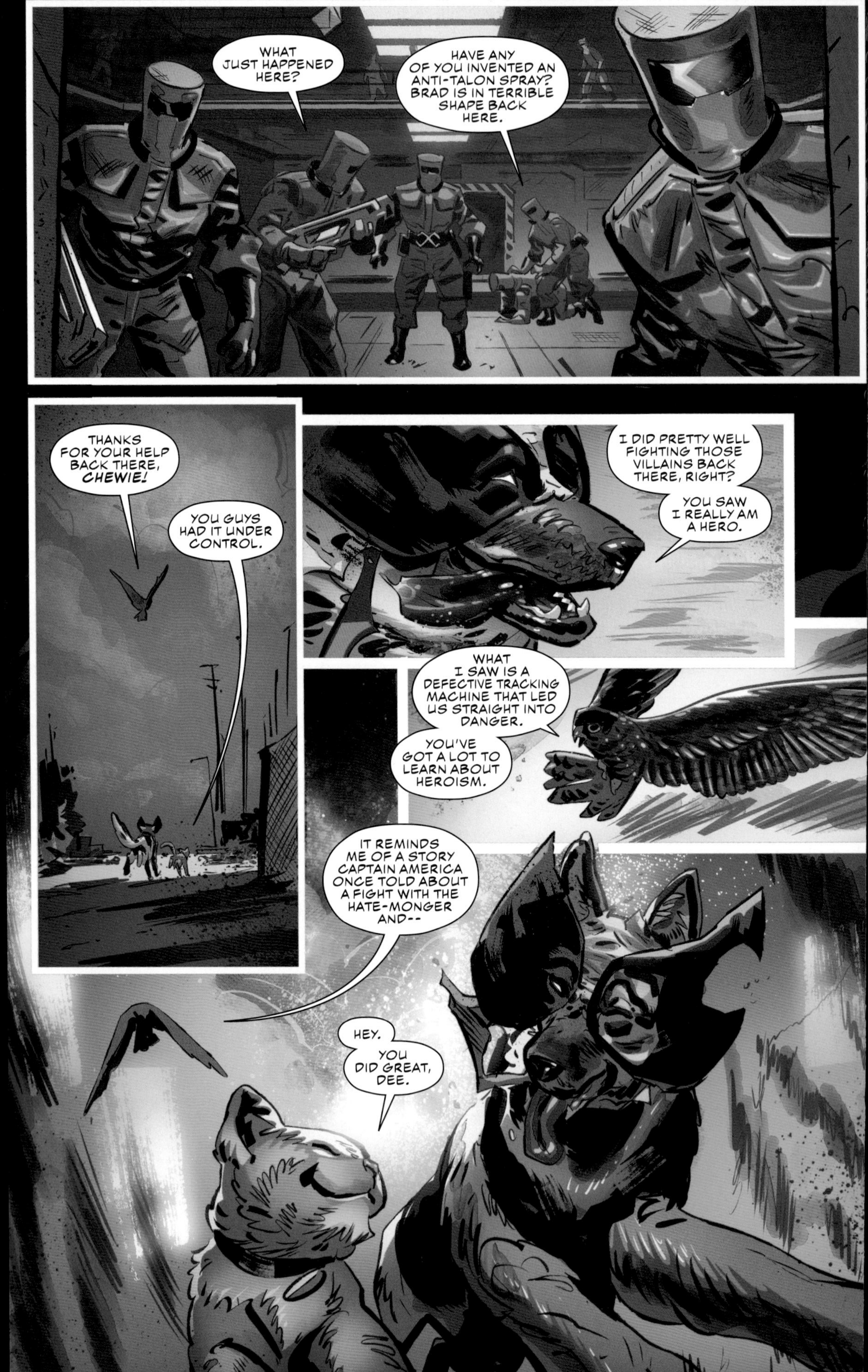
WHAT JUST HAPPENED HERE?
HAVE ANY OF YOU INVENTED AN ANTI-TALON SPRAY? BRAD IS IN TERRIBLE SHAPE BACK HERE.
THANKS FOR YOUR HELP BACK THERE, CHEWIE!
YOU GUYS HAD IT UNDER CONTROL.
I DID PRETTY WELL FIGHTING THOSE VILLAINS BACK THERE, RIGHT?
YOU SAW I REALLY AM A HERO.
WHAT I SAW IS A DEFECTIVE TRACKING MACHINE THAT LED US STRAIGHT INTO DANGER.
YOU'VE GOT A LOT TO LEARN ABOUT HEROISM.
IT REMINDS ME OF A STORY CAPTAIN AMERICA ONCE TOLD ABOUT A FIGHT WITH THE HATE-MONGER AND--
HEY.
YOU DID GREAT, DEE.

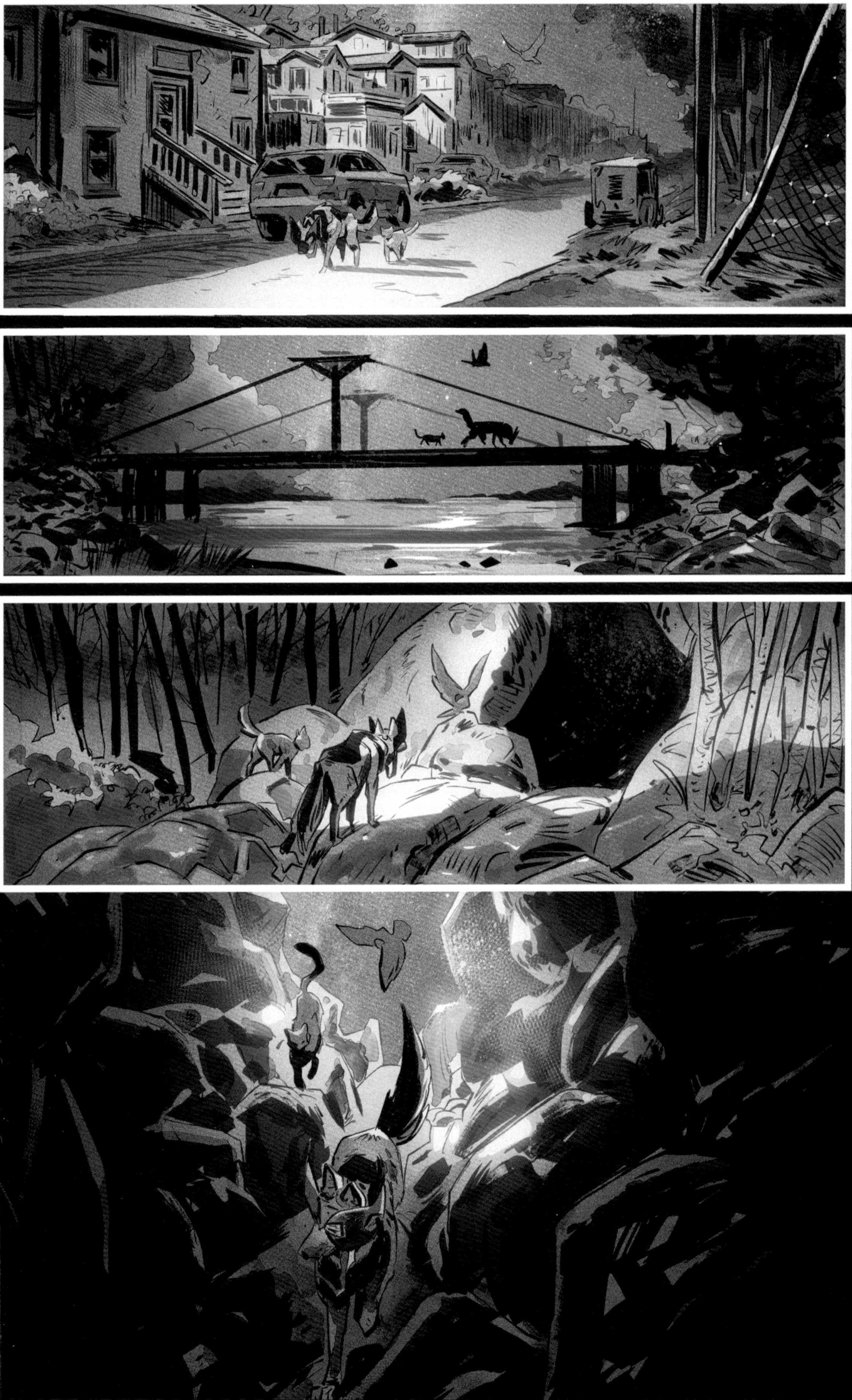

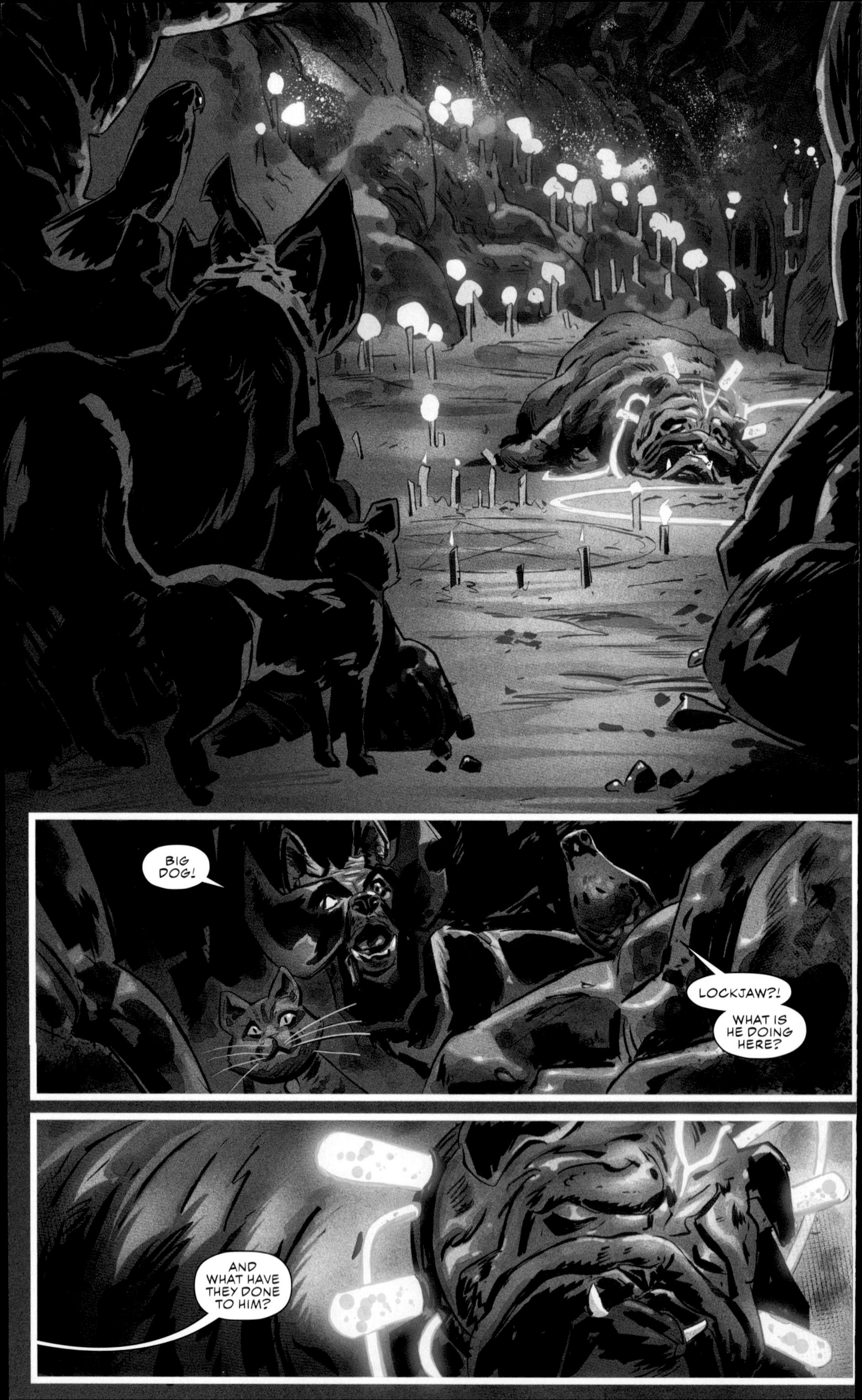
BIG DOG!
LOCKJAW?!
WHAT IS HE DOING HERE?
AND WHAT HAVE THEY DONE TO HIM?

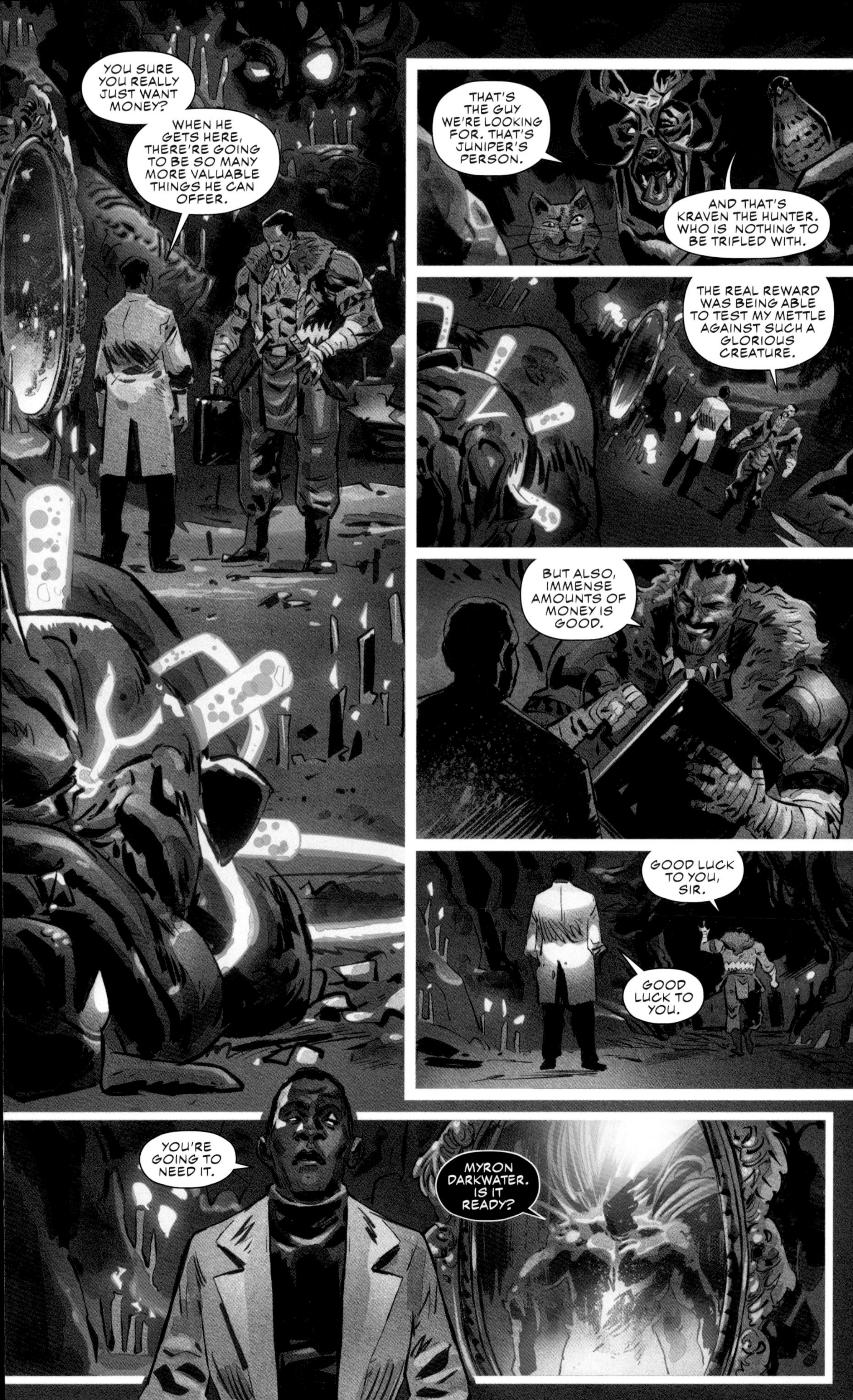
YOU SURE YOU REALLY JUST WANT MONEY?
WHEN HE GETS HERE, THERE'RE GOING TO BE SO MANY MORE VALUABLE THINGS HE CAN OFFER.
THAT'S THE GUY WE'RE LOOKING FOR. THAT'S JUNIPER'S PERSON.
AND THAT'S KRAVEN THE HUNTER. WHO IS NOTHING TO BE TRIFLED WITH.
THE REAL REWARD WAS BEING ABLE TO TEST MY METTLE AGAINST SUCH A GLORIOUS CREATURE.
BUT ALSO, IMMENSE AMOUNTS OF MONEY IS GOOD.
GOOD LUCK TO YOU, SIR.
GOOD LUCK TO YOU.
YOU'RE GOING TO NEED IT.
MYRON DARKWATER. IS IT READY?

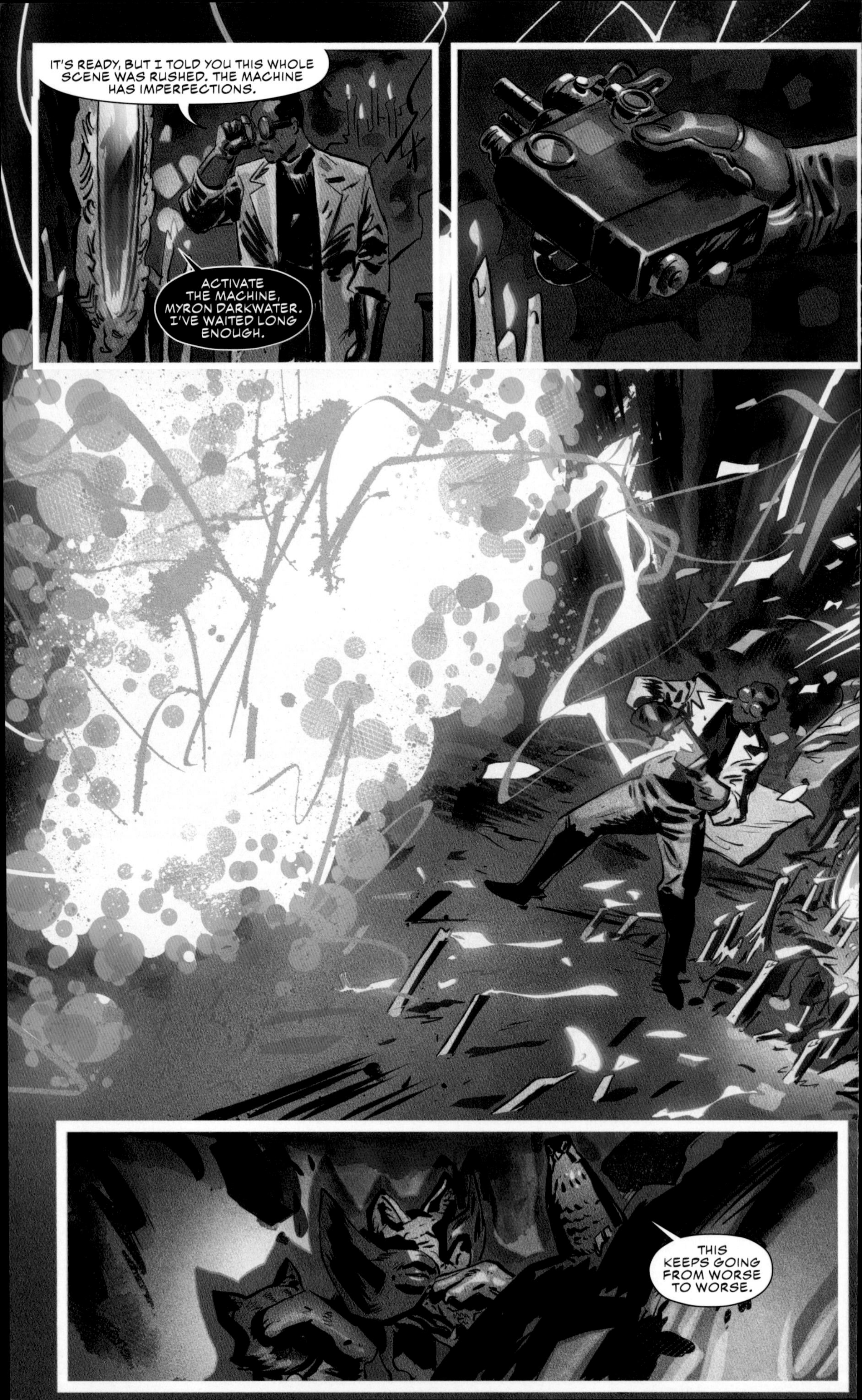
IT'S READY, BUT I TOLD YOU THIS WHOLE SCENE WAS RUSHED. THE MACHINE HAS IMPERFECTIONS.
ACTIVATE THE MACHINE, MYRON DARKWATER. I'VE WAITED LONG ENOUGH.
THIS KEEPS GOING FROM WORSE TO WORSE.

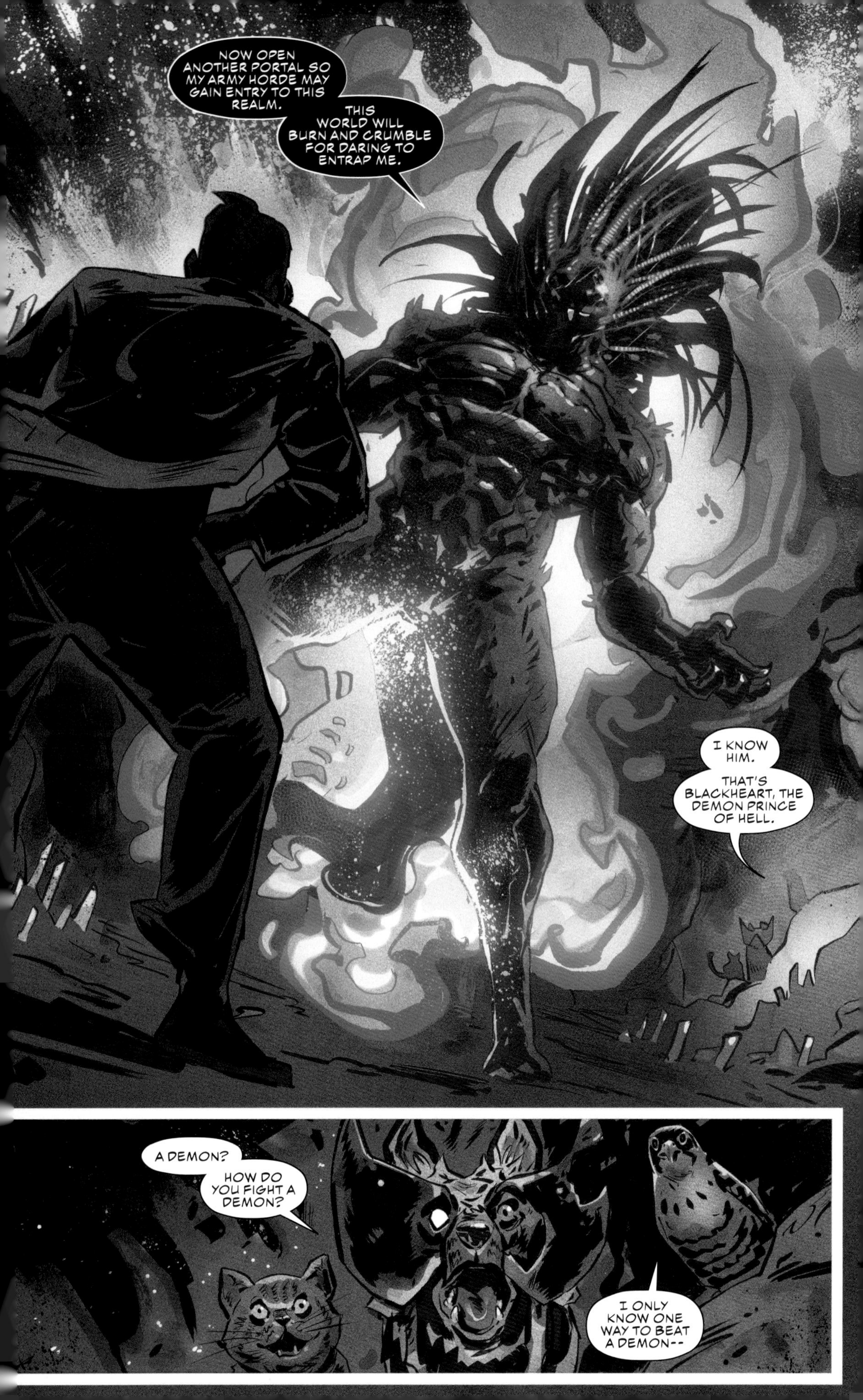
NOW OPEN ANOTHER PORTAL SO MY ARMY HORDE MAY GAIN ENTRY TO THIS REALM.
THIS WORLD WILL BURN AND CRUMBLE FOR DARING TO ENTRAP ME.
I KNOW HIM.
THAT'S BLACKHEART, THE DEMON PRINCE OF HELL.
A DEMON?
HOW DO YOU FIGHT A DEMON?
I ONLY KNOW ONE WAY TO BEAT A DEMON--

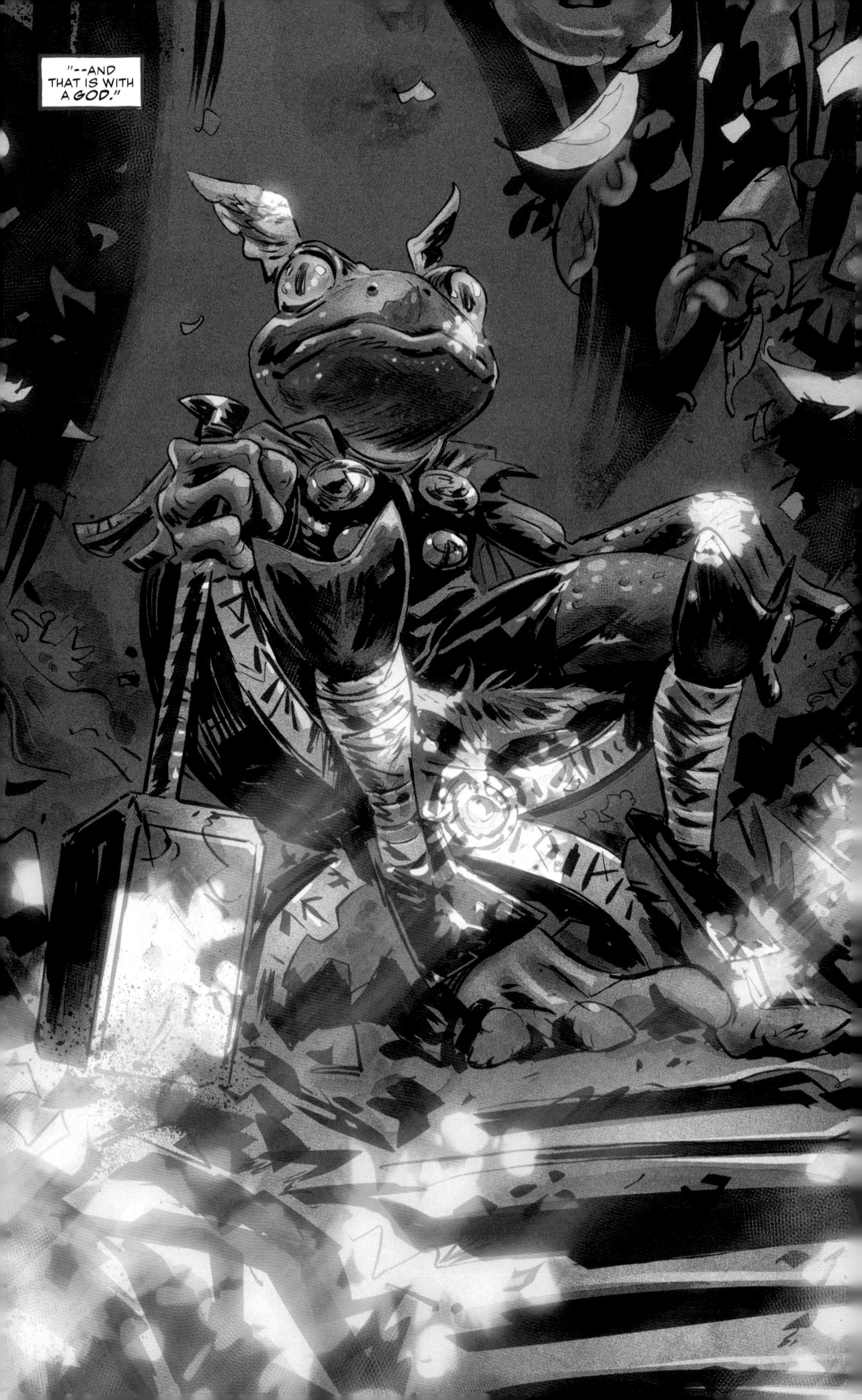
"--AND THAT IS WITH A GOD."

TWO

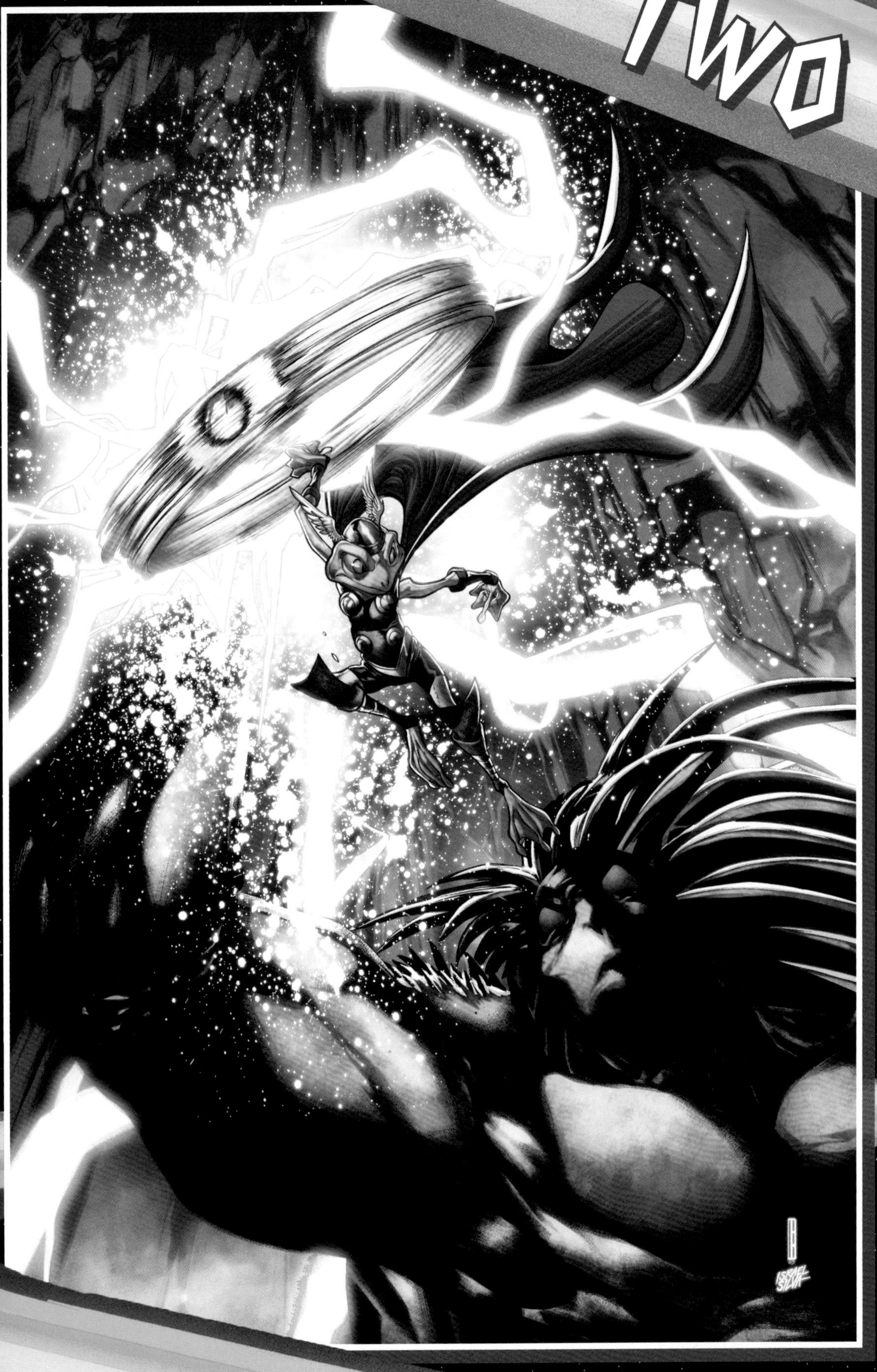

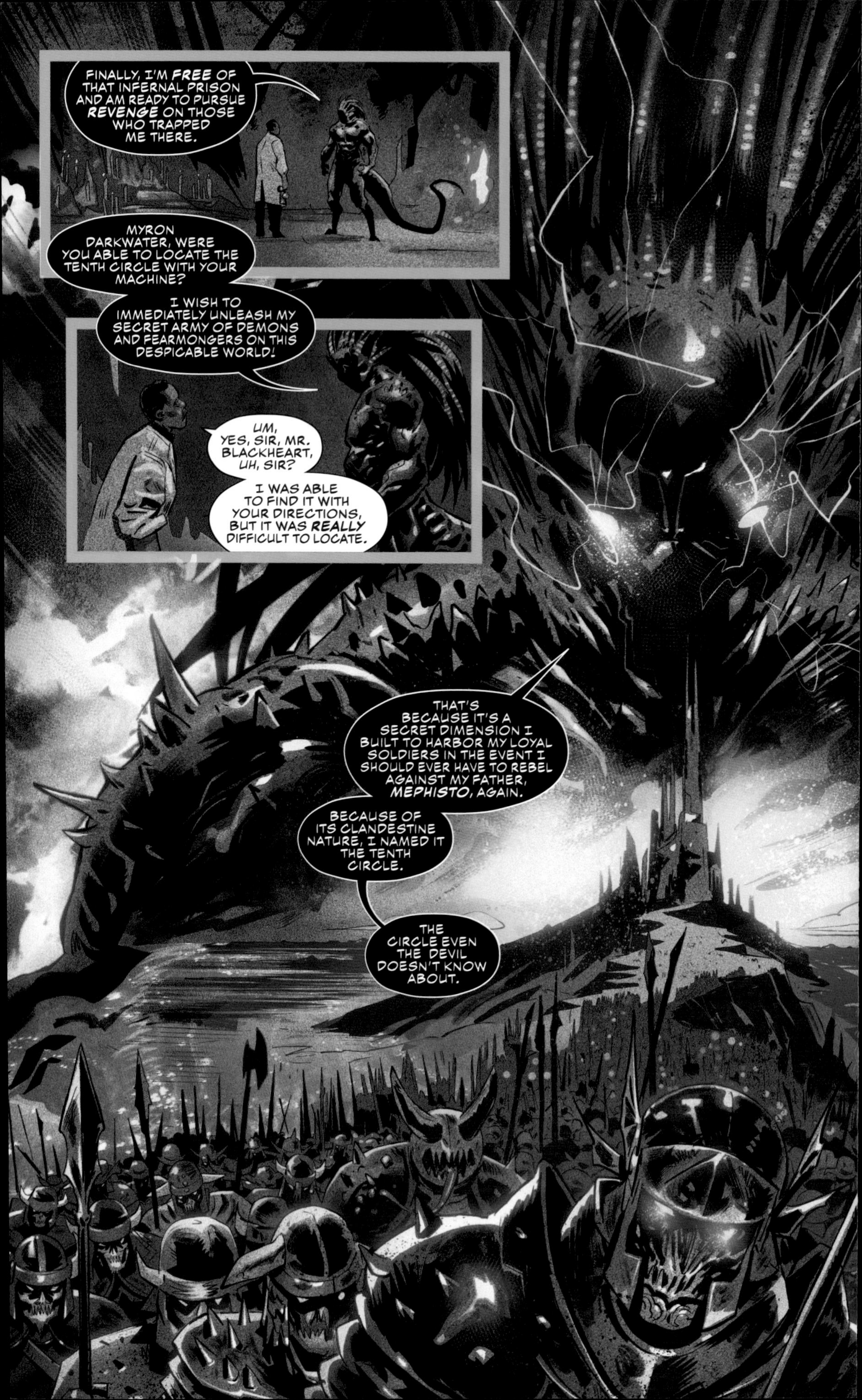
FINALLY, I'M FREE OF THAT INFERNAL PRISON AND AM READY TO PURSUE REVENGE ON THOSE WHO TRAPPED ME THERE.
MYRON DARKWATER, WERE YOU ABLE TO LOCATE THE TENTH CIRCLE WITH YOUR MACHINE?
I WISH TO IMMEDIATELY UNLEASH MY SECRET ARMY OF DEMONS AND FEARMONGERS ON THIS DESPICABLE WORLD!
UM, YES, SIR, MR. BLACKHEART, UH, SIR?
I WAS ABLE TO FIND IT WITH YOUR DIRECTIONS, BUT IT WAS REALLY DIFFICULT TO LOCATE.
THAT'S BECAUSE IT'S A SECRET DIMENSION I BUILT TO HARBOR MY LOYAL SOLDIERS IN THE EVENT I SHOULD EVER HAVE TO REBEL AGAINST MY FATHER, MEPHISTO, AGAIN.
BECAUSE OF ITS CLANDESTINE NATURE, I NAMED IT THE TENTH CIRCLE.
THE CIRCLE EVEN THE DEVIL DOESN'T KNOW ABOUT.

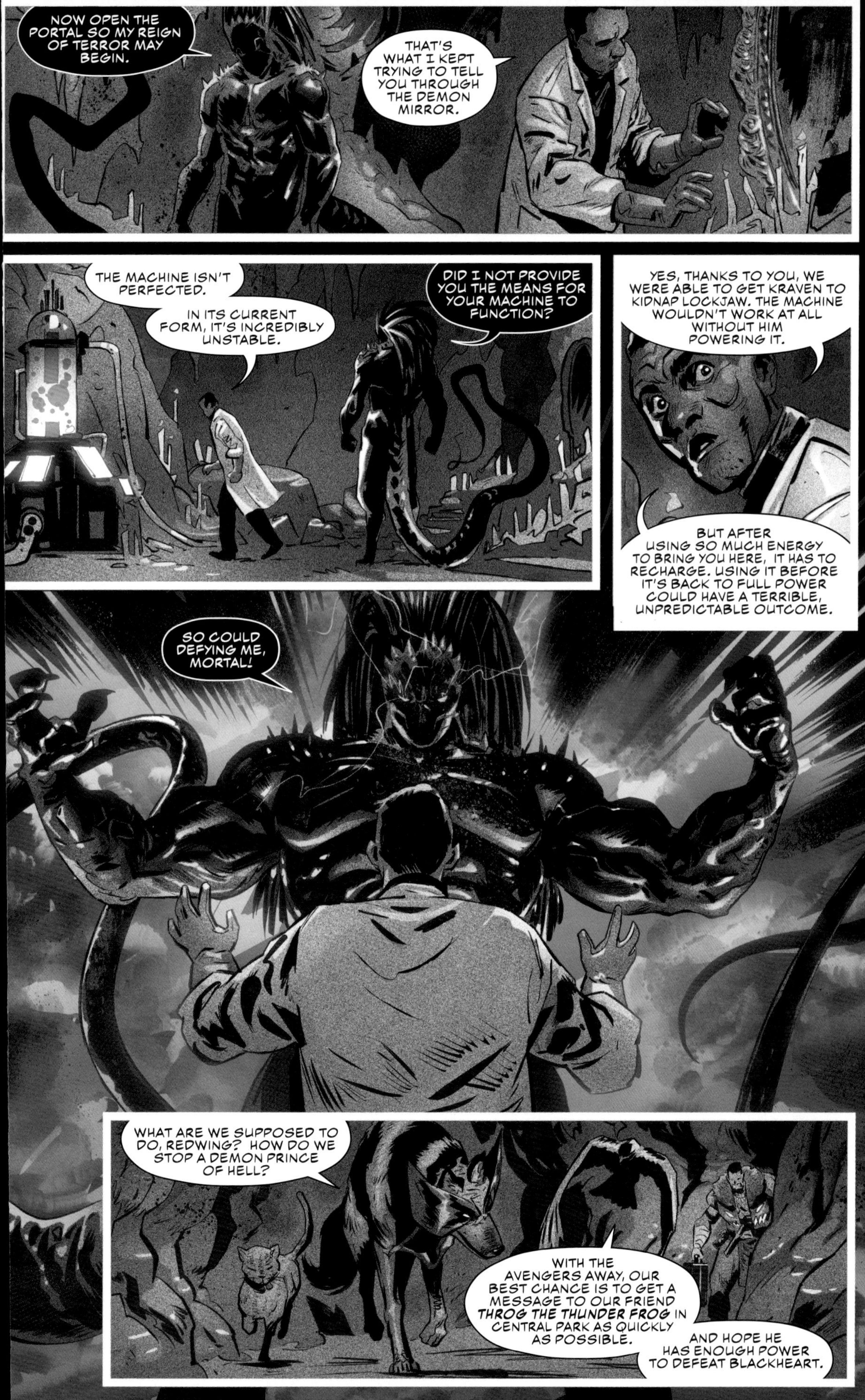
NOW OPEN THE PORTAL SO MY REIGN OF TERROR MAY BEGIN.
THAT'S WHAT I KEPT TRYING TO TELL YOU THROUGH THE DEMON MIRROR.
THE MACHINE ISN'T PERFECTED.
IN ITS CURRENT FORM, IT'S INCREDIBLY UNSTABLE.
DID I NOT PROVIDE YOU THE MEANS FOR YOUR MACHINE TO FUNCTION?
YES, THANKS TO YOU, WE WERE ABLE TO GET KRAVEN TO KIDNAP LOCKJAW. THE MACHINE WOULDN'T WORK AT ALL WITHOUT HIM POWERING IT.
BUT AFTER USING SO MUCH ENERGY TO BRING YOU HERE, IT HAS TO RECHARGE. USING IT BEFORE IT'S BACK TO FULL POWER COULD HAVE A TERRIBLE, UNPREDICTABLE OUTCOME.
SO COULD DEFYING ME, MORTAL!
WHAT ARE WE SUPPOSED TO DO, REDWING? HOW DO WE STOP A DEMON PRINCE OF HELL?
WITH THE AVENGERS AWAY, OUR BEST CHANCE IS TO GET A MESSAGE TO OUR FRIEND ***THROG THE THUNDER FROG*** IN CENTRAL PARK AS QUICKLY AS POSSIBLE.
AND HOPE HE HAS ENOUGH POWER TO DEFEAT BLACKHEART.

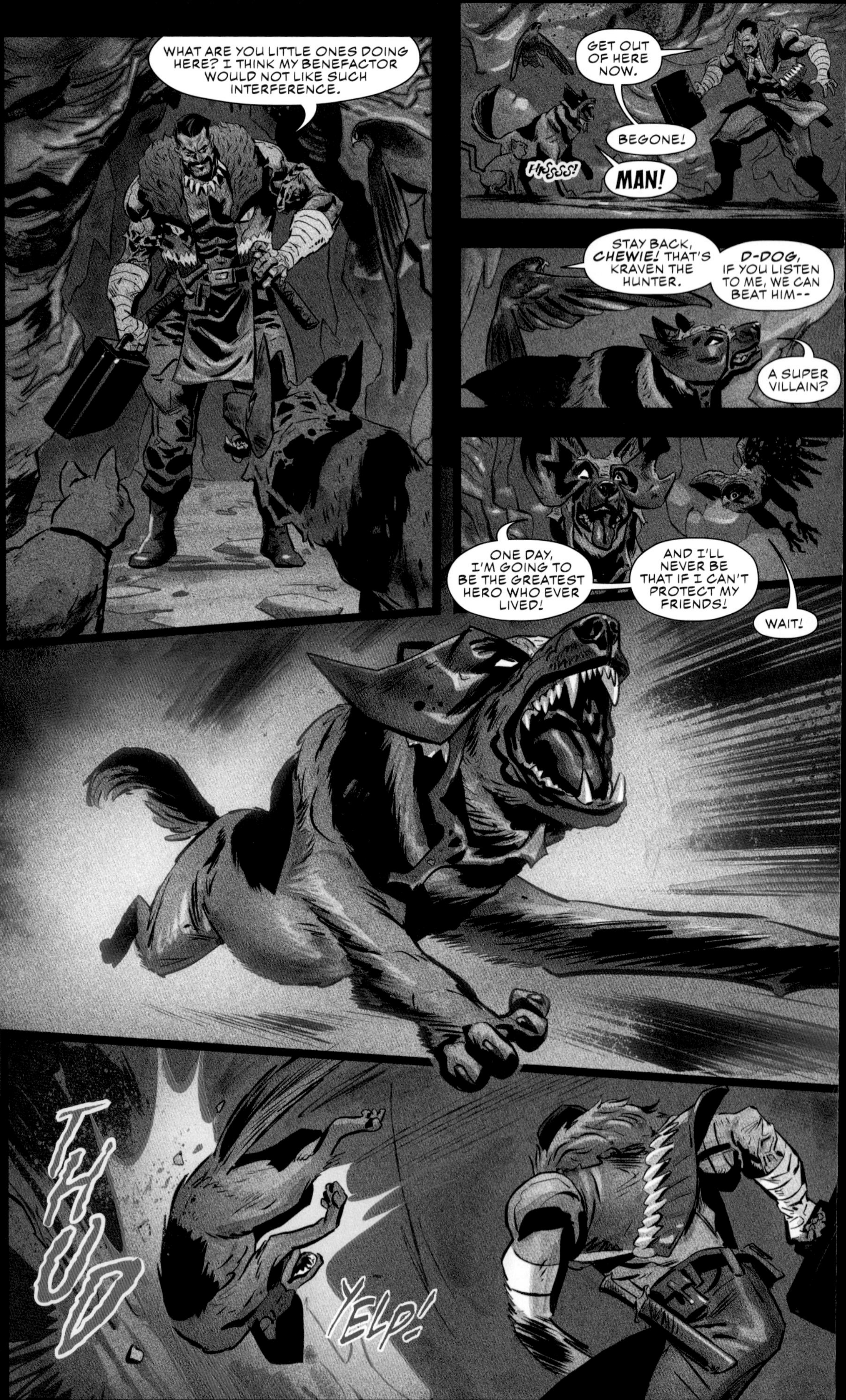

WHAT ARE YOU LITTLE ONES DOING HERE? I THINK MY BENEFACTOR WOULD NOT LIKE SUCH INTERFERENCE.
GET OUT OF HERE NOW.
BEGONE!
HSSSS!
MAN!
STAY BACK, CHEWIE! THAT'S KRAVEN THE HUNTER.
D-DOG, IF YOU LISTEN TO ME, WE CAN BEAT HIM--
A SUPER VILLAIN?
ONE DAY, I'M GOING TO BE THE GREATEST HERO WHO EVER LIVED!
AND I'LL NEVER BE THAT IF I CAN'T PROTECT MY FRIENDS!
WAIT!
THUD
YELP!

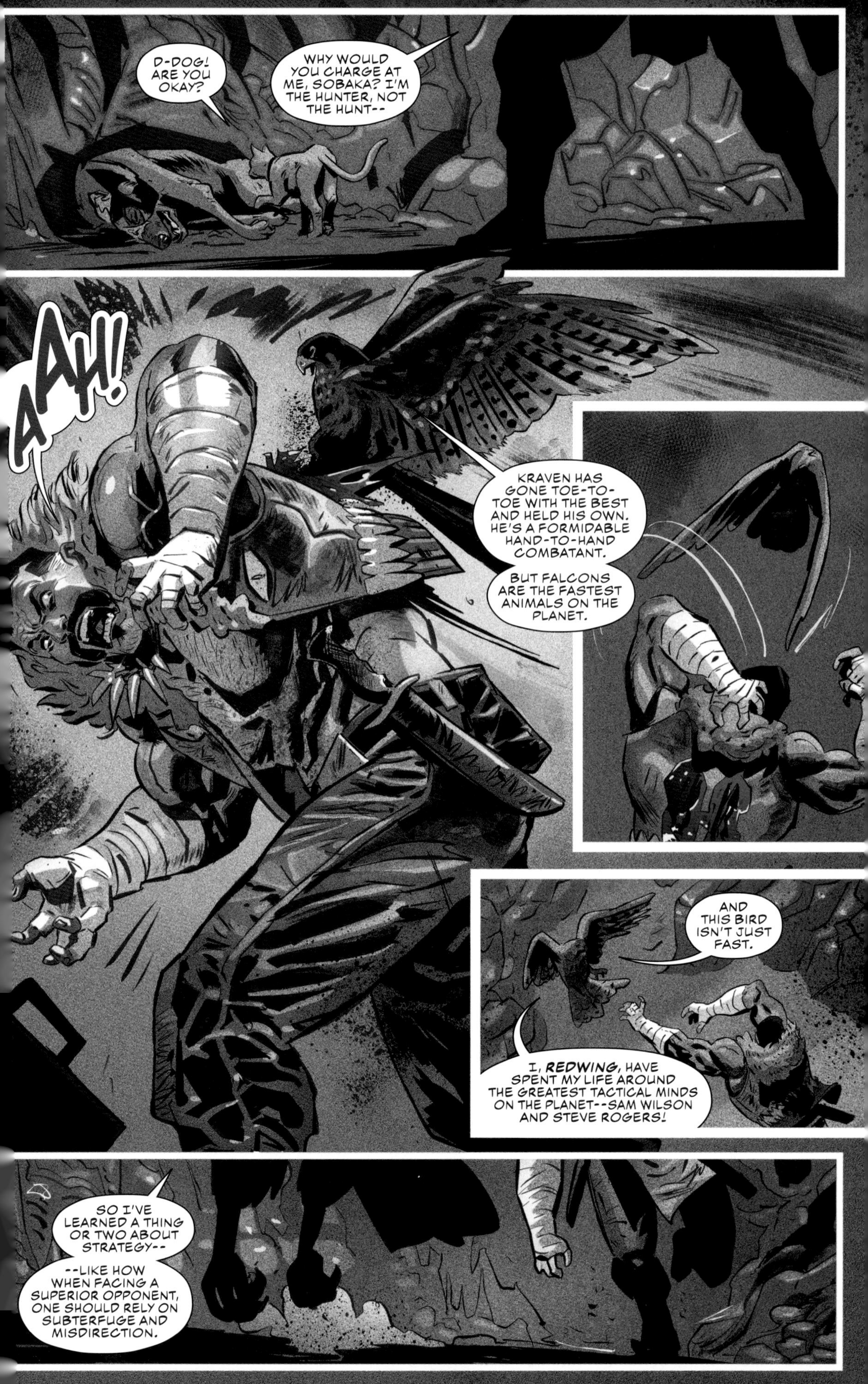
D-DOG! ARE YOU OKAY?
WHY WOULD YOU CHARGE AT ME, SOBAKA? I'M THE HUNTER, NOT THE HUNT--
AAH!
KRAVEN HAS GONE TOE-TO-TOE WITH THE BEST AND HELD HIS OWN. HE'S A FORMIDABLE HAND-TO-HAND COMBATANT.
BUT FALCONS ARE THE FASTEST ANIMALS ON THE PLANET.
AND THIS BIRD ISN'T JUST FAST.
I, **REDWING**, HAVE SPENT MY LIFE AROUND THE GREATEST TACTICAL MINDS ON THE PLANET--SAM WILSON AND STEVE ROGERS!
SO I'VE LEARNED A THING OR TWO ABOUT STRATEGY--
--LIKE HOW WHEN FACING A SUPERIOR OPPONENT, ONE SHOULD RELY ON SUBTERFUGE AND MISDIRECTION.

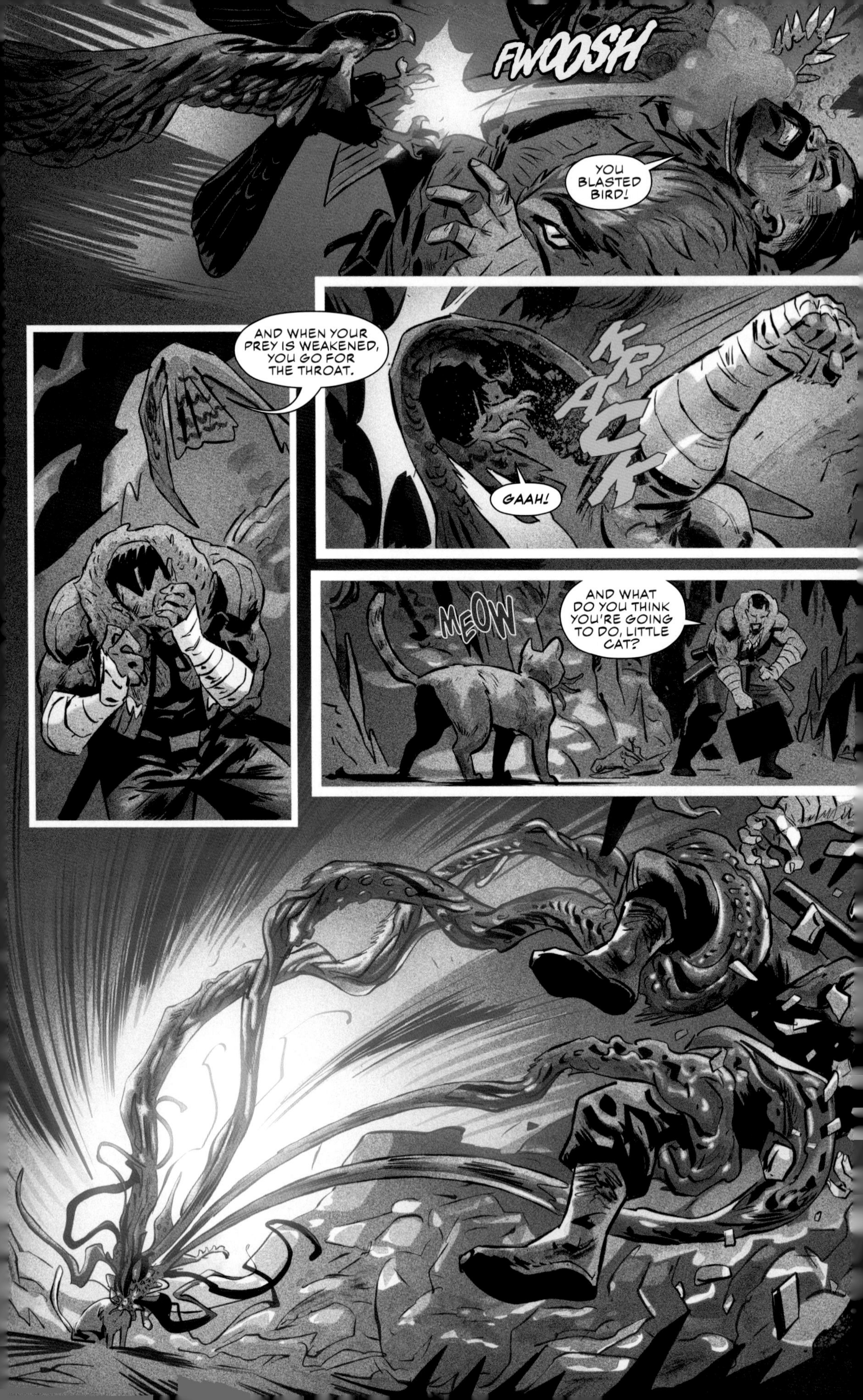
FWOOSH
YOU BLASTED BIRD!
AND WHEN YOUR PREY IS WEAKENED, YOU GO FOR THE THROAT.
KRACK
GAAH!
MEOW
AND WHAT DO YOU THINK YOU'RE GOING TO DO, LITTLE CAT?

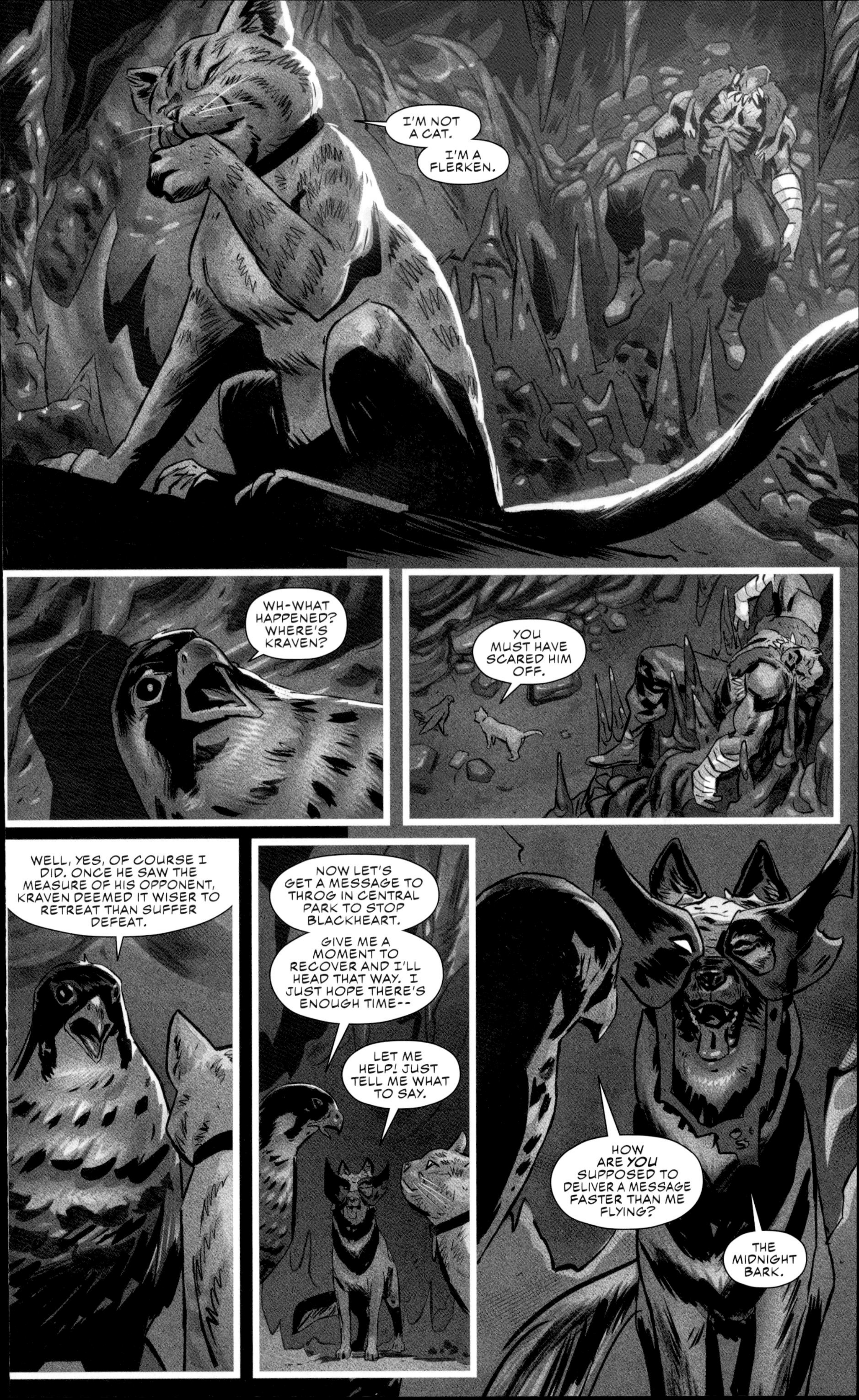
I'M NOT A CAT.
I'M A FLERKEN.
WH-WHAT HAPPENED? WHERE'S KRAVEN?
YOU MUST HAVE SCARED HIM OFF.
WELL, YES, OF COURSE I DID. ONCE HE SAW THE MEASURE OF HIS OPPONENT, KRAVEN DEEMED IT WISER TO RETREAT THAN SUFFER DEFEAT.
NOW LET'S GET A MESSAGE TO THROG IN CENTRAL PARK TO STOP BLACKHEART.
GIVE ME A MOMENT TO RECOVER AND I'LL HEAD THAT WAY. I JUST HOPE THERE'S ENOUGH TIME--
LET ME HELP! JUST TELL ME WHAT TO SAY.
HOW ARE *YOU* SUPPOSED TO DELIVER A MESSAGE FASTER THAN ME FLYING?
THE MIDNIGHT BARK.

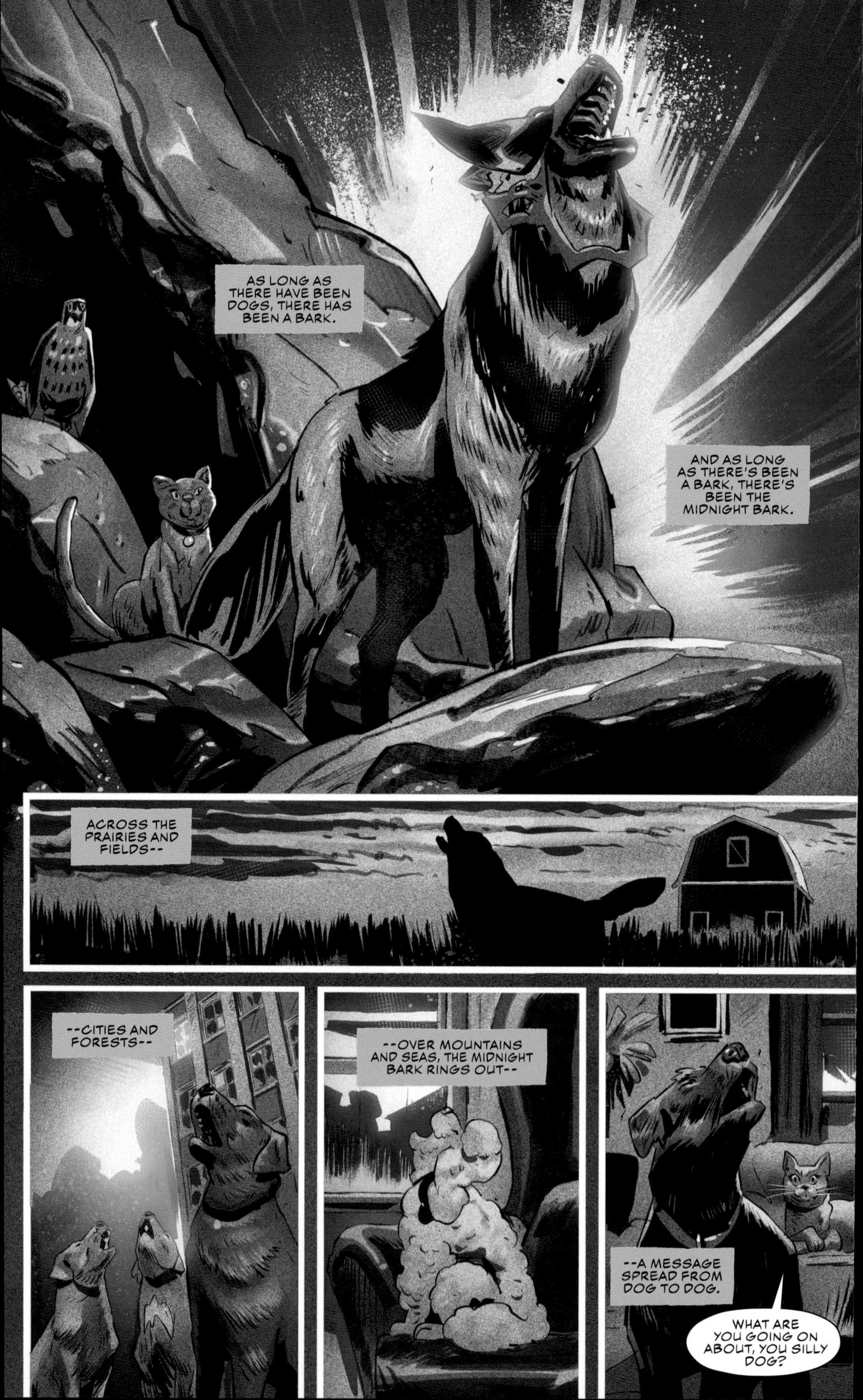
AS LONG AS THERE HAVE BEEN DOGS, THERE HAS BEEN A BARK.
AND AS LONG AS THERE'S BEEN A BARK, THERE'S BEEN THE MIDNIGHT BARK.
ACROSS THE PRAIRIES AND FIELDS--
--CITIES AND FORESTS--
--OVER MOUNTAINS AND SEAS, THE MIDNIGHT BARK RINGS OUT--
--A MESSAGE SPREAD FROM DOG TO DOG.
WHAT ARE YOU GOING ON ABOUT, YOU SILLY DOG?

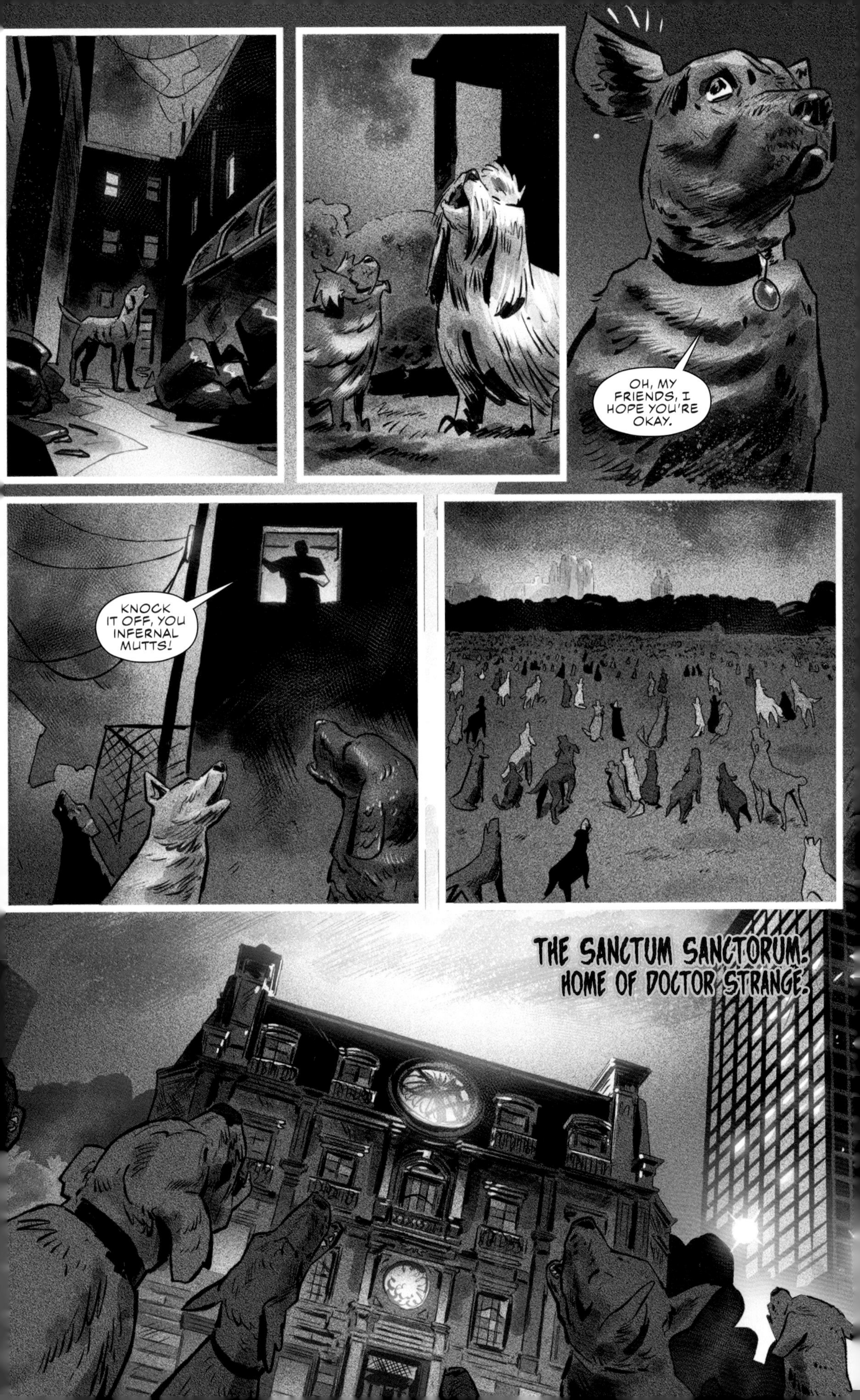
OH, MY FRIENDS, I HOPE YOU'RE OKAY.
KNOCK IT OFF, YOU INFERNAL MUTTS!
THE SANCTUM SANCTORUM. HOME OF DOCTOR STRANGE.

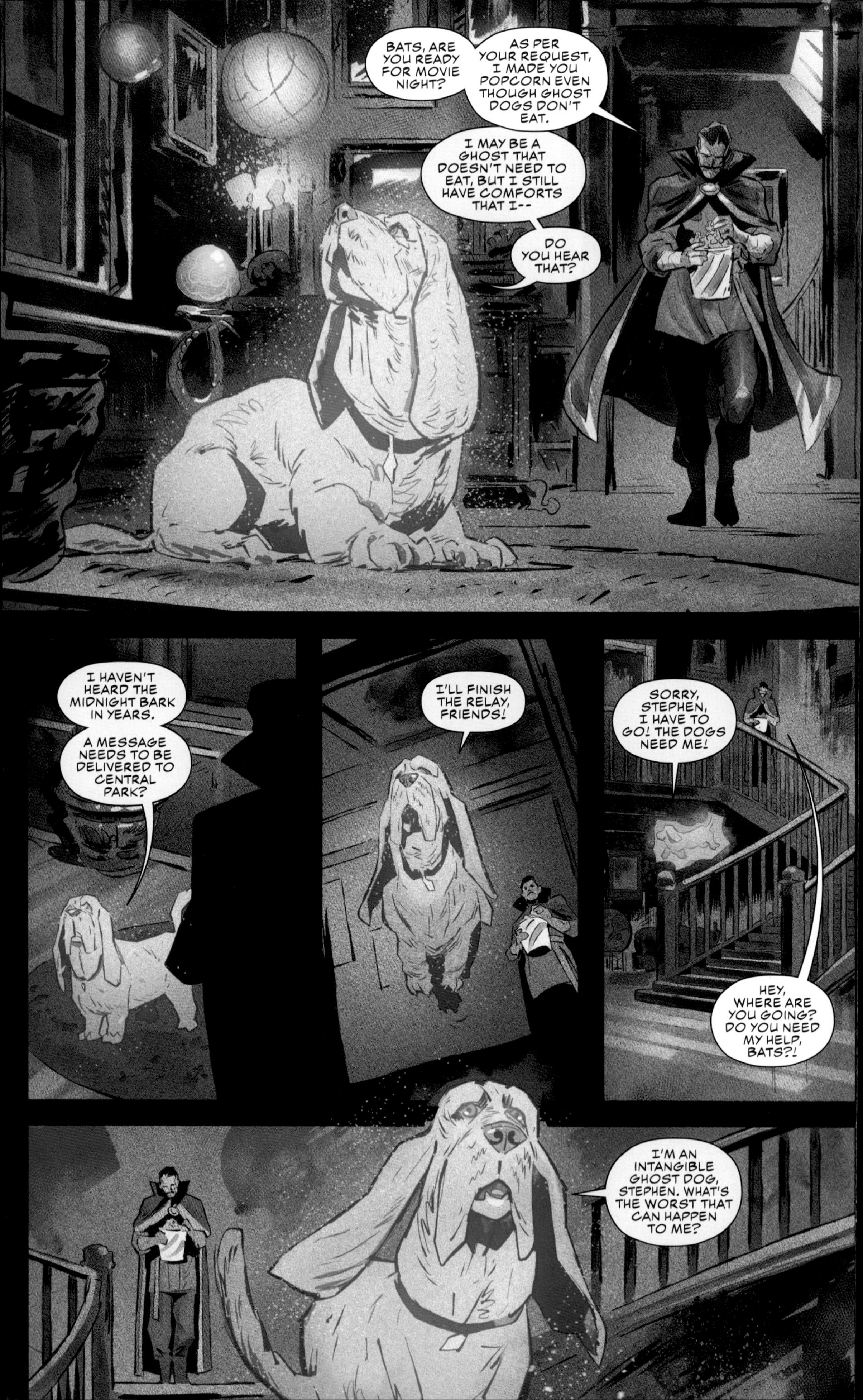

BATS, ARE YOU READY FOR MOVIE NIGHT?
AS PER YOUR REQUEST, I MADE YOU POPCORN EVEN THOUGH GHOST DOGS DON'T EAT.
I MAY BE A GHOST THAT DOESN'T NEED TO EAT, BUT I STILL HAVE COMFORTS THAT I--
DO YOU HEAR THAT?
I HAVEN'T HEARD THE MIDNIGHT BARK IN YEARS.
A MESSAGE NEEDS TO BE DELIVERED TO CENTRAL PARK?
I'LL FINISH THE RELAY, FRIENDS!
SORRY, STEPHEN, I HAVE TO GO! THE DOGS NEED ME!
HEY, WHERE ARE YOU GOING? DO YOU NEED MY HELP, BATS?!
I'M AN INTANGIBLE GHOST DOG, STEPHEN. WHAT'S THE WORST THAT CAN HAPPEN TO ME?

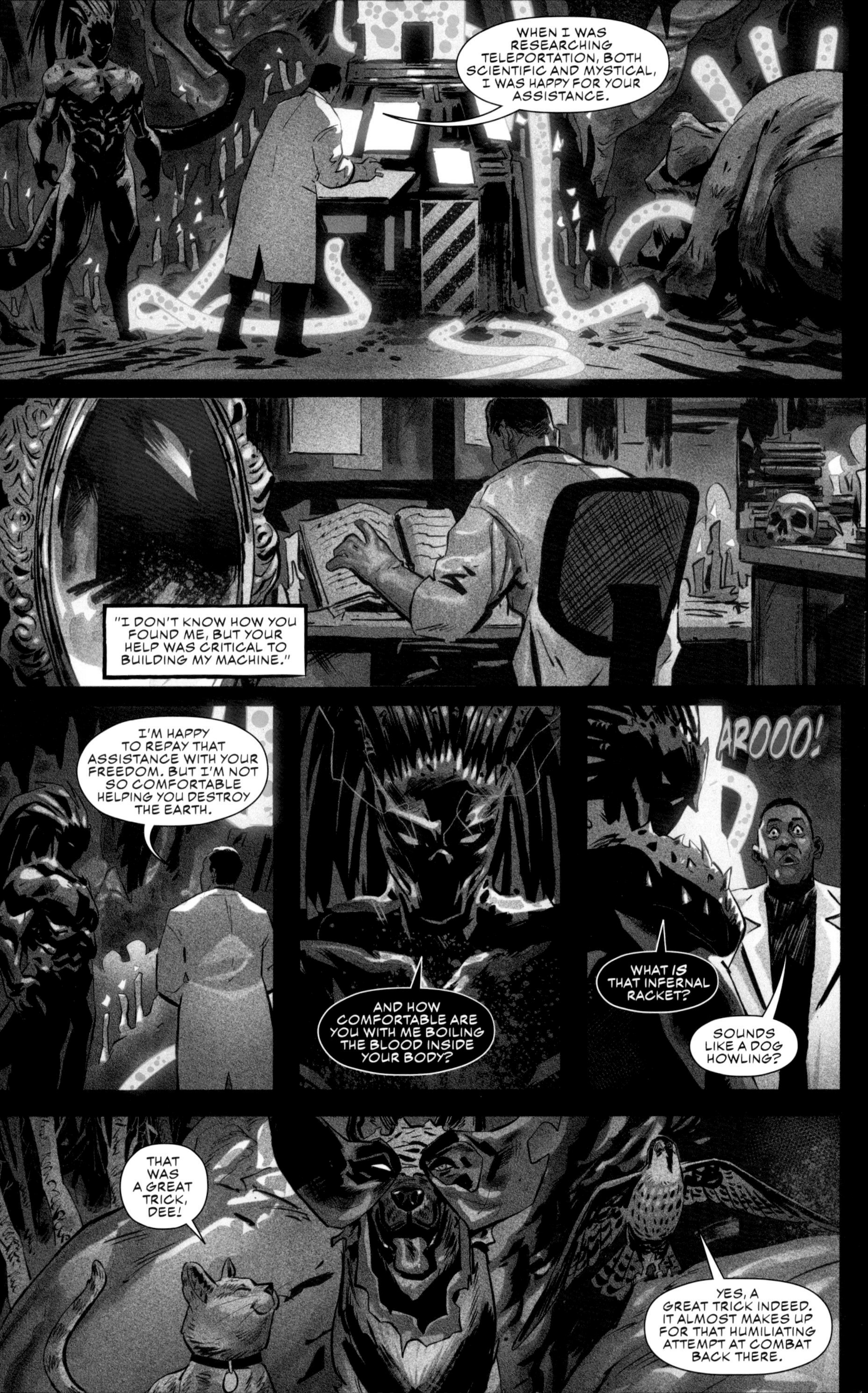
WHEN I WAS RESEARCHING TELEPORTATION, BOTH SCIENTIFIC AND MYSTICAL, I WAS HAPPY FOR YOUR ASSISTANCE.
"I DON'T KNOW HOW YOU FOUND ME, BUT YOUR HELP WAS CRITICAL TO BUILDING MY MACHINE."
I'M HAPPY TO REPAY THAT ASSISTANCE WITH YOUR FREEDOM. BUT I'M NOT SO COMFORTABLE HELPING YOU DESTROY THE EARTH.
AND HOW COMFORTABLE ARE YOU WITH ME BOILING THE BLOOD INSIDE YOUR BODY?
AROOO!
WHAT *IS* THAT INFERNAL RACKET?
SOUNDS LIKE A DOG HOWLING?
THAT WAS A GREAT TRICK, DEE!
YES, A GREAT TRICK INDEED. IT ALMOST MAKES UP FOR THAT HUMILIATING ATTEMPT AT COMBAT BACK THERE.

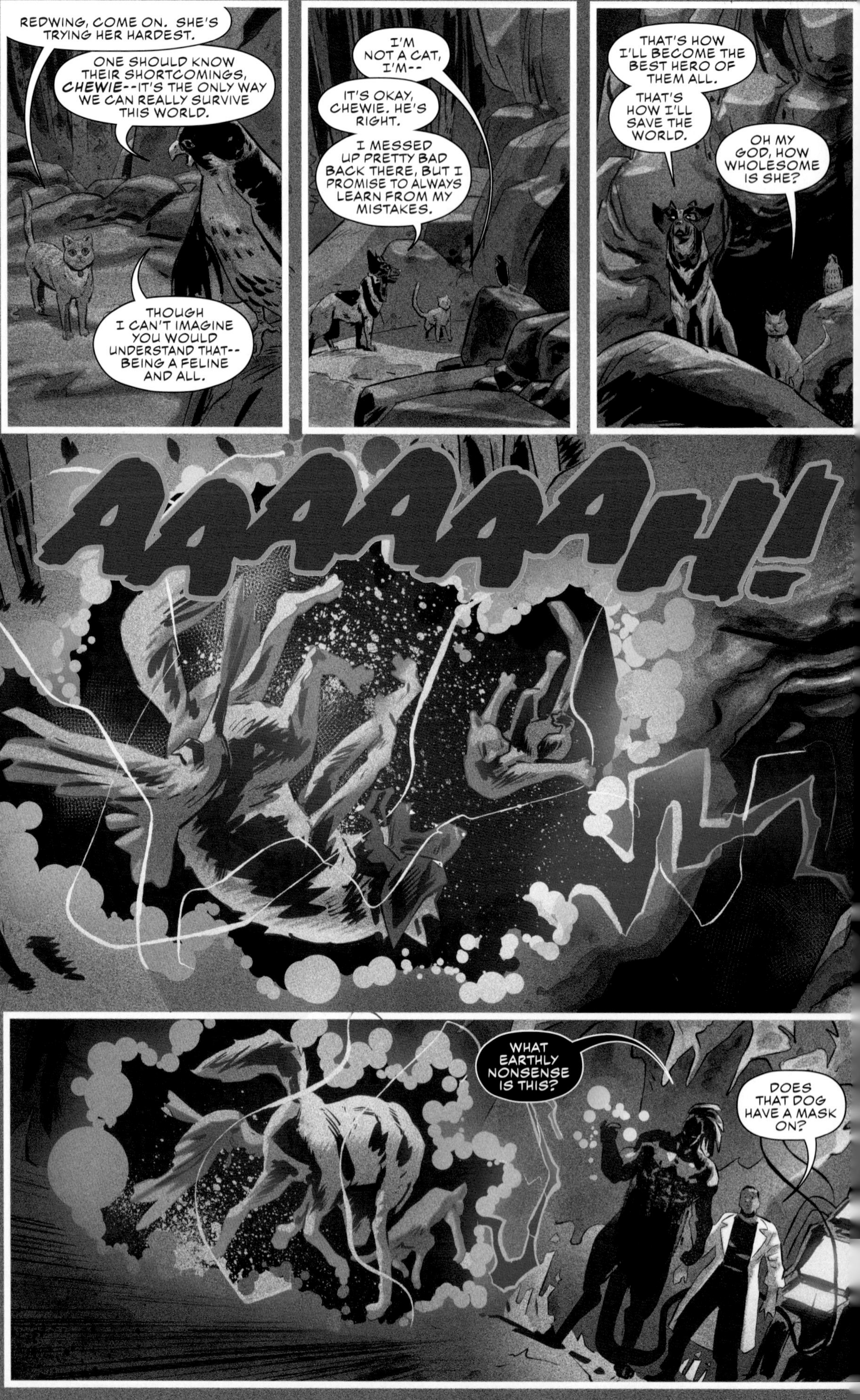
REDWING, COME ON. SHE'S TRYING HER HARDEST.
ONE SHOULD KNOW THEIR SHORTCOMINGS, CHEWIE--IT'S THE ONLY WAY WE CAN REALLY SURVIVE THIS WORLD.
THOUGH I CAN'T IMAGINE YOU WOULD UNDERSTAND THAT--BEING A FELINE AND ALL.
I'M NOT A CAT, I'M--
IT'S OKAY, CHEWIE. HE'S RIGHT.
I MESSED UP PRETTY BAD BACK THERE, BUT I PROMISE TO ALWAYS LEARN FROM MY MISTAKES.
THAT'S HOW I'LL BECOME THE BEST HERO OF THEM ALL.
THAT'S HOW I'LL SAVE THE WORLD.
OH MY GOD, HOW WHOLESOME IS SHE?
AAAAAAH!
WHAT EARTHLY NONSENSE IS THIS?
DOES THAT DOG HAVE A MASK ON?

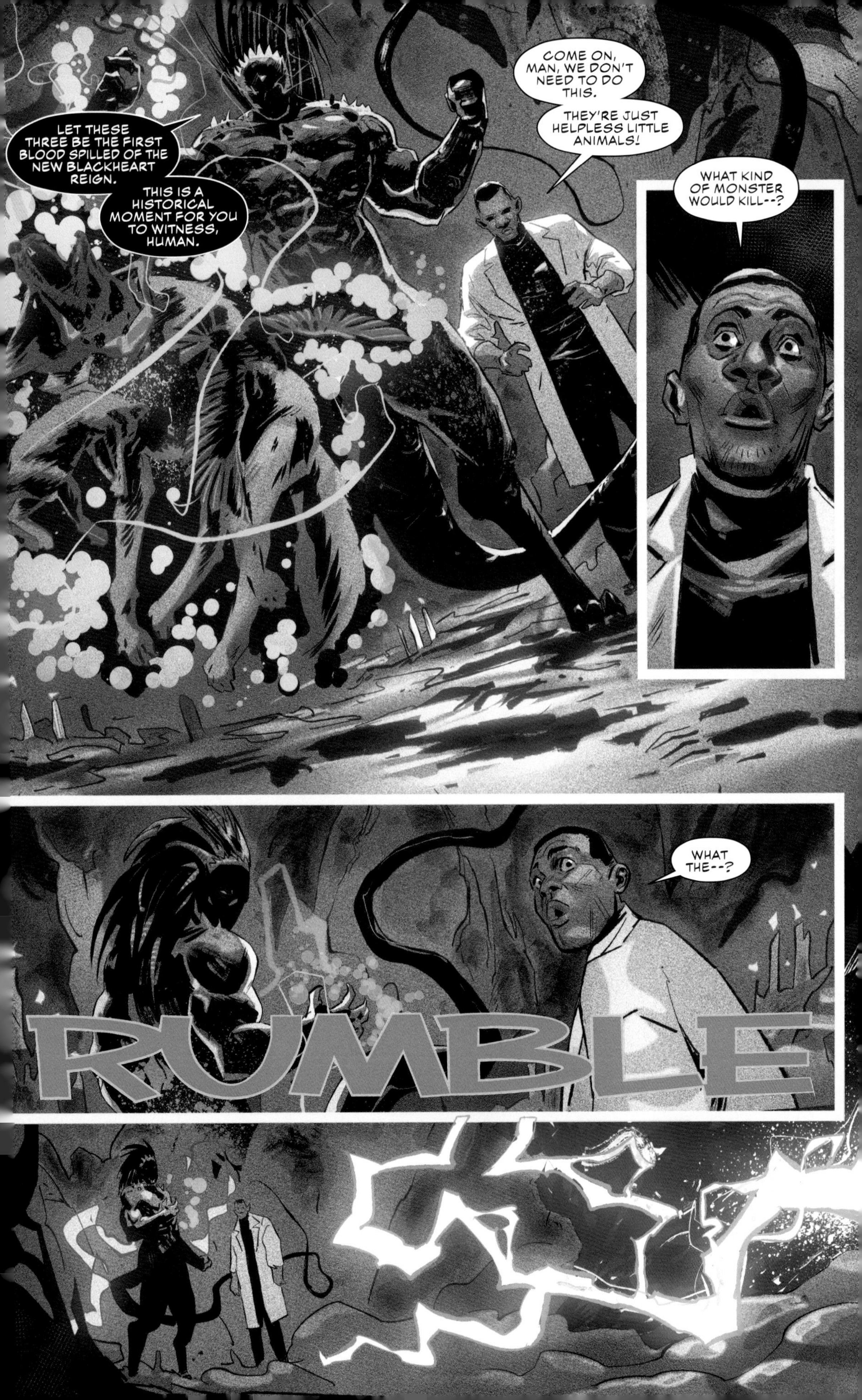
LET THESE THREE BE THE FIRST BLOOD SPILLED OF THE NEW BLACKHEART REIGN.
THIS IS A HISTORICAL MOMENT FOR YOU TO WITNESS, HUMAN.
COME ON, MAN, WE DON'T NEED TO DO THIS.
THEY'RE JUST HELPLESS LITTLE ANIMALS!
WHAT KIND OF MONSTER WOULD KILL--?
WHAT THE--?
RUMBLE

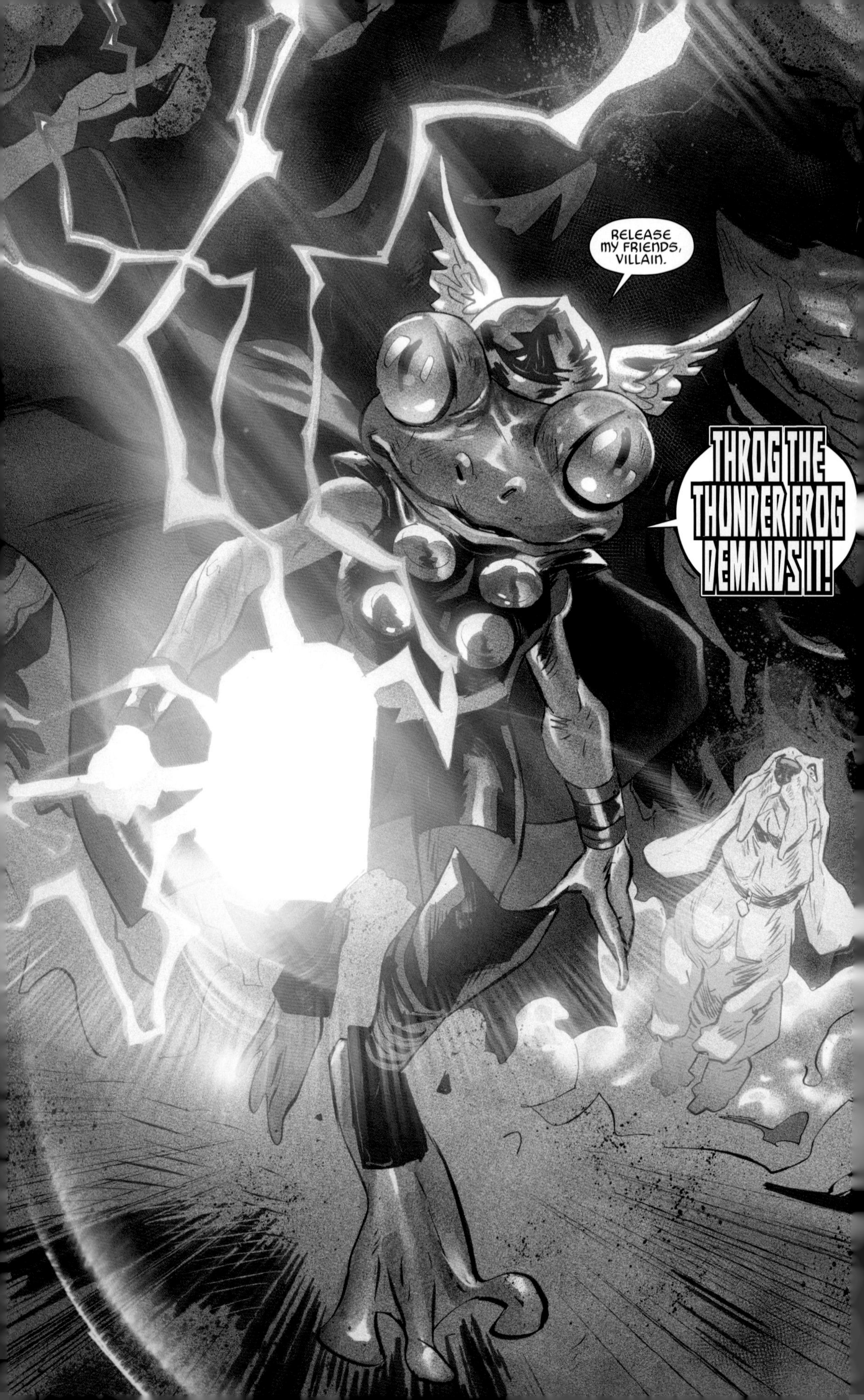
RELEASE MY FRIENDS, VILLAIN.
THROG THE THUNDER FROG DEMANDS IT!

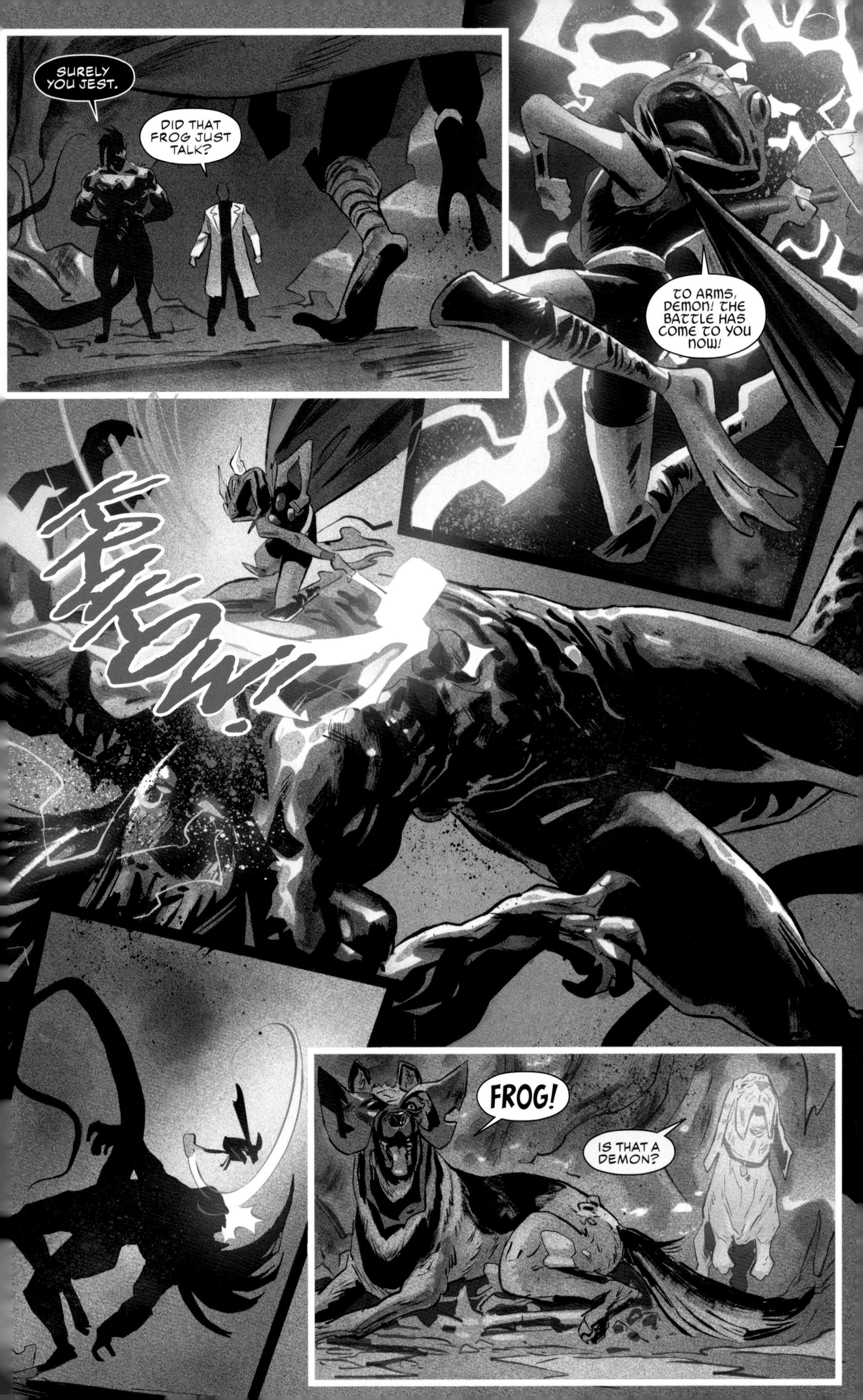
SURELY YOU JEST.
DID THAT FROG JUST TALK?
TO ARMS, DEMON! THE BATTLE HAS COME TO YOU NOW!
KRAKOW!
FROG!
IS THAT A DEMON?

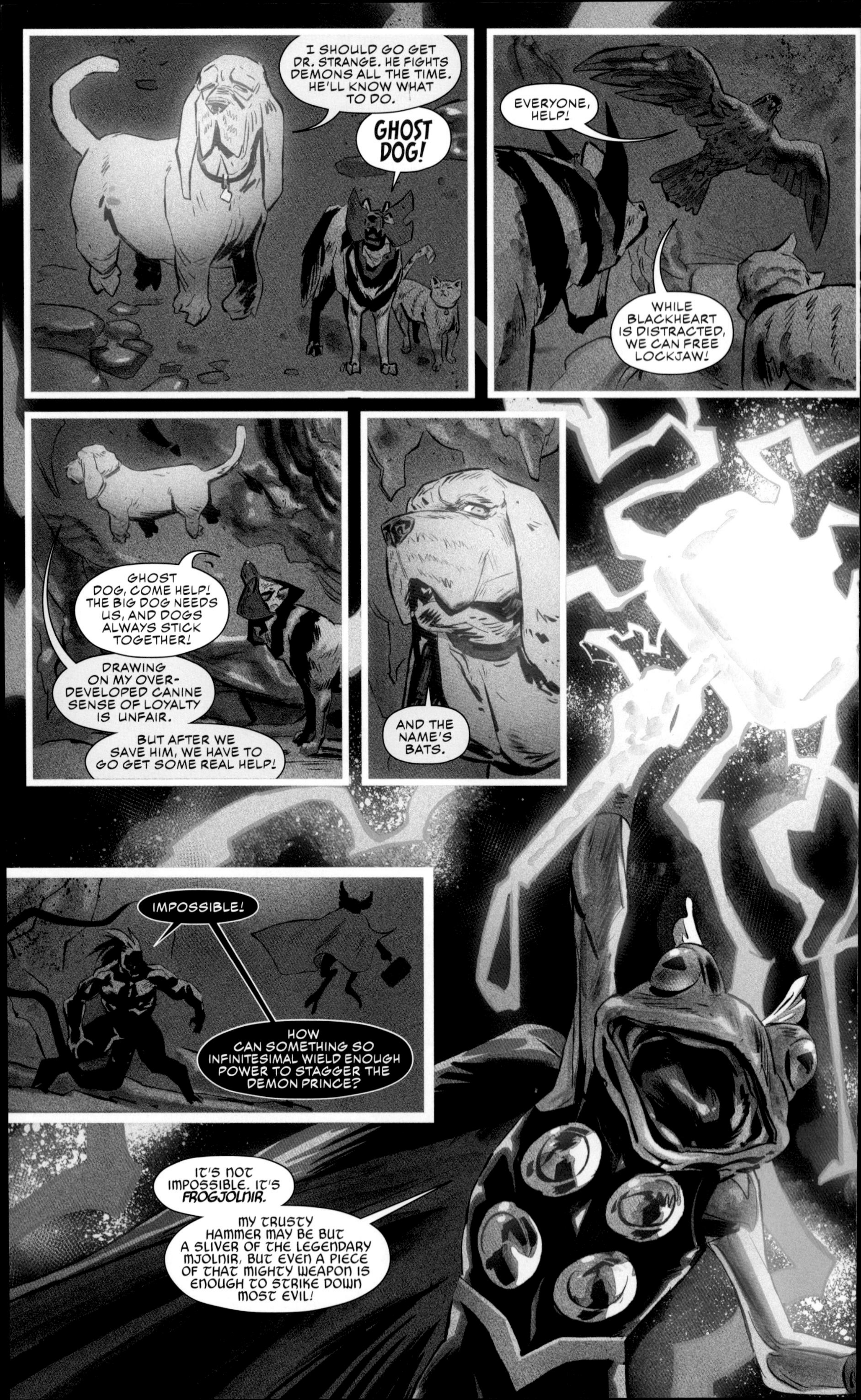

I SHOULD GO GET DR. STRANGE. HE FIGHTS DEMONS ALL THE TIME. HE'LL KNOW WHAT TO DO.
GHOST DOG!
EVERYONE, HELP!
WHILE BLACKHEART IS DISTRACTED, WE CAN FREE LOCKJAW!
GHOST DOG, COME HELP! THE BIG DOG NEEDS US, AND DOGS ALWAYS STICK TOGETHER!
DRAWING ON MY OVER-DEVELOPED CANINE SENSE OF LOYALTY IS UNFAIR.
BUT AFTER WE SAVE HIM, WE HAVE TO GO GET SOME REAL HELP!
AND THE NAME'S BATS.
IMPOSSIBLE!
HOW CAN SOMETHING SO INFINITESIMAL WIELD ENOUGH POWER TO STAGGER THE DEMON PRINCE?
IT'S NOT IMPOSSIBLE. IT'S FROGJOLNIR.
MY TRUSTY HAMMER MAY BE BUT A SLIVER OF THE LEGENDARY MJOLNIR, BUT EVEN A PIECE OF THAT MIGHTY WEAPON IS ENOUGH TO STRIKE DOWN MOST EVIL!

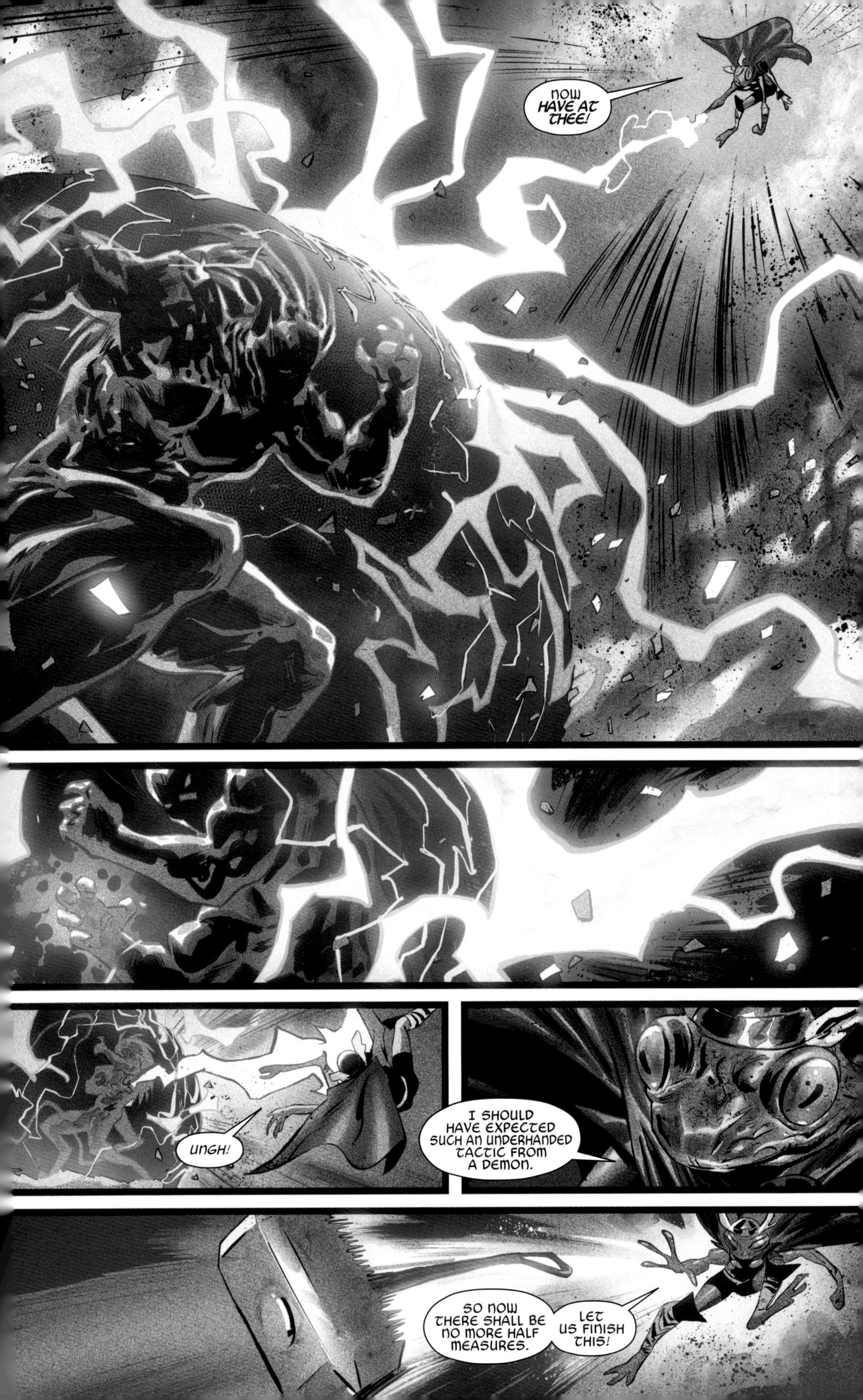
NOW HAVE AT THEE!
UNGH!
I SHOULD HAVE EXPECTED SUCH AN UNDERHANDED TACTIC FROM A DEMON.
SO NOW THERE SHALL BE NO MORE HALF MEASURES.
LET US FINISH THIS!

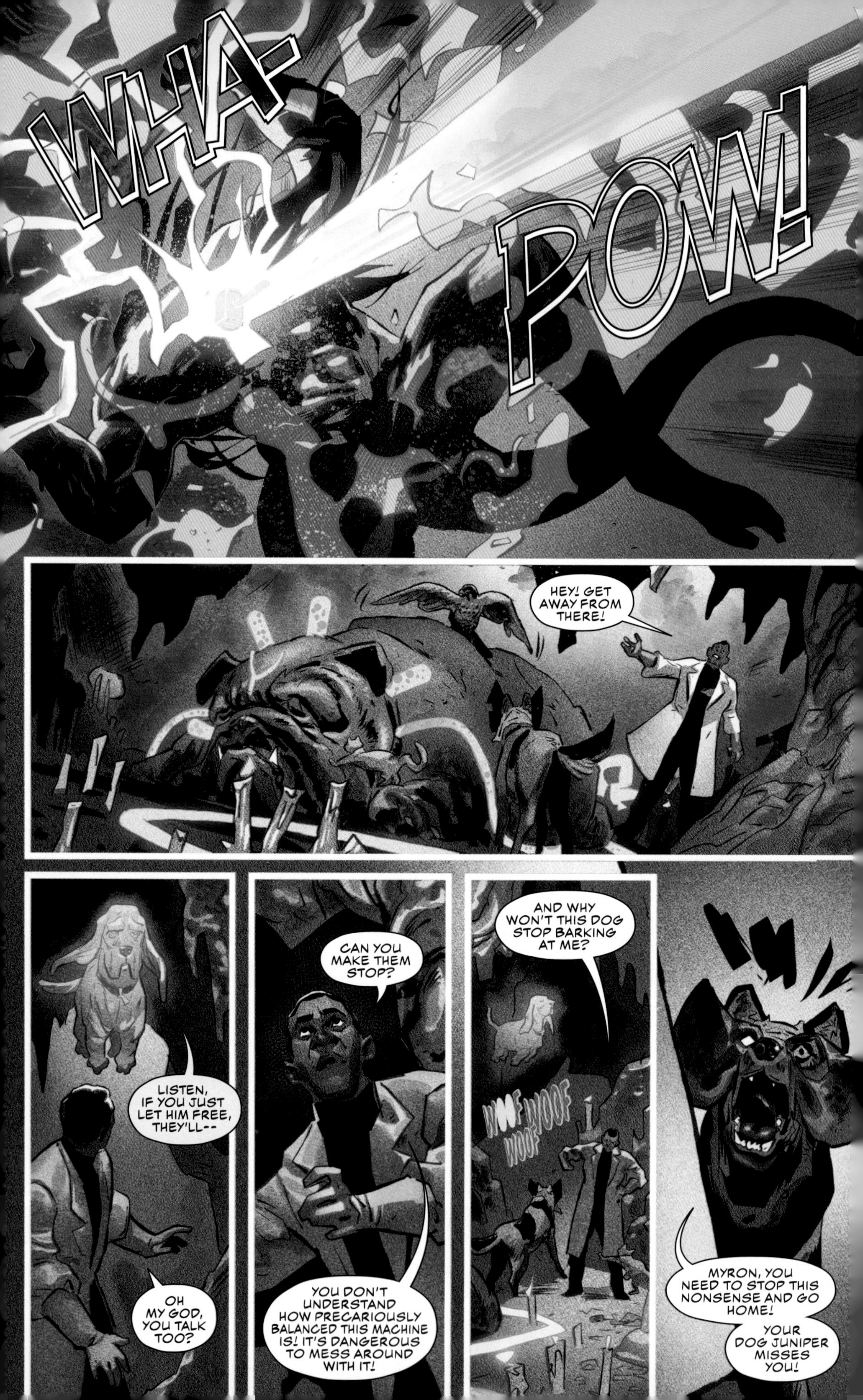
WHA-
POW!
HEY! GET AWAY FROM THERE!
LISTEN, IF YOU JUST LET HIM FREE, THEY'LL--
OH MY GOD, YOU TALK TOO?
CAN YOU MAKE THEM STOP?
YOU DON'T UNDERSTAND HOW PRECARIOUSLY BALANCED THIS MACHINE IS! IT'S DANGEROUS TO MESS AROUND WITH IT!
AND WHY WON'T THIS DOG STOP BARKING AT ME?
WOOF WOOF
WOOF
MYRON, YOU NEED TO STOP THIS NONSENSE AND GO HOME!
YOUR DOG JUNIPER MISSES YOU!

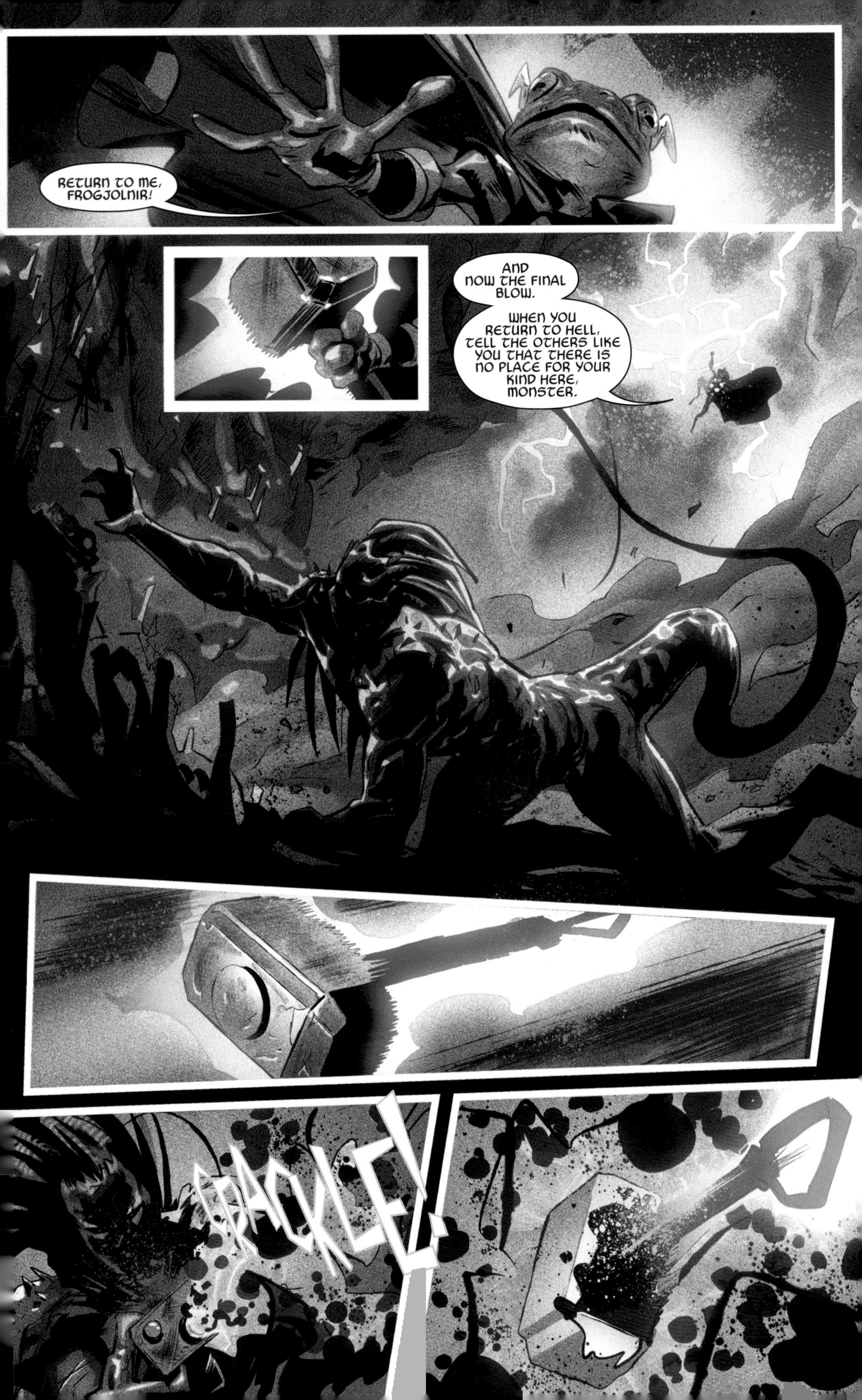
RETURN TO ME, FROGJOLNIR!
AND NOW THE FINAL BLOW.
WHEN YOU RETURN TO HELL, TELL THE OTHERS LIKE YOU THAT THERE IS NO PLACE FOR YOUR KIND HERE, MONSTER.
CRACKLE!

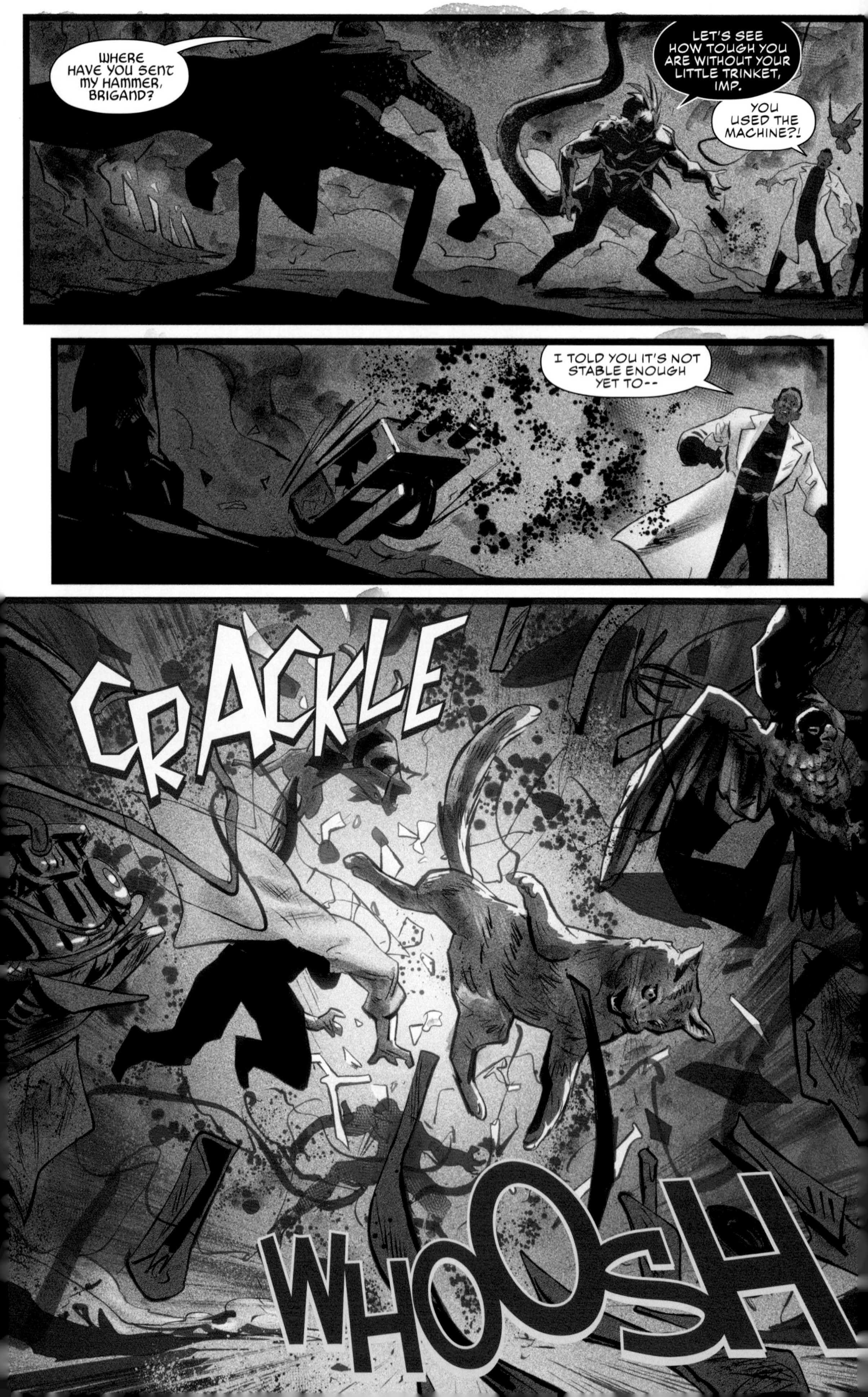
WHERE HAVE YOU SENT MY HAMMER, BRIGAND?
LET'S SEE HOW TOUGH YOU ARE WITHOUT YOUR LITTLE TRINKET, IMP.
YOU USED THE MACHINE?!
I TOLD YOU IT'S NOT STABLE ENOUGH YET TO--
CRACKLE
WHOOSH

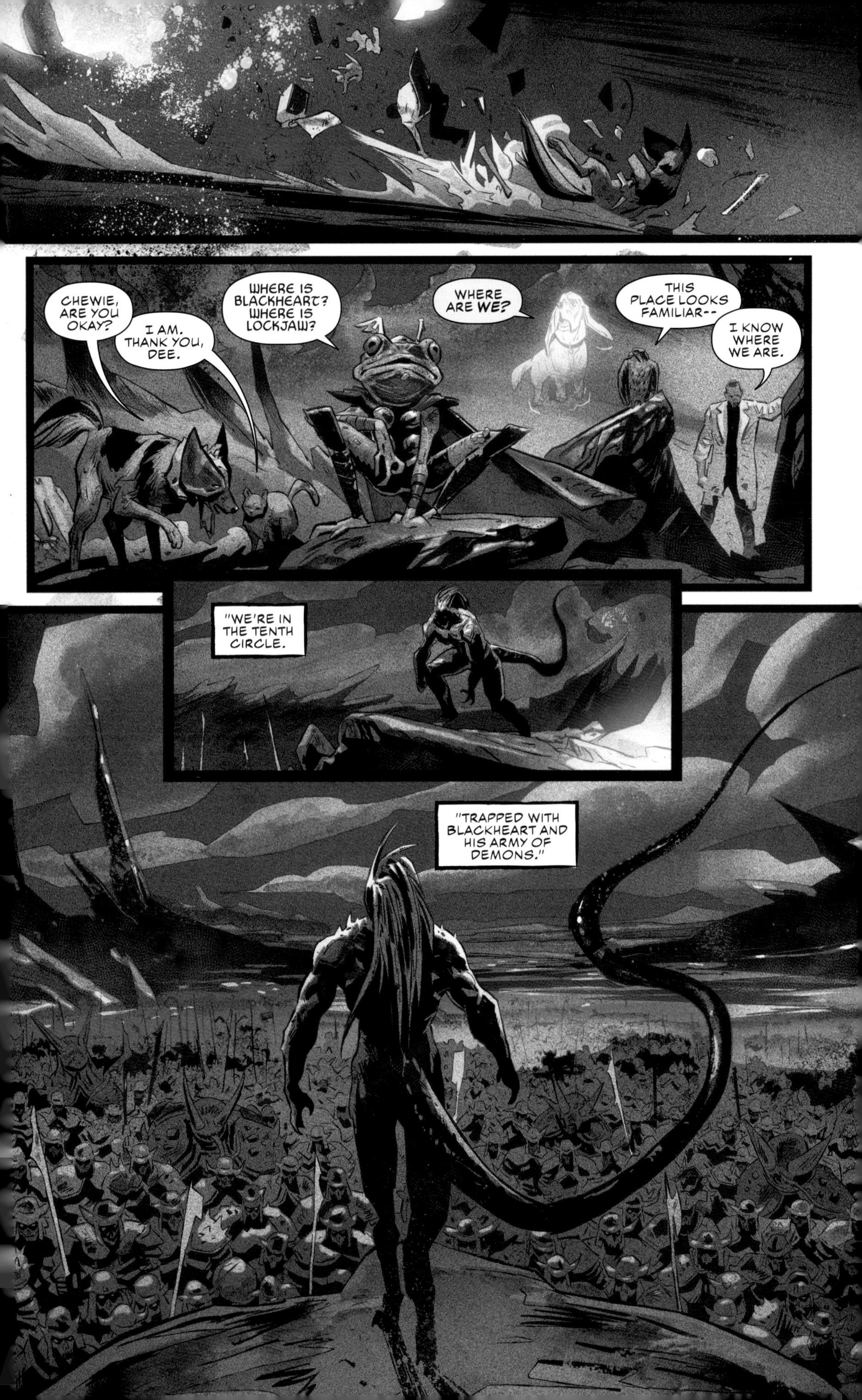
CHEWIE, ARE YOU OKAY?
I AM. THANK YOU, DEE.
WHERE IS BLACKHEART? WHERE IS LOCKJAW?
WHERE ARE WE?
THIS PLACE LOOKS FAMILIAR--
I KNOW WHERE WE ARE.
"WE'RE IN THE TENTH CIRCLE.
"TRAPPED WITH BLACKHEART AND HIS ARMY OF DEMONS."

THREE

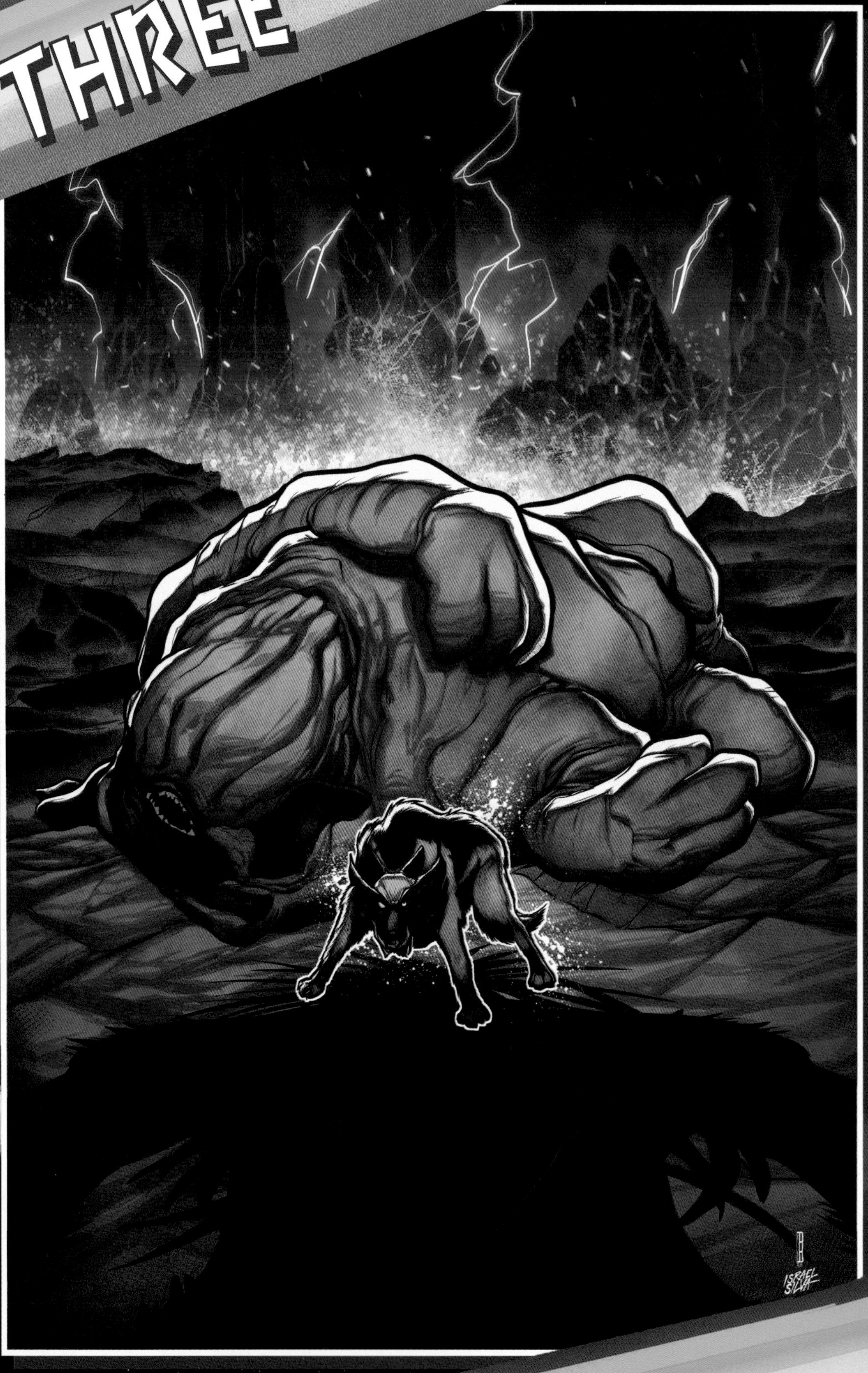

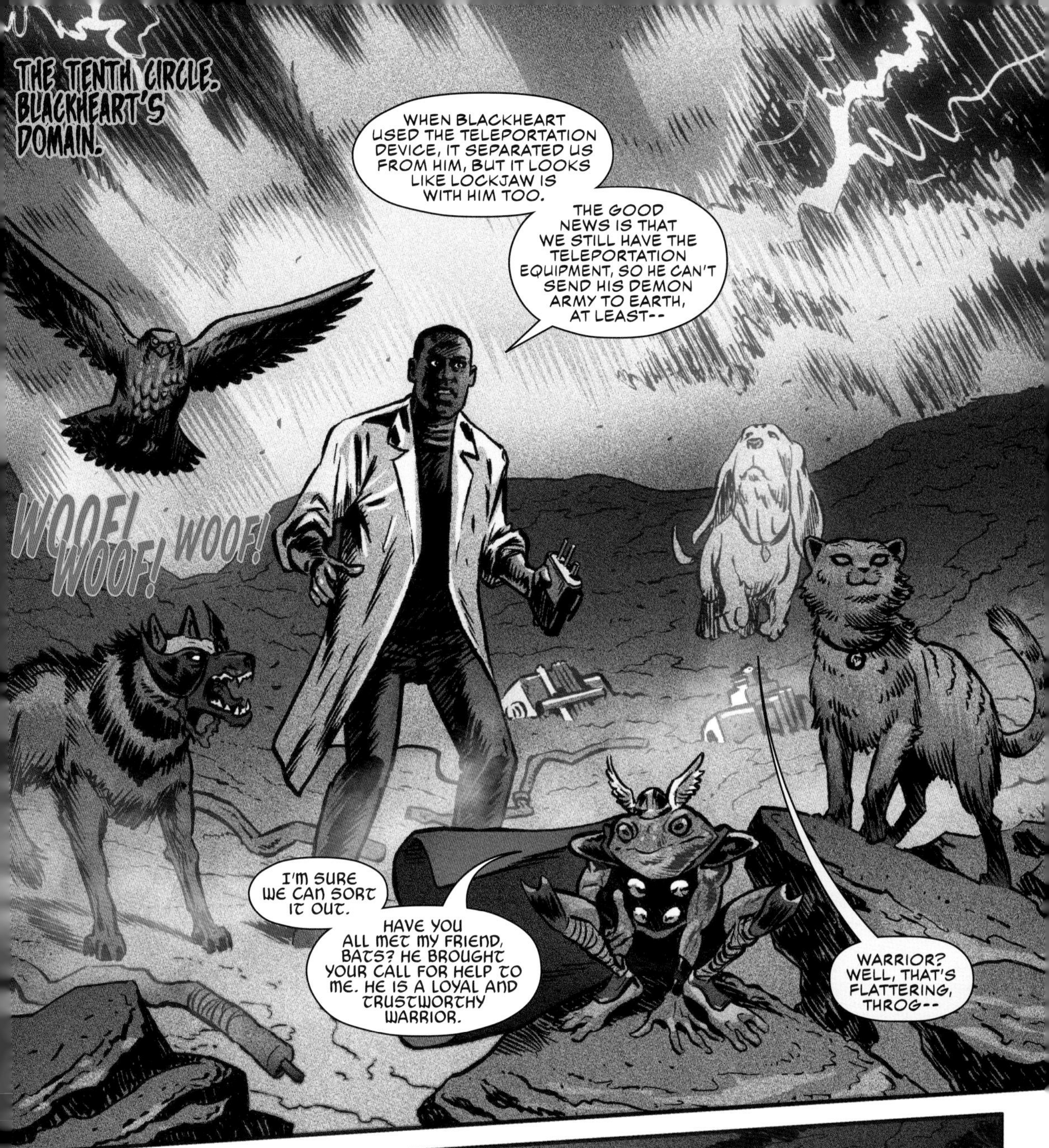
THE TENTH CIRCLE. BLACKHEART'S DOMAIN.
WHEN BLACKHEART USED THE TELEPORTATION DEVICE, IT SEPARATED US FROM HIM, BUT IT LOOKS LIKE LOCKJAW IS WITH HIM TOO.
THE GOOD NEWS IS THAT WE STILL HAVE THE TELEPORTATION EQUIPMENT, SO HE CAN'T SEND HIS DEMON ARMY TO EARTH, AT LEAST--
WOOF! WOOF! WOOF!
I'M SURE WE CAN SORT IT OUT.
HAVE YOU ALL MET MY FRIEND, BATS? HE BROUGHT YOUR CALL FOR HELP TO ME. HE IS A LOYAL AND TRUSTWORTHY WARRIOR.
WARRIOR? WELL, THAT'S FLATTERING, THROG--

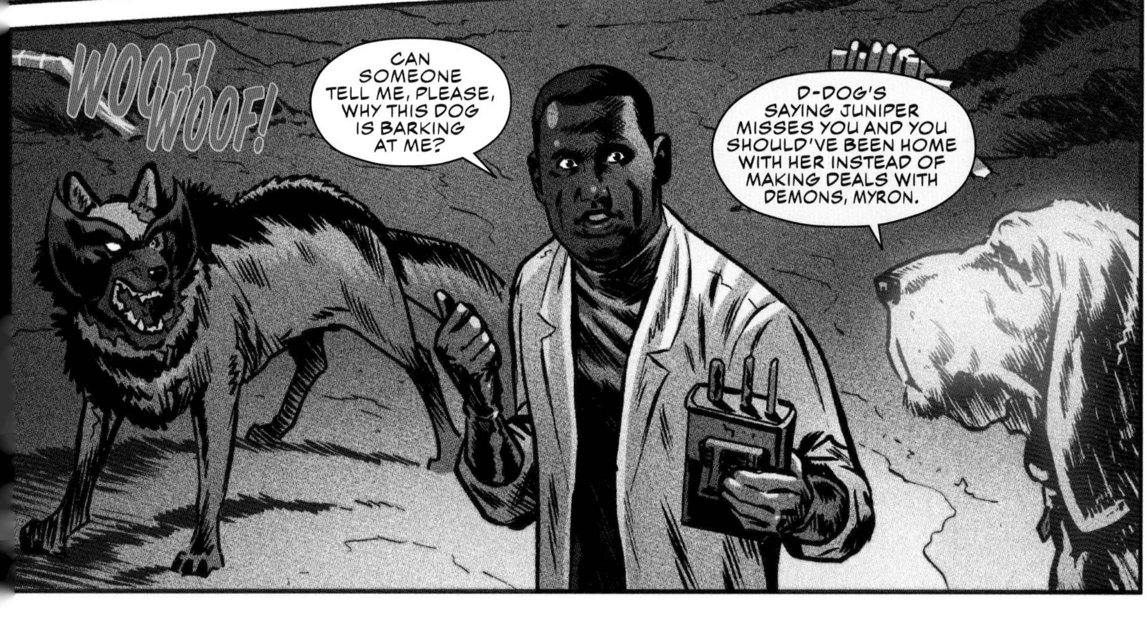
WOOF! WOOF!
CAN SOMEONE TELL ME, PLEASE, WHY THIS DOG IS BARKING AT ME?
D-DOG'S SAYING JUNIPER MISSES YOU AND YOU SHOULD'VE BEEN HOME WITH HER INSTEAD OF MAKING DEALS WITH DEMONS, MYRON.

OH MY GOD, I LEFT JUNIPER ALL ALONE.

I'M THE **WORST** PET OWNER.

OWNER?

GRR

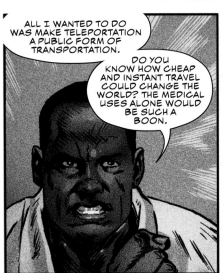

ALL I WANTED TO DO WAS MAKE TELEPORTATION A PUBLIC FORM OF TRANSPORTATION.

DO YOU KNOW HOW CHEAP AND INSTANT TRAVEL COULD CHANGE THE WORLD? THE MEDICAL USES ALONE WOULD BE SUCH A BOON.

"I KNEW THE FOLKS AT A.I.M. WEREN'T NECESSARILY GOOD PEOPLE, BUT I JOINED UP TO GET ACCESS TO THEIR RESOURCES AND LABS.

"I WASN'T MAKING THE PROGRESS I WOULD'VE LIKED, SO I ASKED MYSELF: WHAT WOULD VICTOR VON DOOM DO?

"HE'S BEEN KNOWN TO DALLY IN THE MYSTIC ELEMENTS, AND I SURMISED MY SOLUTION WOULDN'T BE SOLELY SCIENTIFIC IN NATURE.

"BUT NEXT THING YOU KNOW, I'M BEING CONTACTED BY THIS **PRESENCE** AND IT HELPED ME WITH MY RESEARCH.

"IT HELPED A LOT.

"I DIDN'T REALIZE WHAT I WAS GETTING TIED UP IN! I DIDN'T KNOW IT WAS **BLACKHEART** TRYING TO **DESTROY** THE EARTH!"

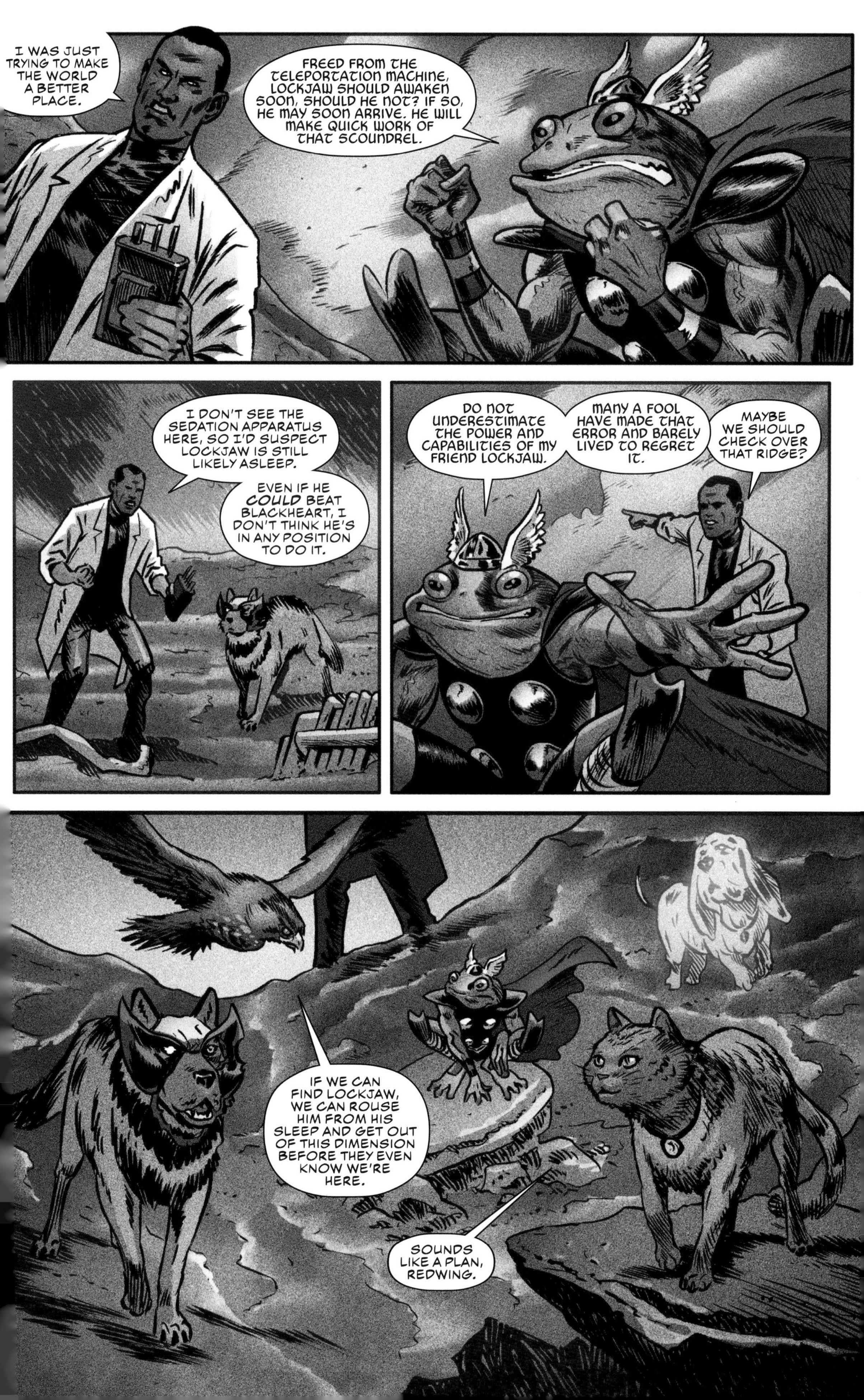
I WAS JUST TRYING TO MAKE THE WORLD A BETTER PLACE.
FREED FROM THE TELEPORTATION MACHINE, LOCKJAW SHOULD AWAKEN SOON, SHOULD HE NOT? IF SO, HE MAY SOON ARRIVE. HE WILL MAKE QUICK WORK OF THAT SCOUNDREL.
I DON'T SEE THE SEDATION APPARATUS HERE, SO I'D SUSPECT LOCKJAW IS STILL LIKELY ASLEEP.
EVEN IF HE COULD BEAT BLACKHEART, I DON'T THINK HE'S IN ANY POSITION TO DO IT.
DO NOT UNDERESTIMATE THE POWER AND CAPABILITIES OF MY FRIEND LOCKJAW.
MANY A FOOL HAVE MADE THAT ERROR AND BARELY LIVED TO REGRET IT.
MAYBE WE SHOULD CHECK OVER THAT RIDGE?
IF WE CAN FIND LOCKJAW, WE CAN ROUSE HIM FROM HIS SLEEP AND GET OUT OF THIS DIMENSION BEFORE THEY EVEN KNOW WE'RE HERE.
SOUNDS LIKE A PLAN, REDWING.

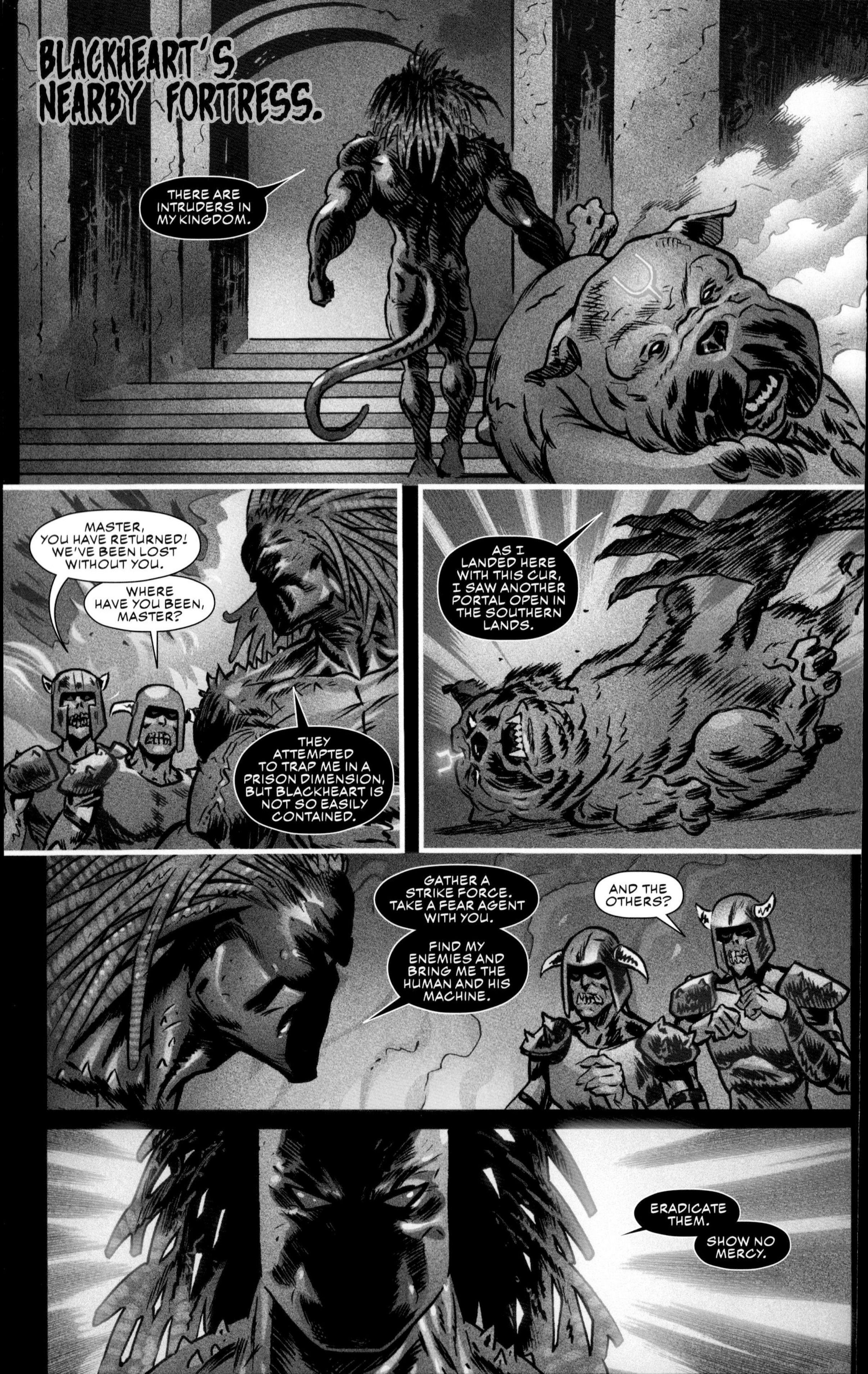
BLACKHEART'S NEARBY FORTRESS.
THERE ARE INTRUDERS IN MY KINGDOM.
MASTER, YOU HAVE RETURNED! WE'VE BEEN LOST WITHOUT YOU.
WHERE HAVE YOU BEEN, MASTER?
THEY ATTEMPTED TO TRAP ME IN A PRISON DIMENSION, BUT BLACKHEART IS NOT SO EASILY CONTAINED.
AS I LANDED HERE WITH THIS CUR, I SAW ANOTHER PORTAL OPEN IN THE SOUTHERN LANDS.
GATHER A STRIKE FORCE. TAKE A FEAR AGENT WITH YOU.
FIND MY ENEMIES AND BRING ME THE HUMAN AND HIS MACHINE.
AND THE OTHERS?
ERADICATE THEM.
SHOW NO MERCY.

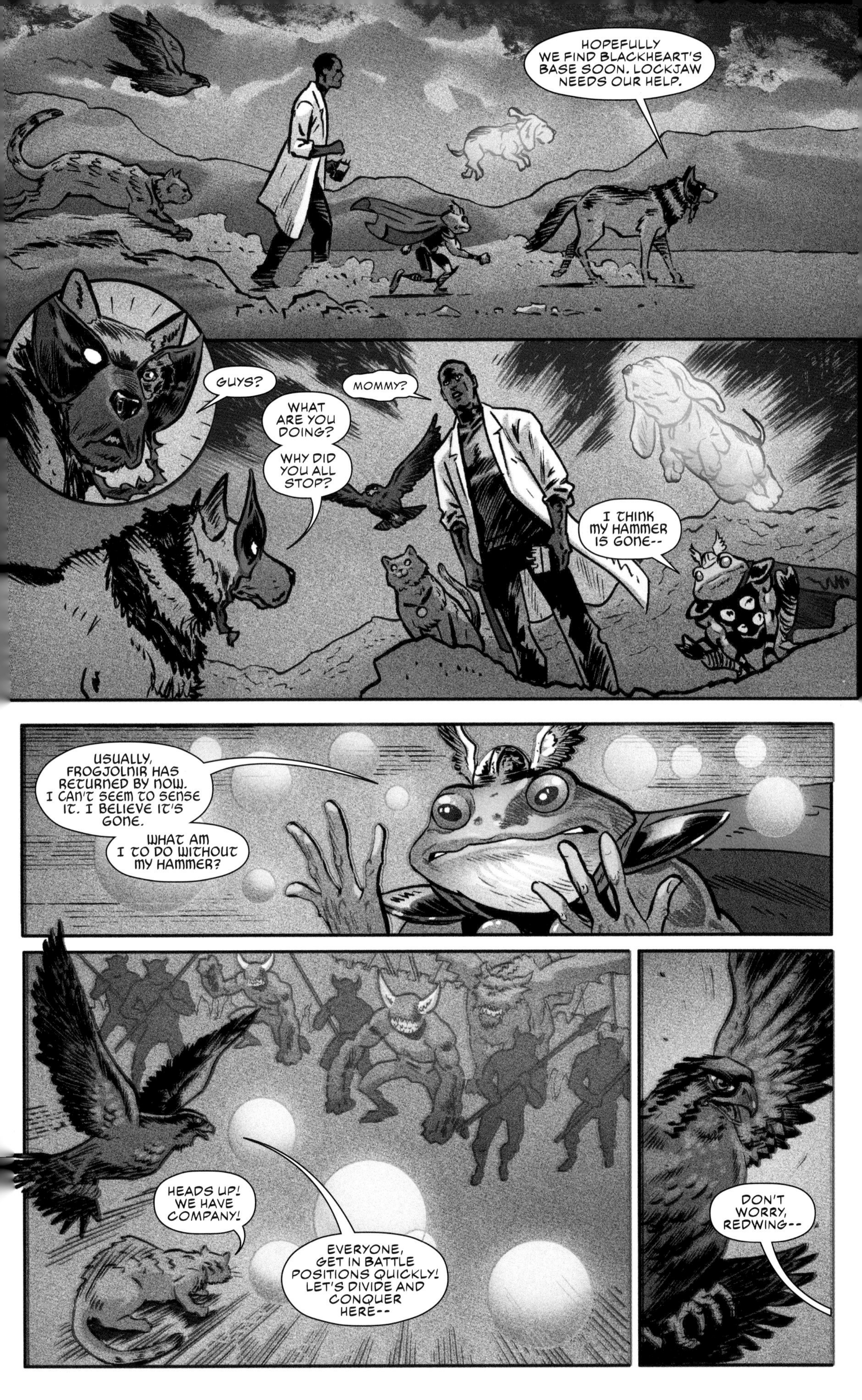
HOPEFULLY WE FIND BLACKHEART'S BASE SOON. LOCKJAW NEEDS OUR HELP.
GUYS?
WHAT ARE YOU DOING?
WHY DID YOU ALL STOP?
MOMMY?
I THINK MY HAMMER IS GONE--
USUALLY, FROGJOLNIR HAS RETURNED BY NOW. I CAN'T SEEM TO SENSE IT. I BELIEVE IT'S GONE.
WHAT AM I TO DO WITHOUT MY HAMMER?
HEADS UP! WE HAVE COMPANY!
EVERYONE, GET IN BATTLE POSITIONS QUICKLY! LET'S DIVIDE AND CONQUER HERE--
DON'T WORRY, REDWING--

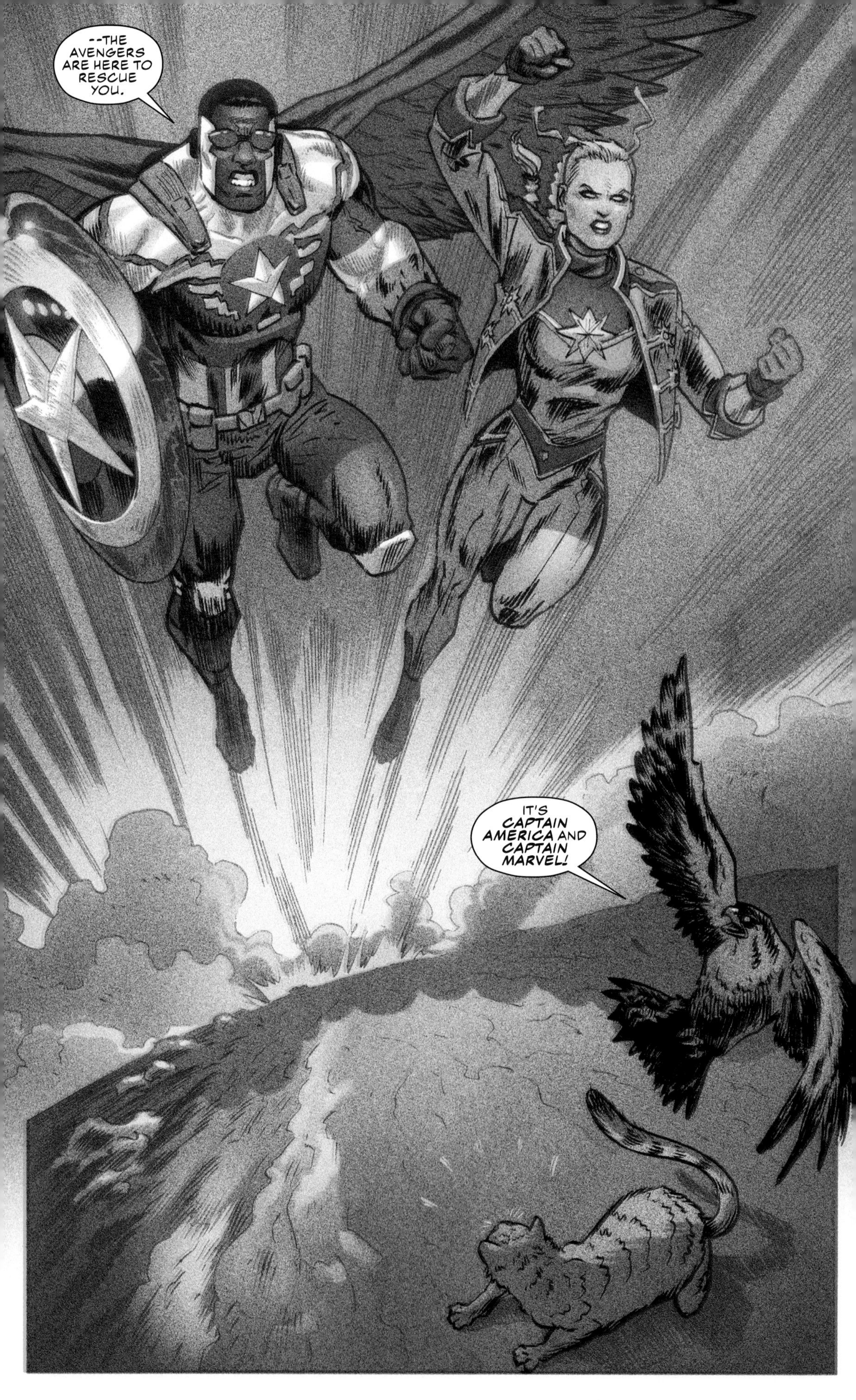
--THE AVENGERS ARE HERE TO RESCUE YOU.
IT'S CAPTAIN AMERICA AND CAPTAIN MARVEL!

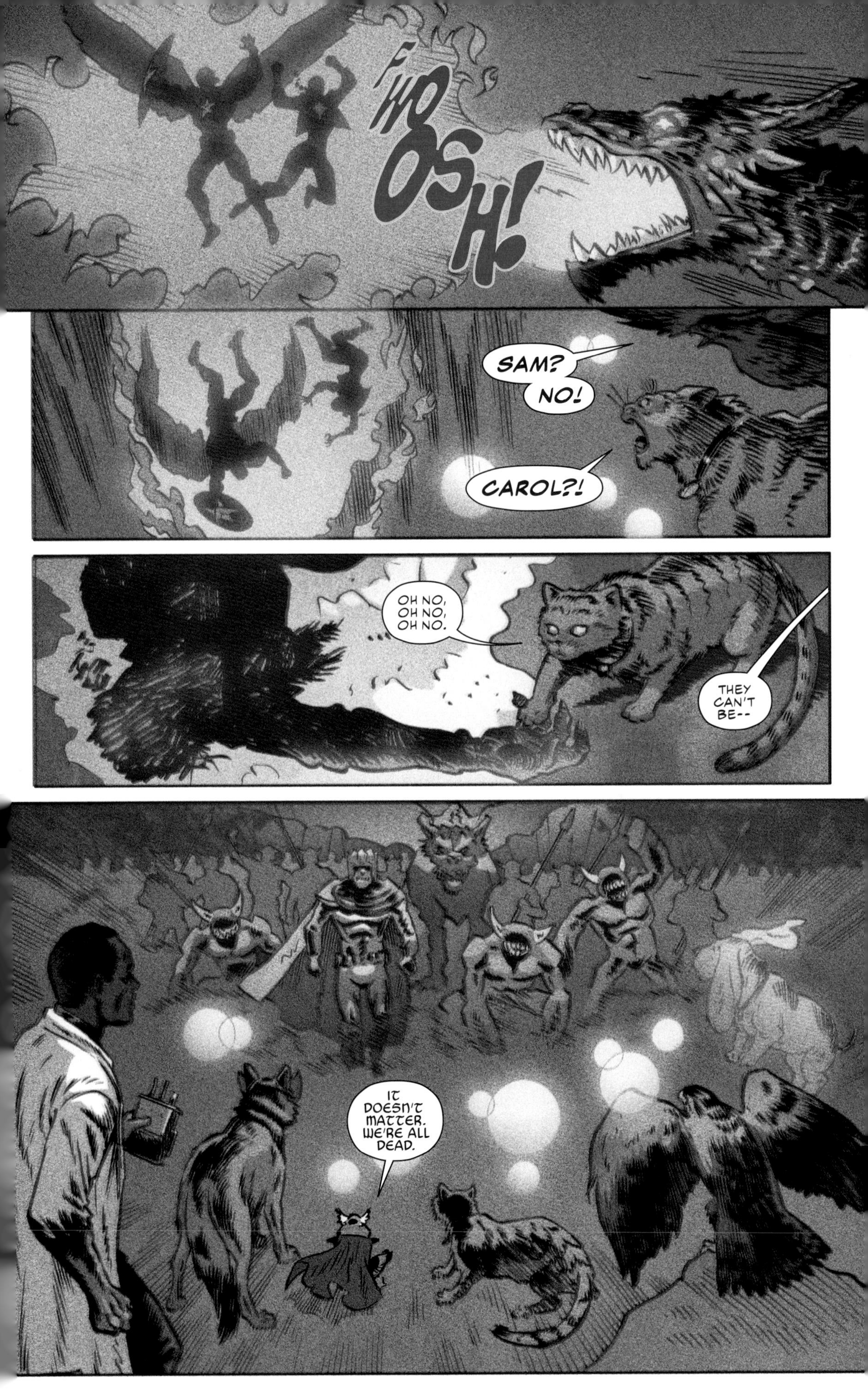
FWOOSH!
SAM?
NO!
CAROL?!
OH NO, OH NO, OH NO.
THEY CAN'T BE--
IT DOESN'T MATTER. WE'RE ALL DEAD.

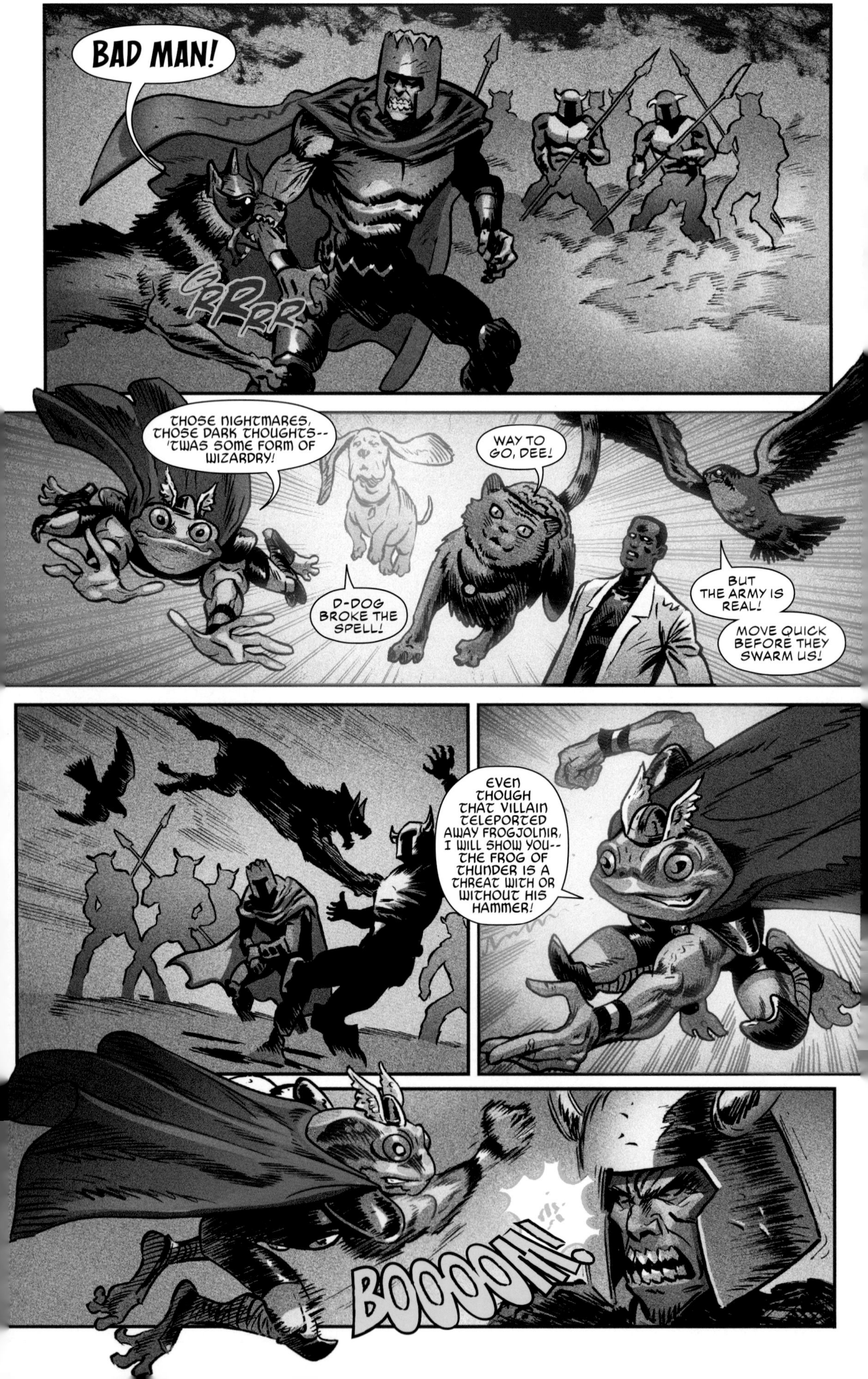
BAD MAN!
GRRRRR
THOSE NIGHTMARES, THOSE DARK THOUGHTS-- 'TWAS SOME FORM OF WIZARDRY!
D-DOG BROKE THE SPELL!
WAY TO GO, DEE!
BUT THE ARMY IS REAL!
MOVE QUICK BEFORE THEY SWARM US!
EVEN THOUGH THAT VILLAIN TELEPORTED AWAY FROGJOLNIR, I WILL SHOW YOU-- THE FROG OF THUNDER IS A THREAT WITH OR WITHOUT HIS HAMMER!
BOOOOM!!

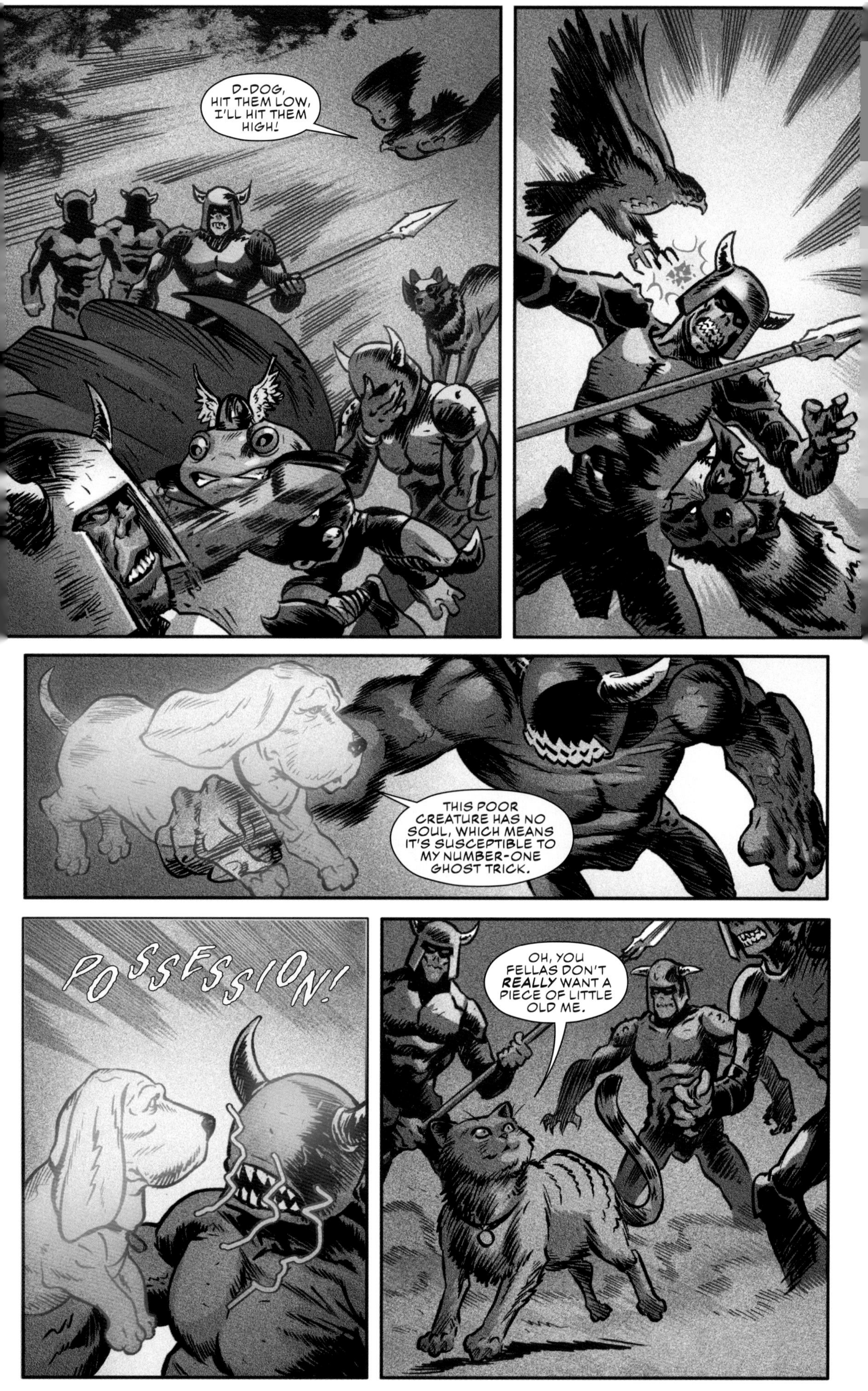
D-DOG, HIT THEM LOW, I'LL HIT THEM HIGH!
THIS POOR CREATURE HAS NO SOUL, WHICH MEANS IT'S SUSCEPTIBLE TO MY NUMBER-ONE GHOST TRICK.
POSSESSION!
OH, YOU FELLAS DON'T REALLY WANT A PIECE OF LITTLE OLD ME.

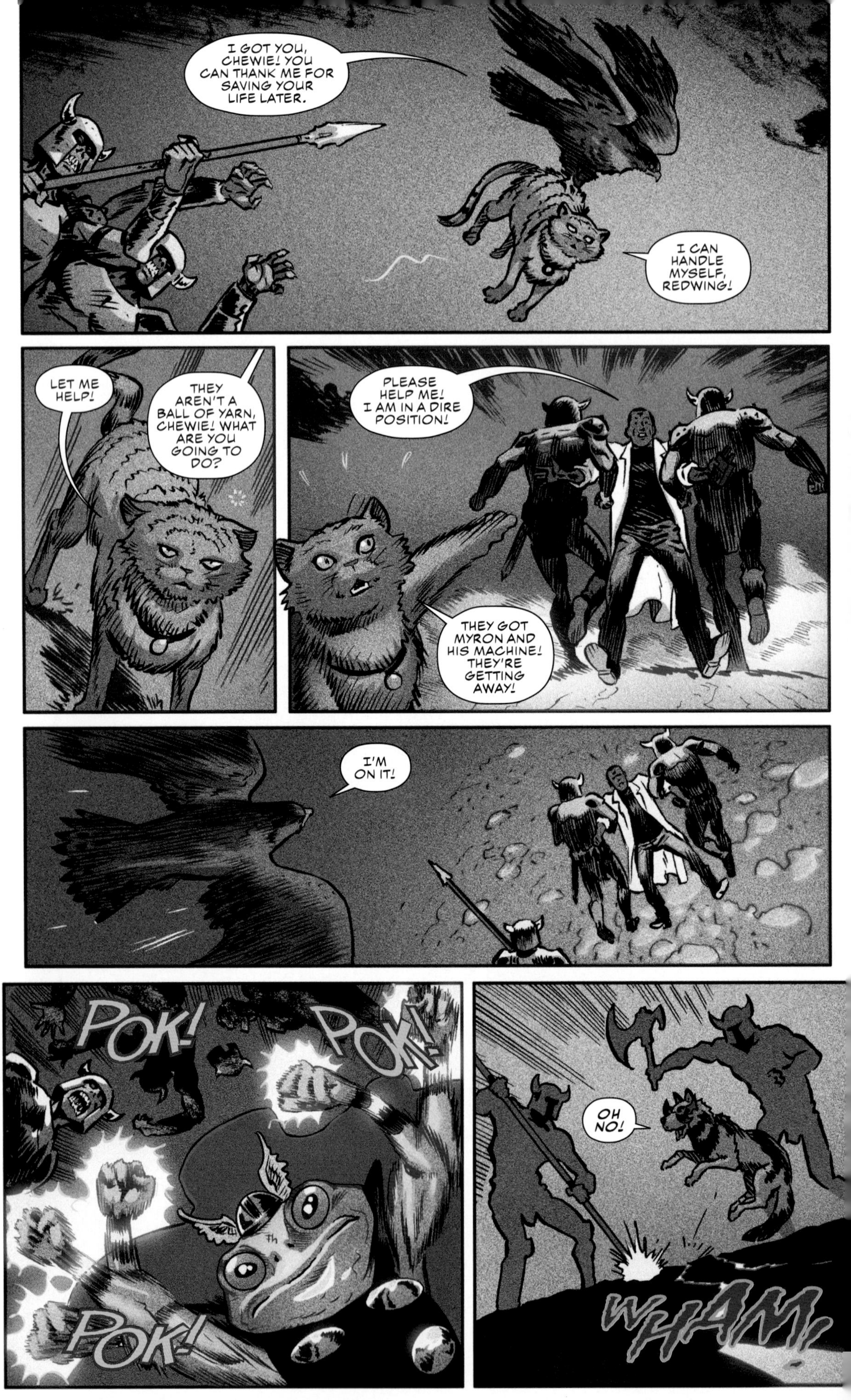
I GOT YOU, CHEWIE! YOU CAN THANK ME FOR SAVING YOUR LIFE LATER.
I CAN HANDLE MYSELF, REDWING!
LET ME HELP!
THEY AREN'T A BALL OF YARN, CHEWIE! WHAT ARE YOU GOING TO DO?
PLEASE HELP ME! I AM IN A DIRE POSITION!
THEY GOT MYRON AND HIS MACHINE! THEY'RE GETTING AWAY!
I'M ON IT!
POK!
POK!
POK!
OH NO!
WHAM!

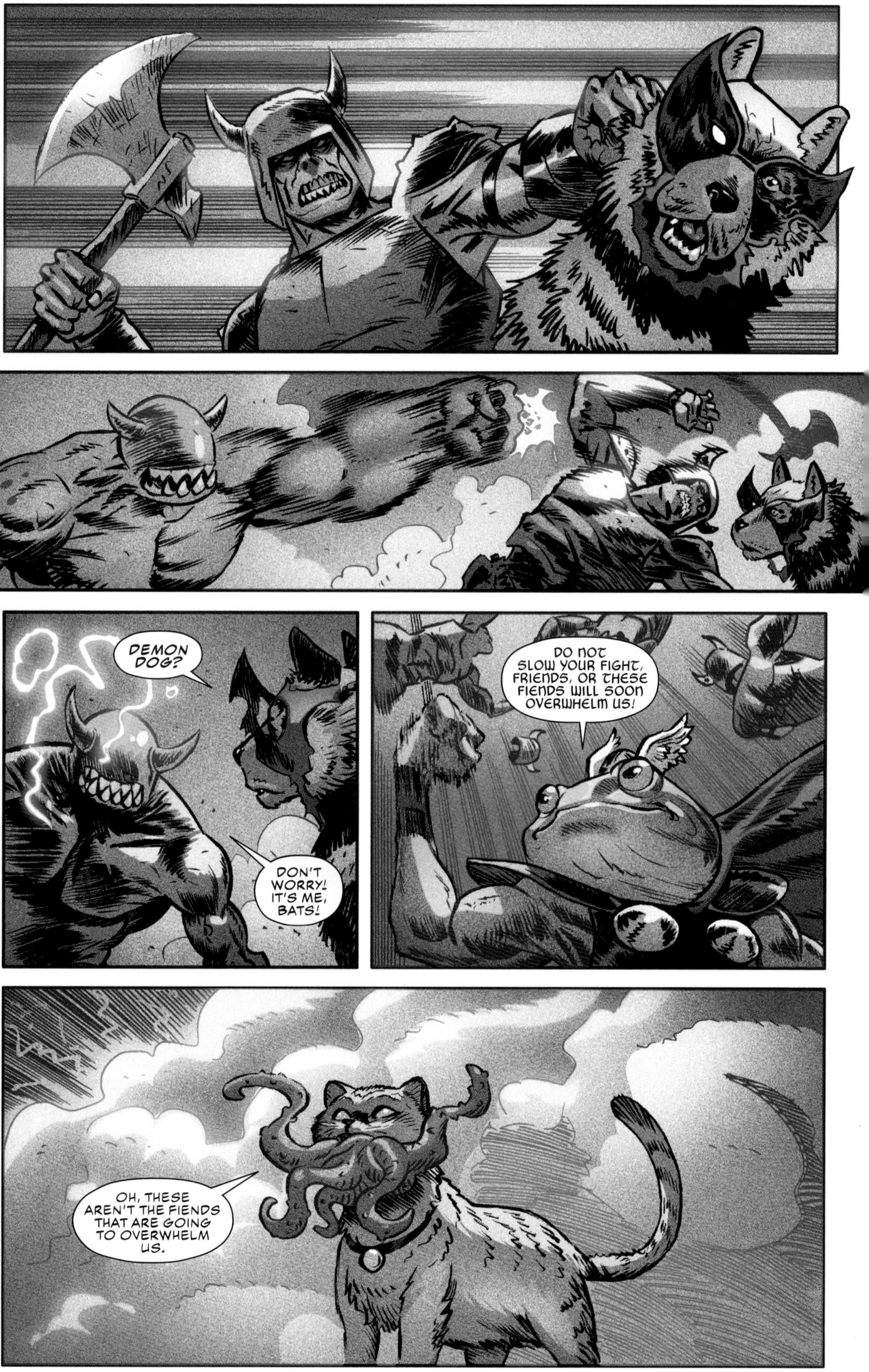
DEMON DOG?
DON'T WORRY! IT'S ME, BATS!
DO NOT SLOW YOUR FIGHT, FRIENDS, OR THESE FIENDS WILL SOON OVERWHELM US!
OH, THESE AREN'T THE FIENDS THAT ARE GOING TO OVERWHELM US.

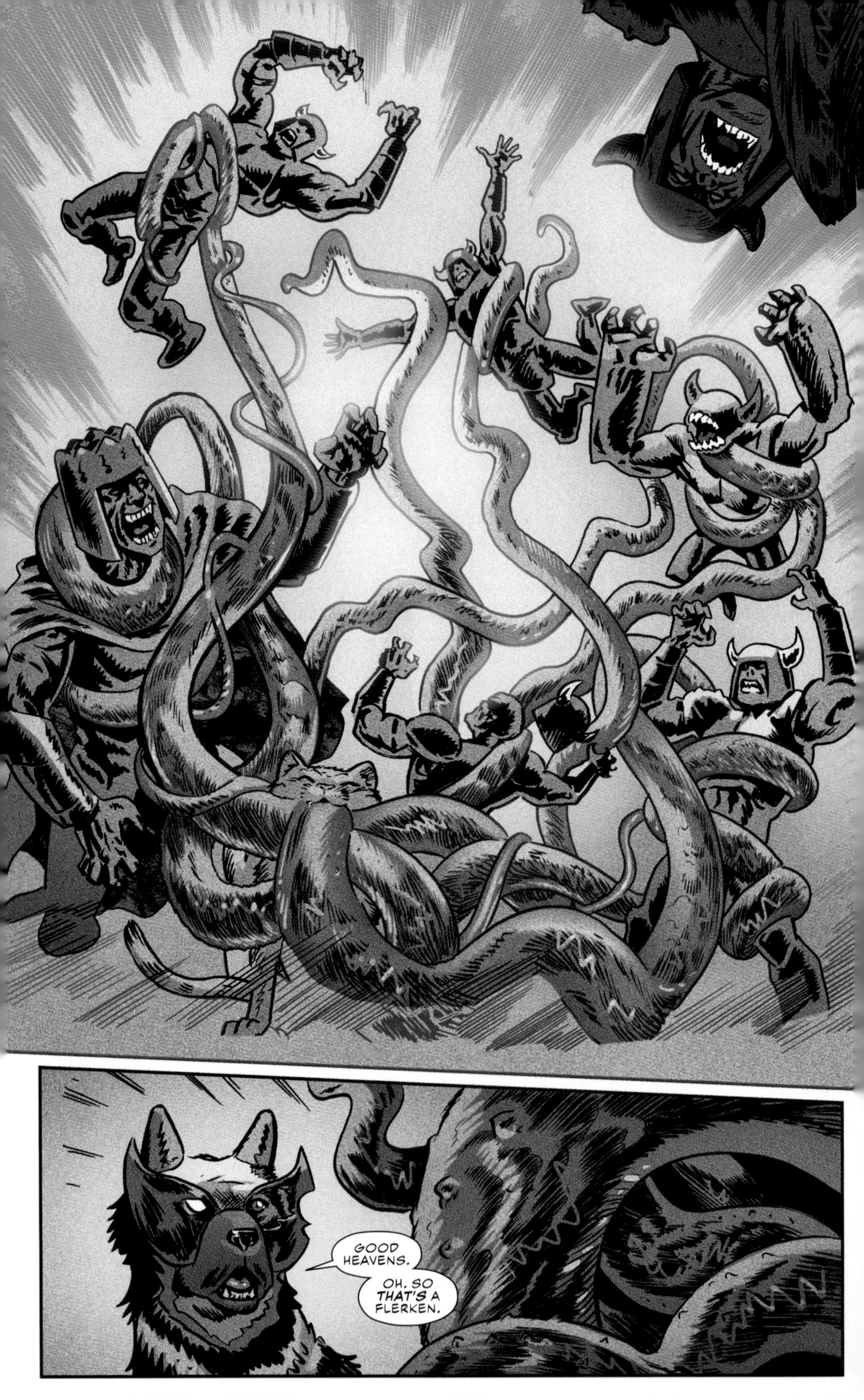
GOOD HEAVENS.
OH. SO THAT'S A FLERKEN.

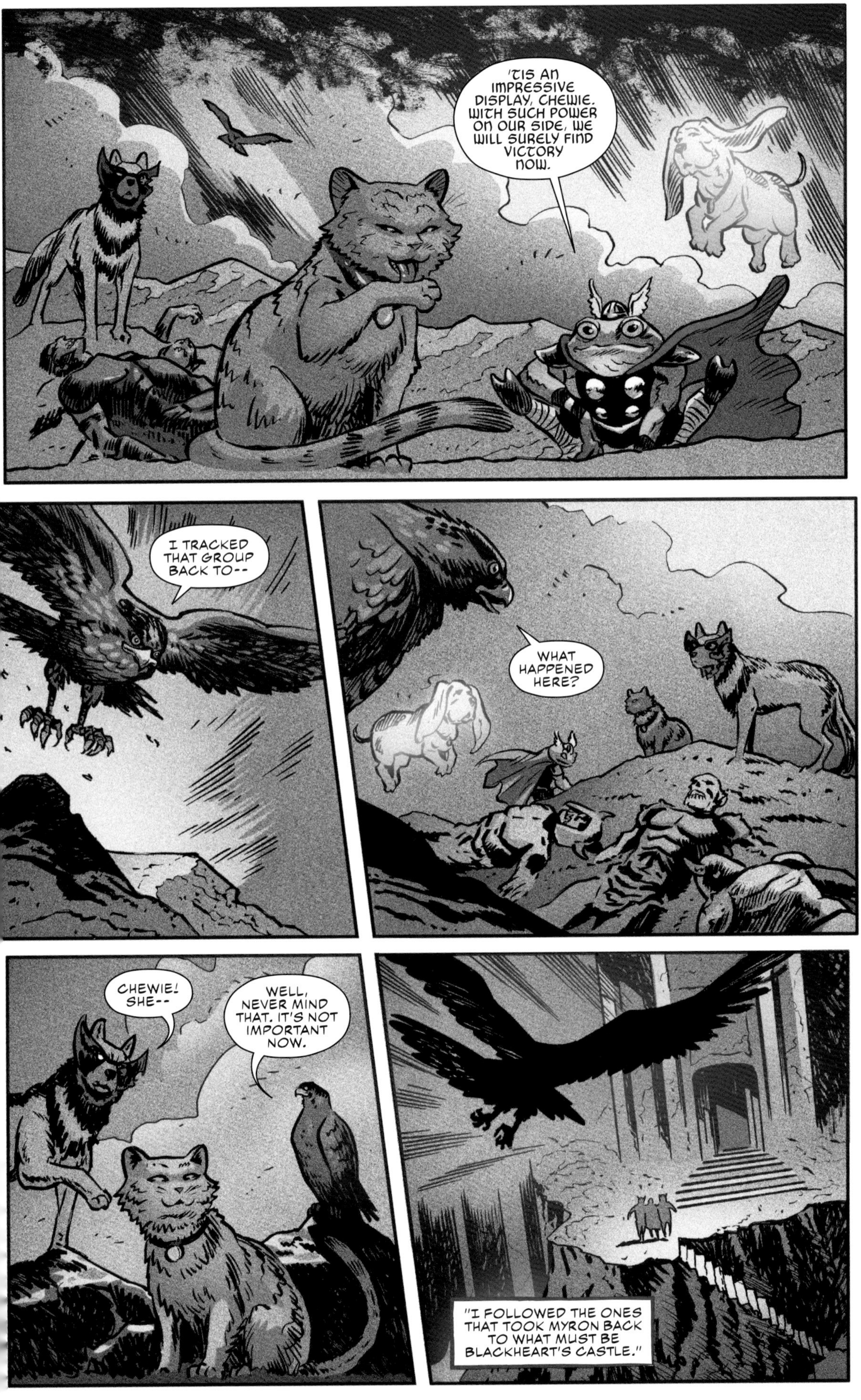
'TIS AN IMPRESSIVE DISPLAY, CHEWIE. WITH SUCH POWER ON OUR SIDE, WE WILL SURELY FIND VICTORY NOW.
I TRACKED THAT GROUP BACK TO--
WHAT HAPPENED HERE?
CHEWIE! SHE--
WELL, NEVER MIND THAT. IT'S NOT IMPORTANT NOW.
"I FOLLOWED THE ONES THAT TOOK MYRON BACK TO WHAT MUST BE BLACKHEART'S CASTLE."

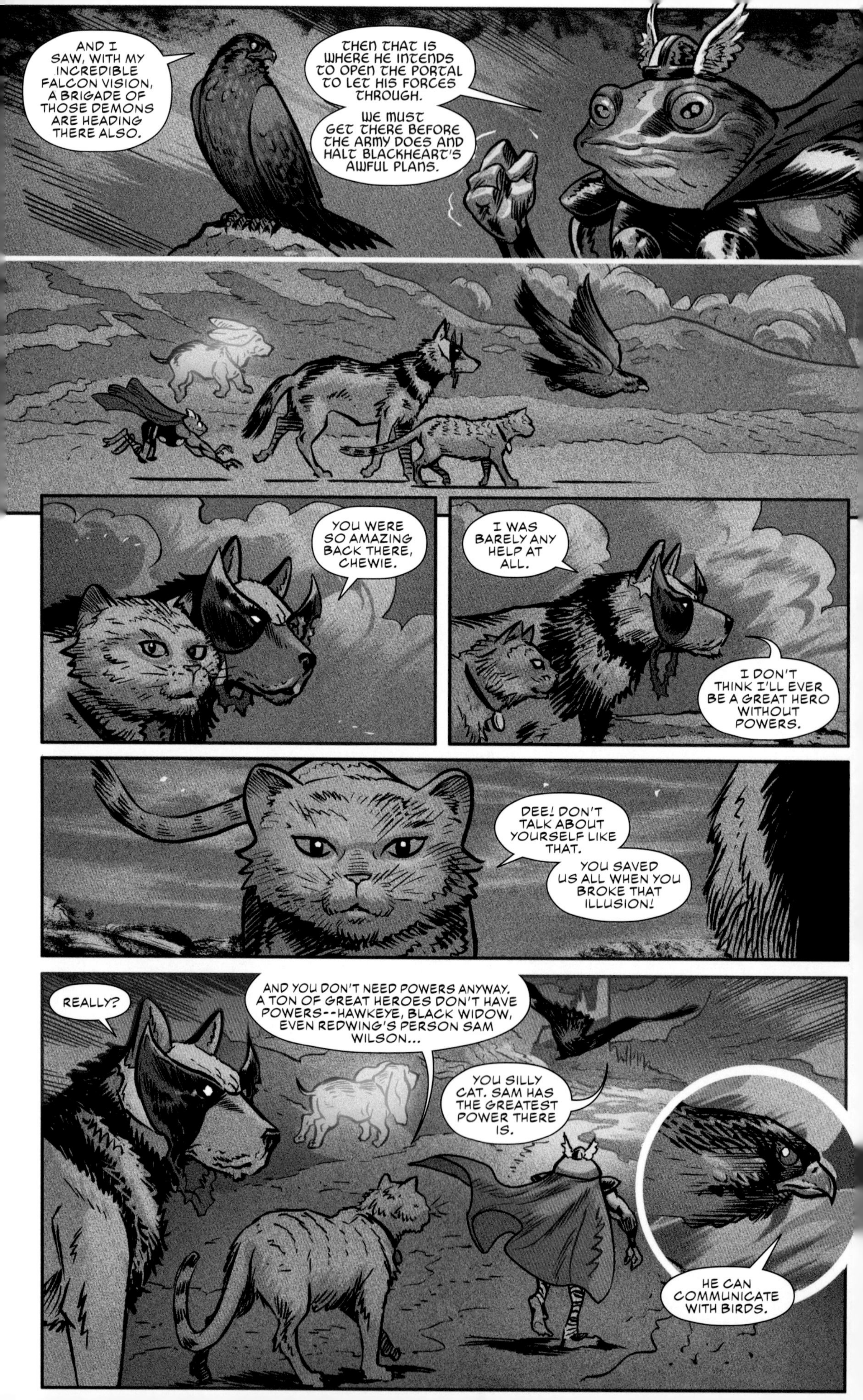
AND I SAW, WITH MY INCREDIBLE FALCON VISION, A BRIGADE OF THOSE DEMONS ARE HEADING THERE ALSO.
THEN THAT IS WHERE HE INTENDS TO OPEN THE PORTAL TO LET HIS FORCES THROUGH.
WE MUST GET THERE BEFORE THE ARMY DOES AND HALT BLACKHEART'S AWFUL PLANS.
YOU WERE SO AMAZING BACK THERE, CHEWIE.
I WAS BARELY ANY HELP AT ALL.
I DON'T THINK I'LL EVER BE A GREAT HERO WITHOUT POWERS.
DEE! DON'T TALK ABOUT YOURSELF LIKE THAT.
YOU SAVED US ALL WHEN YOU BROKE THAT ILLUSION!
REALLY?
AND YOU DON'T NEED POWERS ANYWAY. A TON OF GREAT HEROES DON'T HAVE POWERS--HAWKEYE, BLACK WIDOW, EVEN REDWING'S PERSON SAM WILSON...
YOU SILLY CAT. SAM HAS THE GREATEST POWER THERE IS.
HE CAN COMMUNICATE WITH BIRDS.

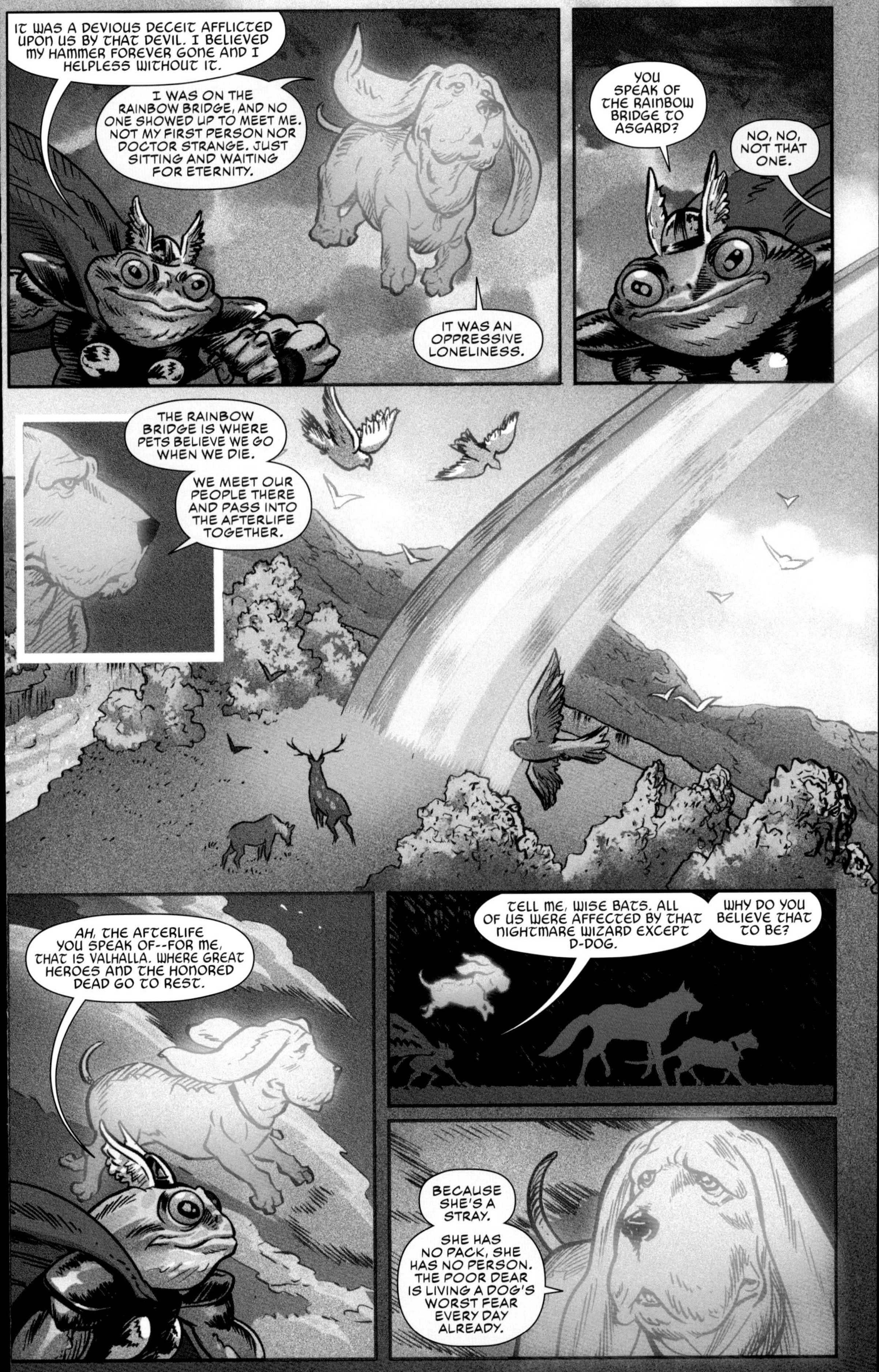
IT WAS A DEVIOUS DECEIT AFFLICTED UPON US BY THAT DEVIL. I BELIEVED MY HAMMER FOREVER GONE AND I HELPLESS WITHOUT IT.
I WAS ON THE RAINBOW BRIDGE, AND NO ONE SHOWED UP TO MEET ME. NOT MY FIRST PERSON NOR DOCTOR STRANGE. JUST SITTING AND WAITING FOR ETERNITY.
IT WAS AN OPPRESSIVE LONELINESS.
YOU SPEAK OF THE RAINBOW BRIDGE TO ASGARD?
NO, NO, NOT THAT ONE.
THE RAINBOW BRIDGE IS WHERE PETS BELIEVE WE GO WHEN WE DIE.
WE MEET OUR PEOPLE THERE AND PASS INTO THE AFTERLIFE TOGETHER.
AH, THE AFTERLIFE YOU SPEAK OF--FOR ME, THAT IS VALHALLA. WHERE GREAT HEROES AND THE HONORED DEAD GO TO REST.
TELL ME, WISE BATS. ALL OF US WERE AFFECTED BY THAT NIGHTMARE WIZARD EXCEPT D-DOG.
WHY DO YOU BELIEVE THAT TO BE?
BECAUSE SHE'S A STRAY.
SHE HAS NO PACK, SHE HAS NO PERSON. THE POOR DEAR IS LIVING A DOG'S WORST FEAR EVERY DAY ALREADY.

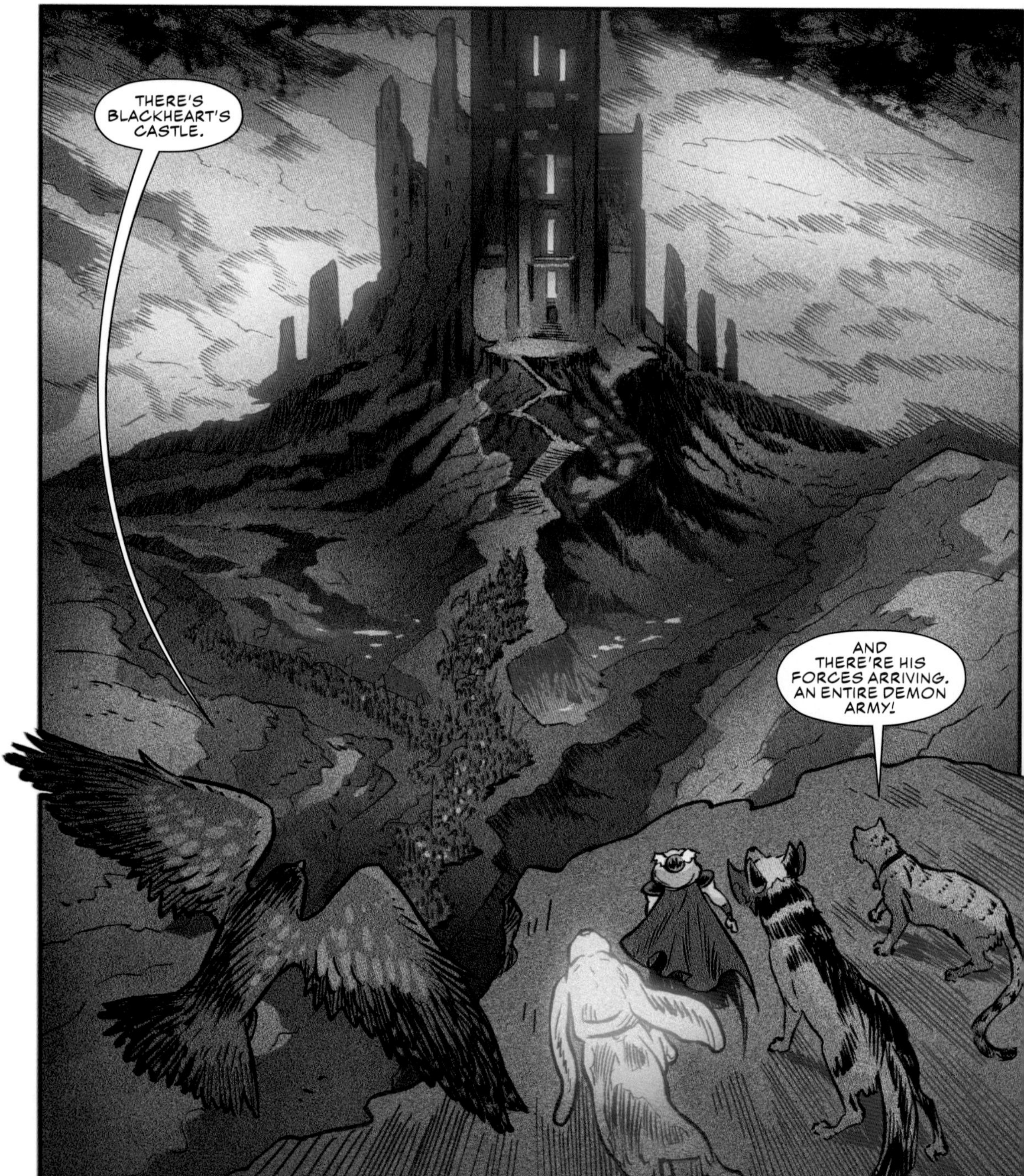
THERE'S BLACKHEART'S CASTLE.
AND THERE'RE HIS FORCES ARRIVING. AN ENTIRE DEMON ARMY!

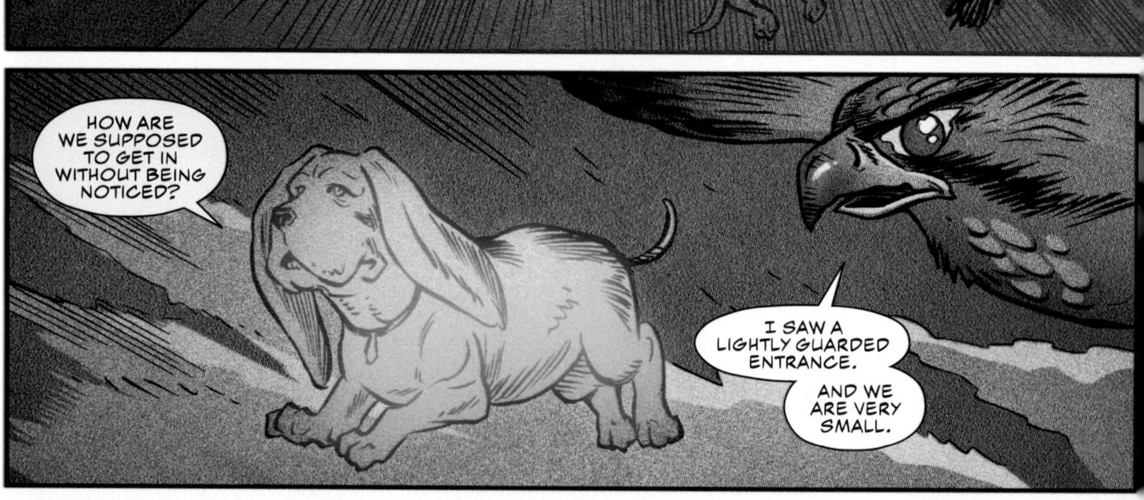
HOW ARE WE SUPPOSED TO GET IN WITHOUT BEING NOTICED?
I SAW A LIGHTLY GUARDED ENTRANCE.
AND WE ARE VERY SMALL.

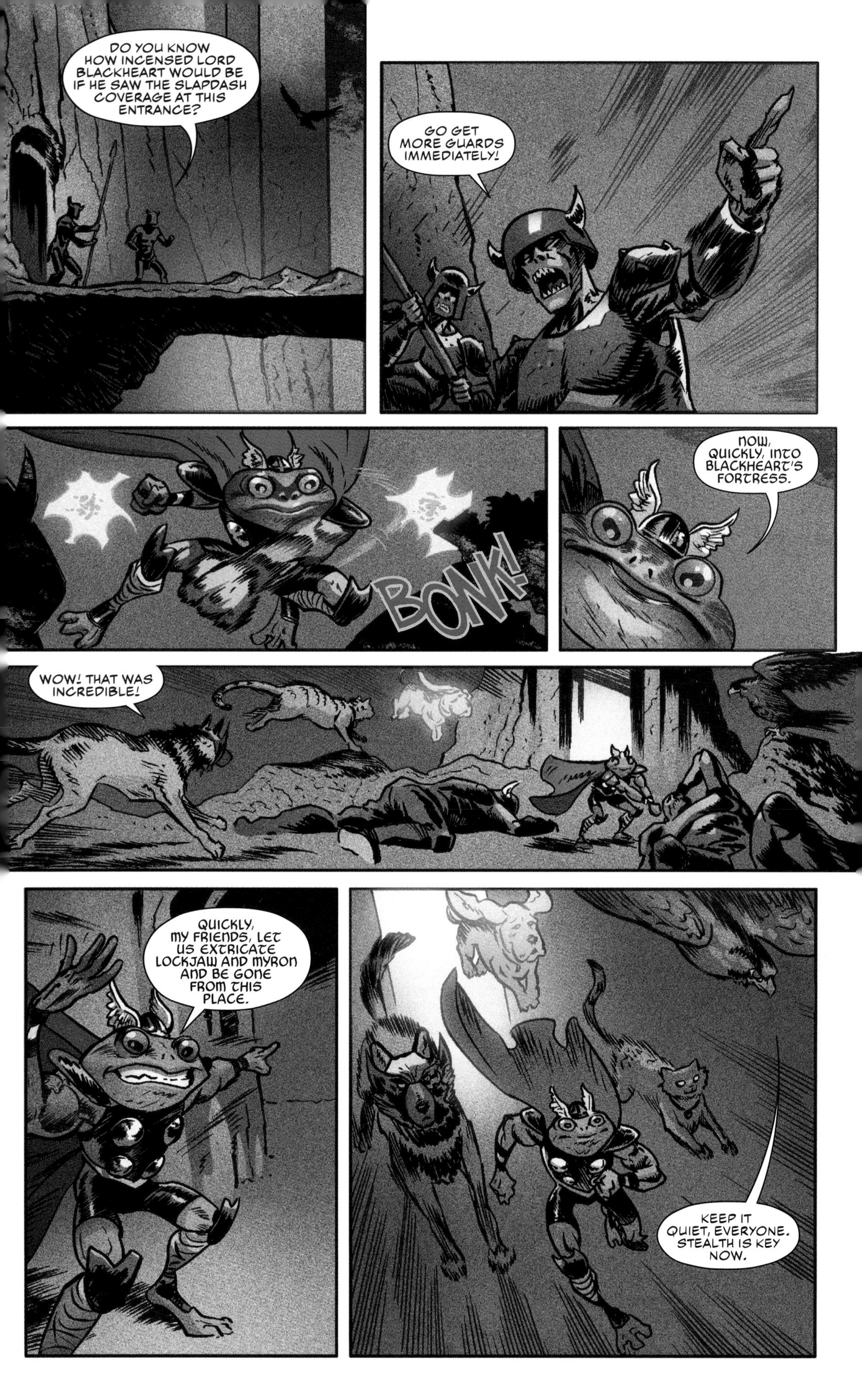
DO YOU KNOW HOW INCENSED LORD BLACKHEART WOULD BE IF HE SAW THE SLAPDASH COVERAGE AT THIS ENTRANCE?
GO GET MORE GUARDS IMMEDIATELY!
BONK!
NOW, QUICKLY, INTO BLACKHEART'S FORTRESS.
WOW! THAT WAS INCREDIBLE!
QUICKLY, MY FRIENDS, LET US EXTRICATE LOCKJAW AND MYRON AND BE GONE FROM THIS PLACE.
KEEP IT QUIET, EVERYONE. STEALTH IS KEY NOW.

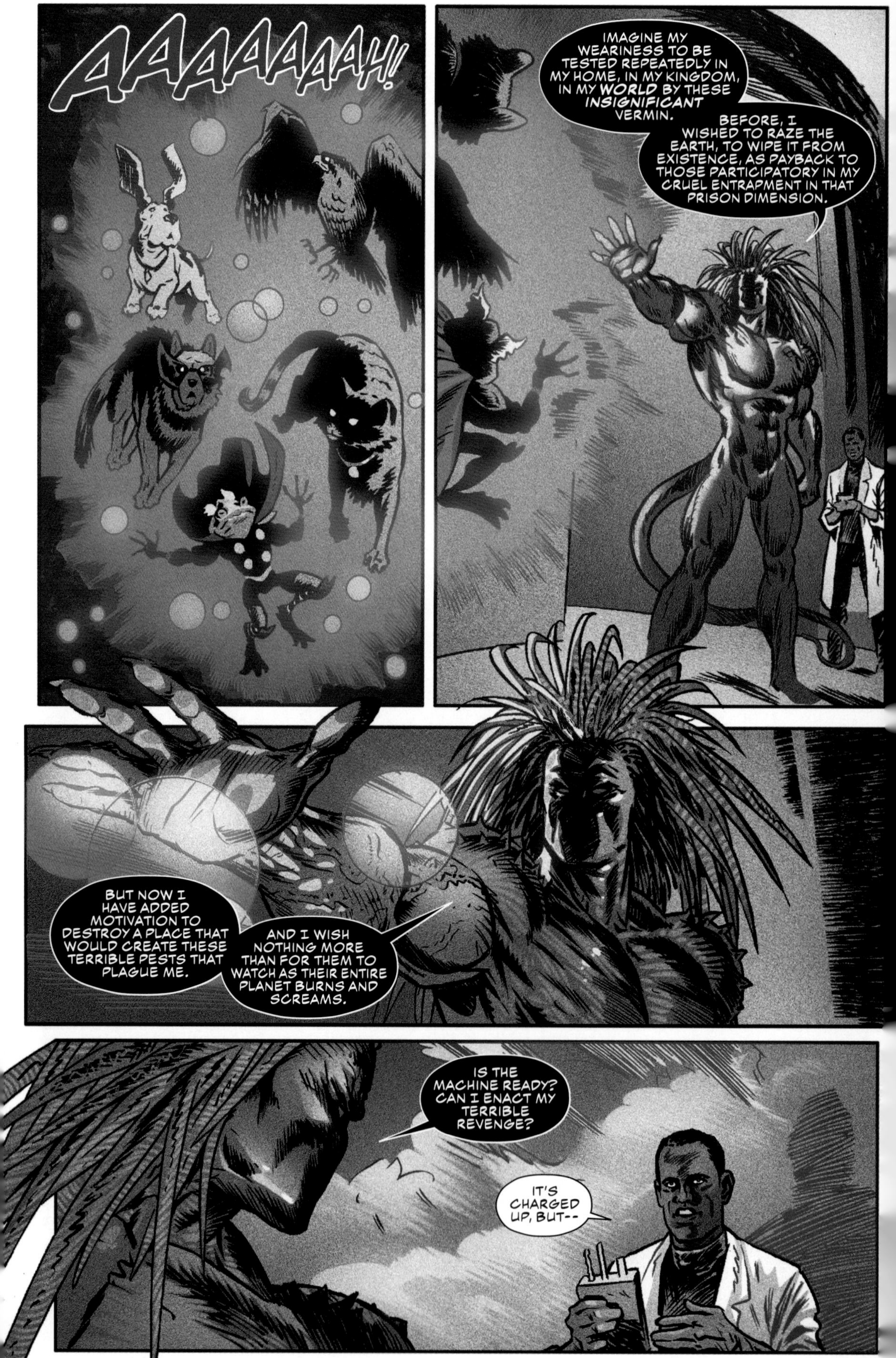
AAAAAAAH!
IMAGINE MY WEARINESS TO BE TESTED REPEATEDLY IN MY HOME, IN MY KINGDOM, IN MY WORLD BY THESE INSIGNIFICANT VERMIN.
BEFORE, I WISHED TO RAZE THE EARTH, TO WIPE IT FROM EXISTENCE, AS PAYBACK TO THOSE PARTICIPATORY IN MY CRUEL ENTRAPMENT IN THAT PRISON DIMENSION.
BUT NOW I HAVE ADDED MOTIVATION TO DESTROY A PLACE THAT WOULD CREATE THESE TERRIBLE PESTS THAT PLAGUE ME.
AND I WISH NOTHING MORE THAN FOR THEM TO WATCH AS THEIR ENTIRE PLANET BURNS AND SCREAMS.
IS THE MACHINE READY? CAN I ENACT MY TERRIBLE REVENGE?
IT'S CHARGED UP, BUT--

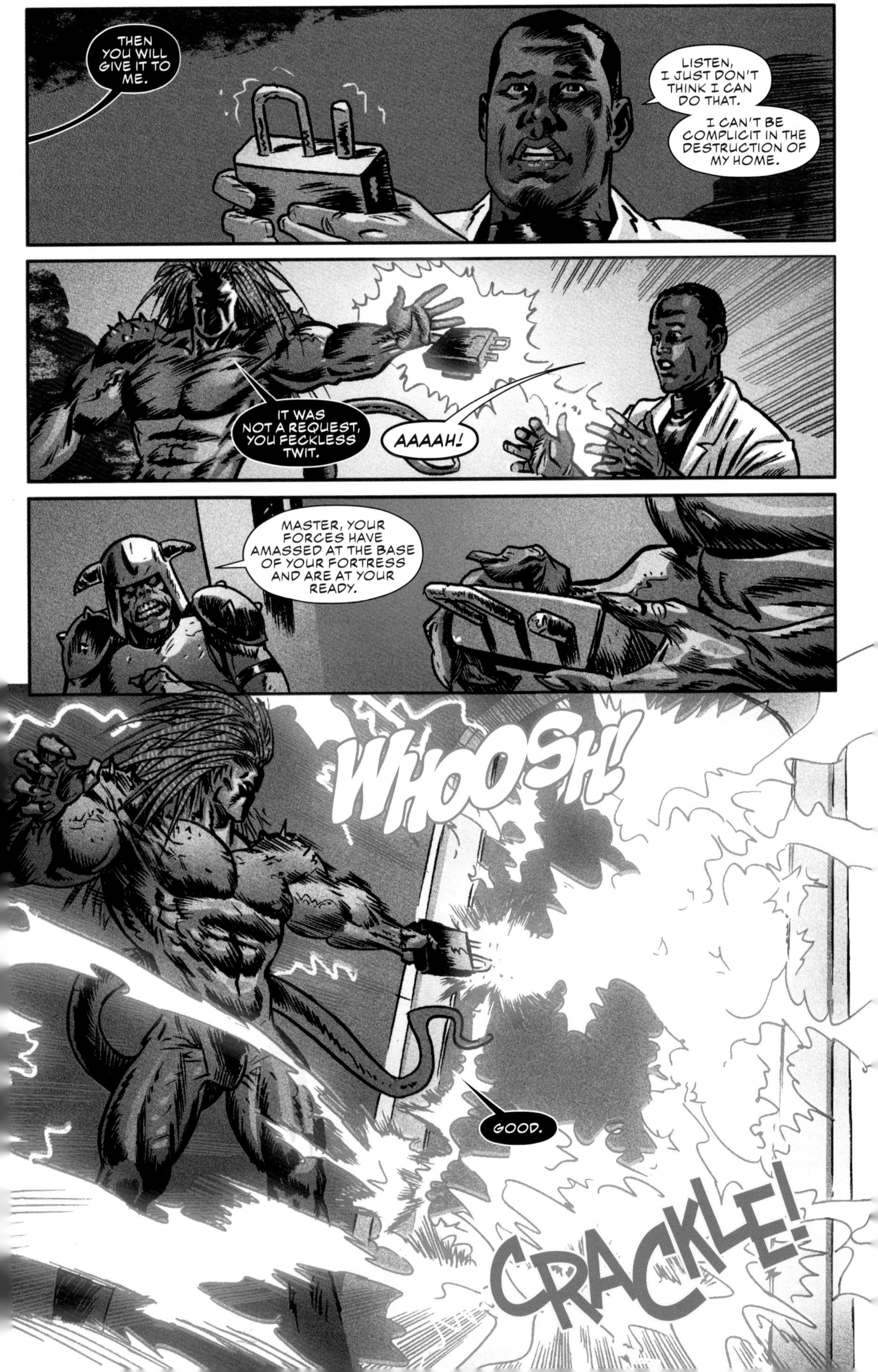
THEN YOU WILL GIVE IT TO ME.
LISTEN, I JUST DON'T THINK I CAN DO THAT.
I CAN'T BE COMPLICIT IN THE DESTRUCTION OF MY HOME.
IT WAS NOT A REQUEST, YOU FECKLESS TWIT.
AAAAH!
MASTER, YOUR FORCES HAVE AMASSED AT THE BASE OF YOUR FORTRESS AND ARE AT YOUR READY.
WHOOSH!
GOOD.
CRACKLE!

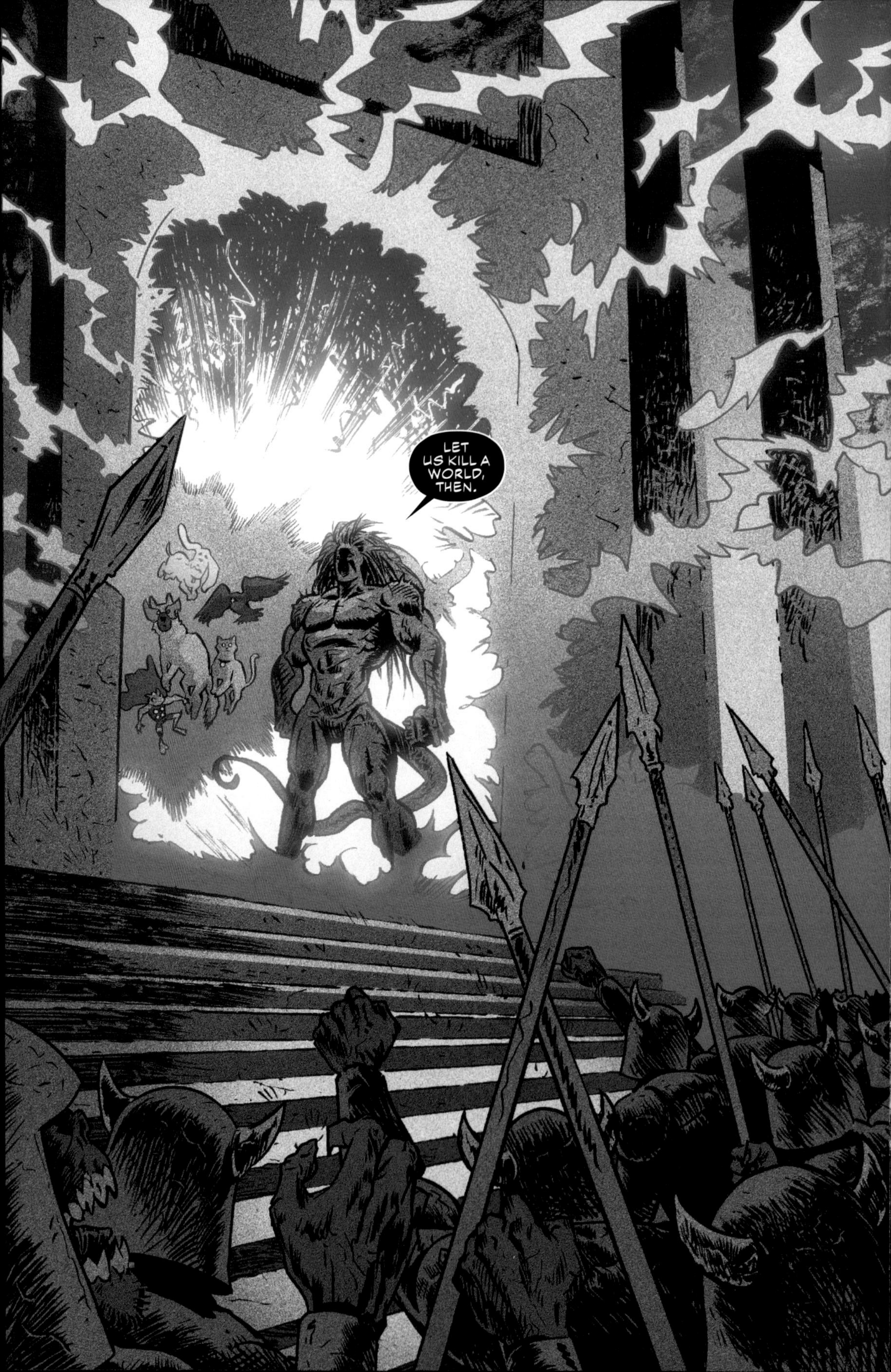
LET US KILL A WORLD, THEN.

FOUR

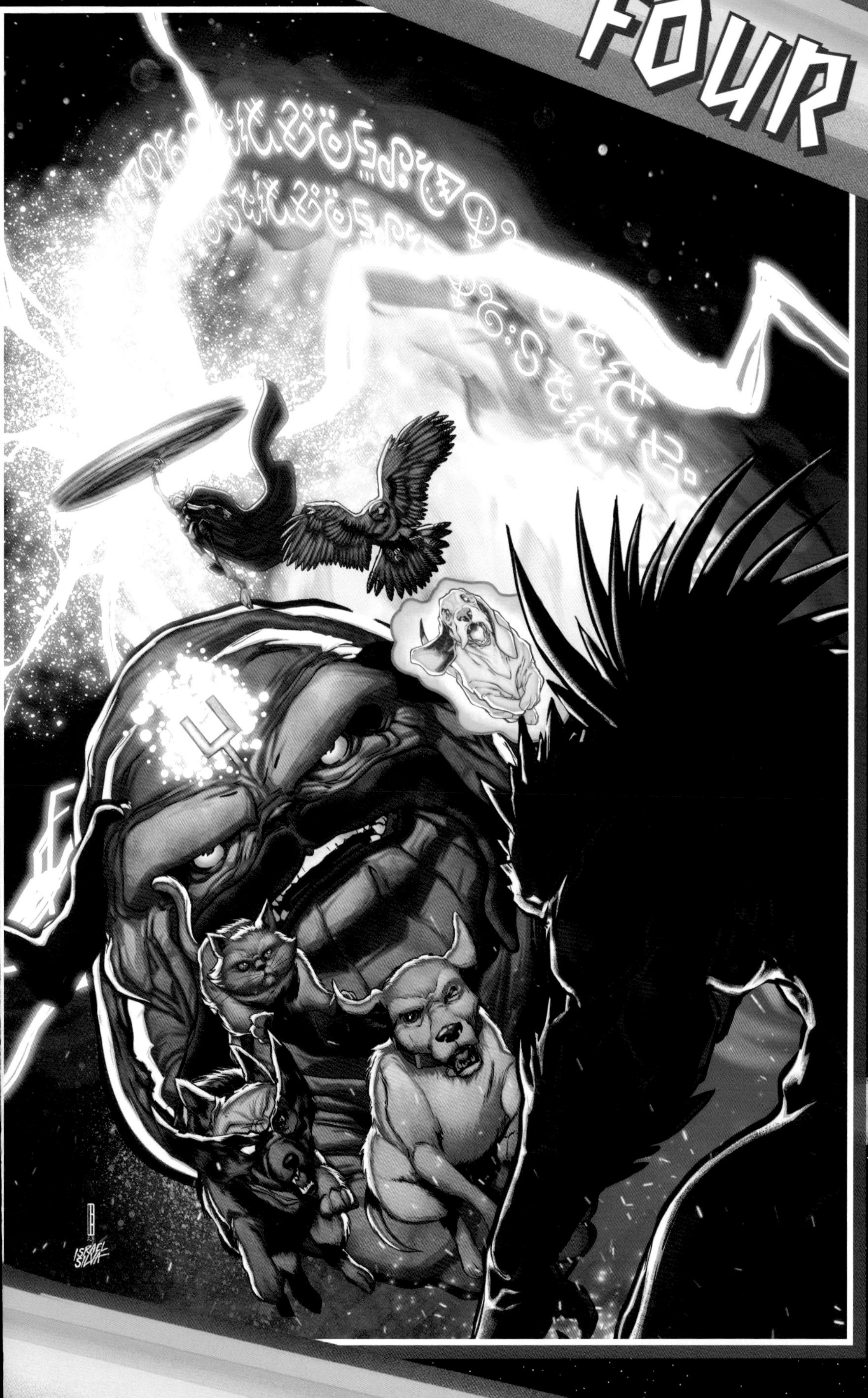

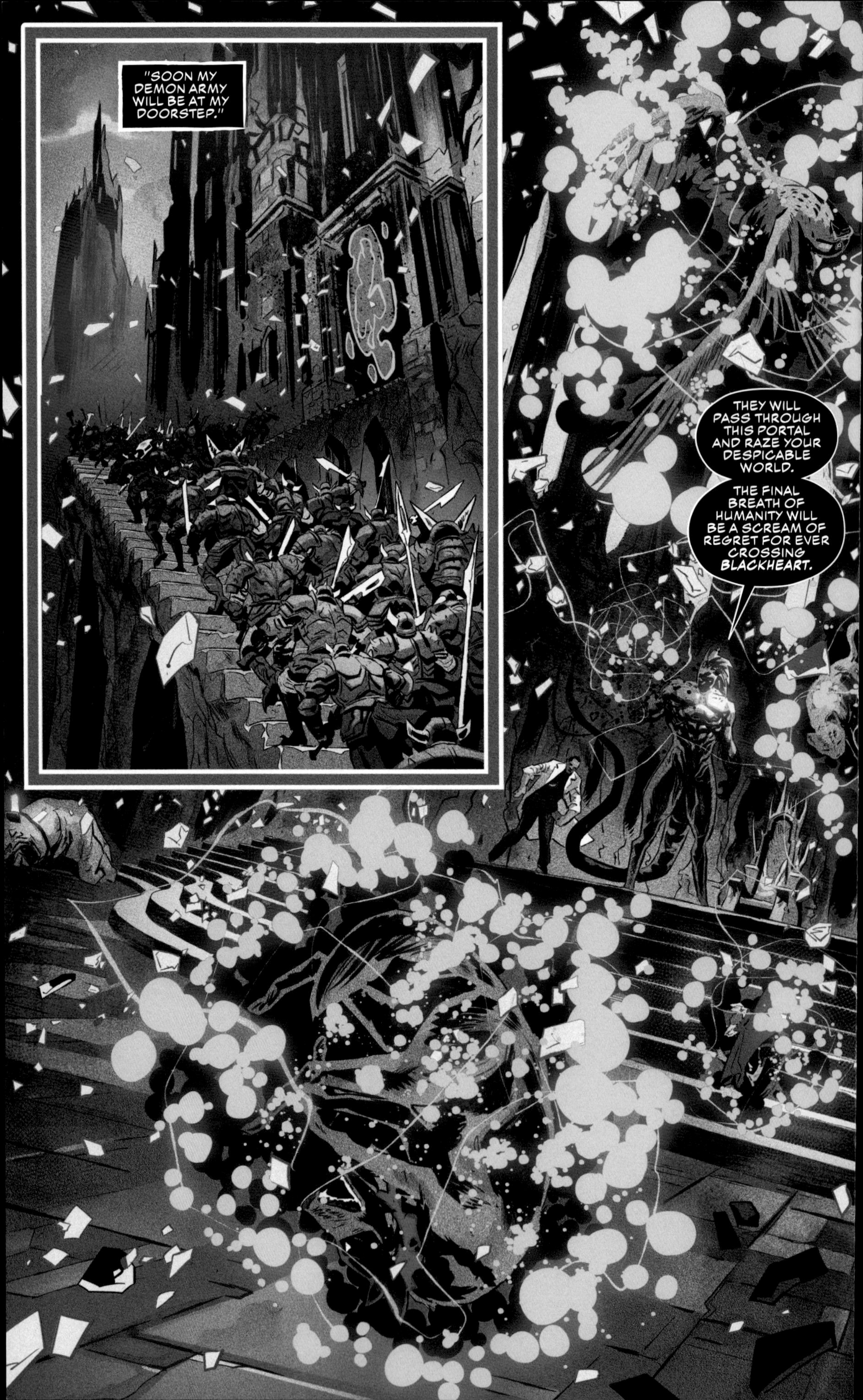

"SOON MY DEMON ARMY WILL BE AT MY DOORSTEP."
THEY WILL PASS THROUGH THIS PORTAL AND RAZE YOUR DESPICABLE WORLD.
THE FINAL BREATH OF HUMANITY WILL BE A SCREAM OF REGRET FOR EVER CROSSING BLACKHEART.

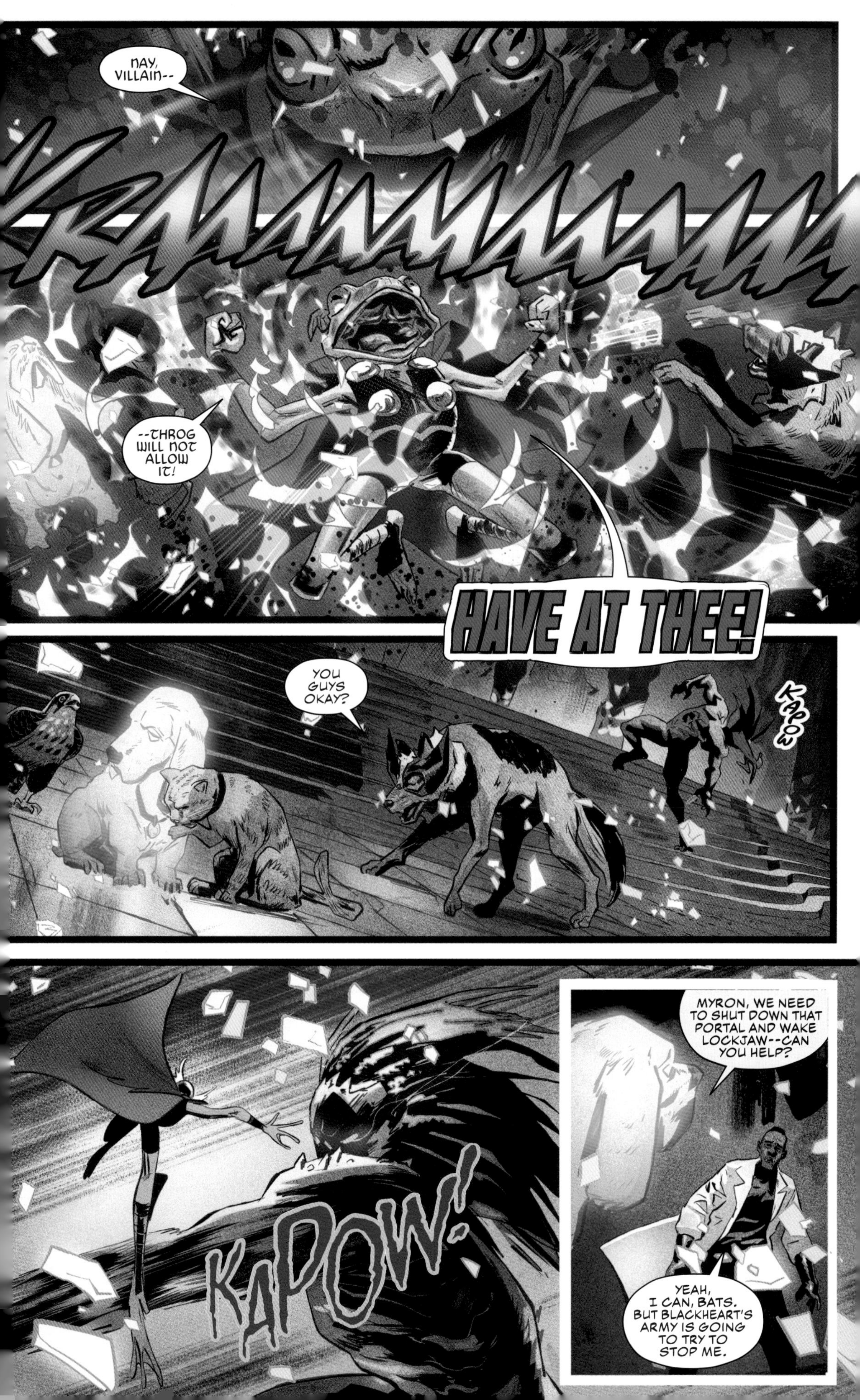
NAY, VILLAIN--
KAAAAAAAAAAAA
--THROG WILL NOT ALLOW IT!
HAVE AT THEE!
YOU GUYS OKAY?
KAPOW
KAPOW!
MYRON, WE NEED TO SHUT DOWN THAT PORTAL AND WAKE LOCKJAW--CAN YOU HELP?
YEAH, I CAN, BATS. BUT BLACKHEART'S ARMY IS GOING TO TRY TO STOP ME.

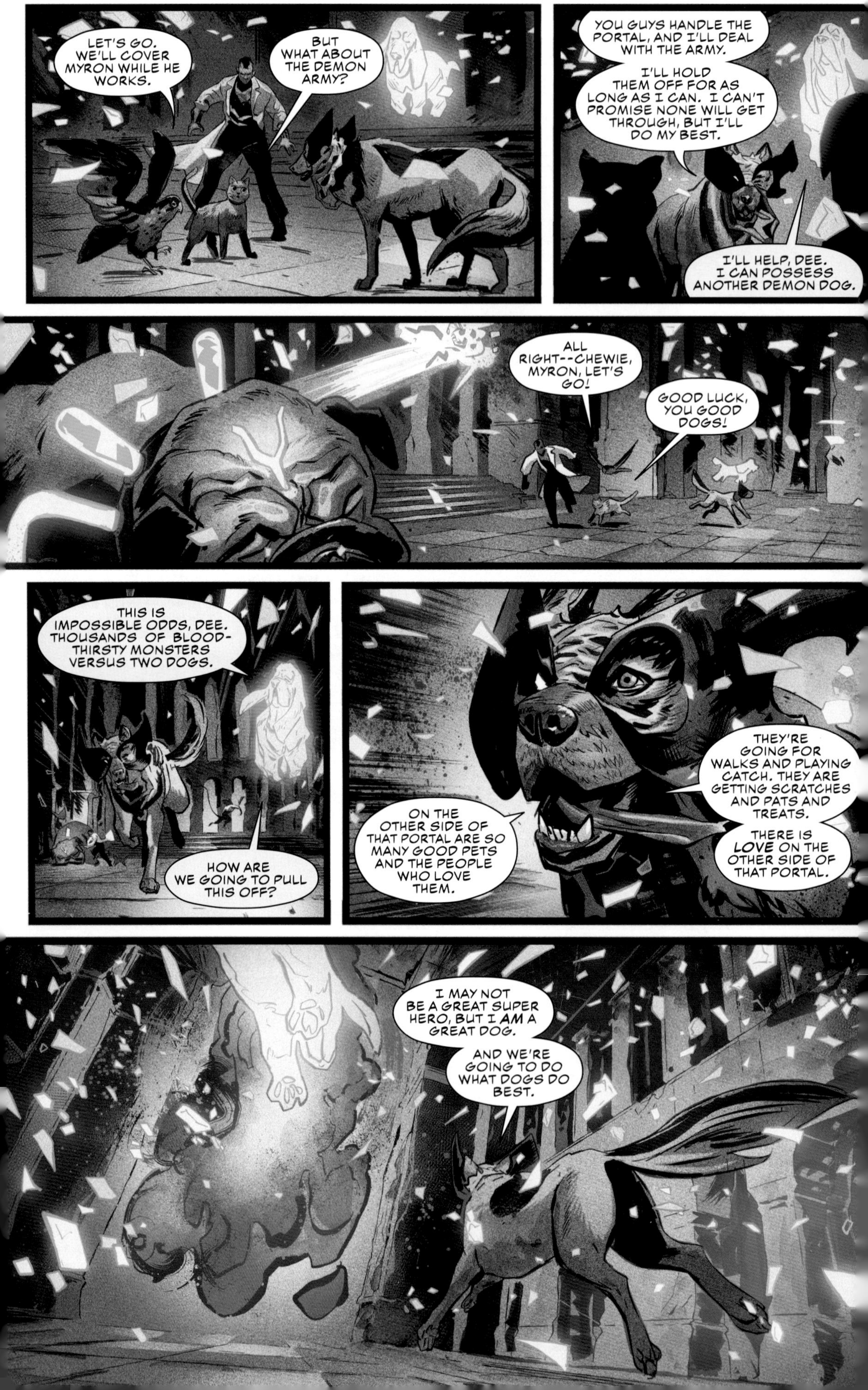
LET'S GO. WE'LL COVER MYRON WHILE HE WORKS.
BUT WHAT ABOUT THE DEMON ARMY?
YOU GUYS HANDLE THE PORTAL, AND I'LL DEAL WITH THE ARMY.
I'LL HOLD THEM OFF FOR AS LONG AS I CAN. I CAN'T PROMISE NONE WILL GET THROUGH, BUT I'LL DO MY BEST.
I'LL HELP, DEE. I CAN POSSESS ANOTHER DEMON DOG.
ALL RIGHT--CHEWIE, MYRON, LET'S GO!
GOOD LUCK, YOU GOOD DOGS!
THIS IS IMPOSSIBLE ODDS, DEE. THOUSANDS OF BLOOD-THIRSTY MONSTERS VERSUS TWO DOGS.
HOW ARE WE GOING TO PULL THIS OFF?
ON THE OTHER SIDE OF THAT PORTAL ARE SO MANY GOOD PETS AND THE PEOPLE WHO LOVE THEM.
THEY'RE GOING FOR WALKS AND PLAYING CATCH. THEY ARE GETTING SCRATCHES AND PATS AND TREATS.
THERE IS LOVE ON THE OTHER SIDE OF THAT PORTAL.
I MAY NOT BE A GREAT SUPER HERO, BUT I AM A GREAT DOG.
AND WE'RE GOING TO DO WHAT DOGS DO BEST.

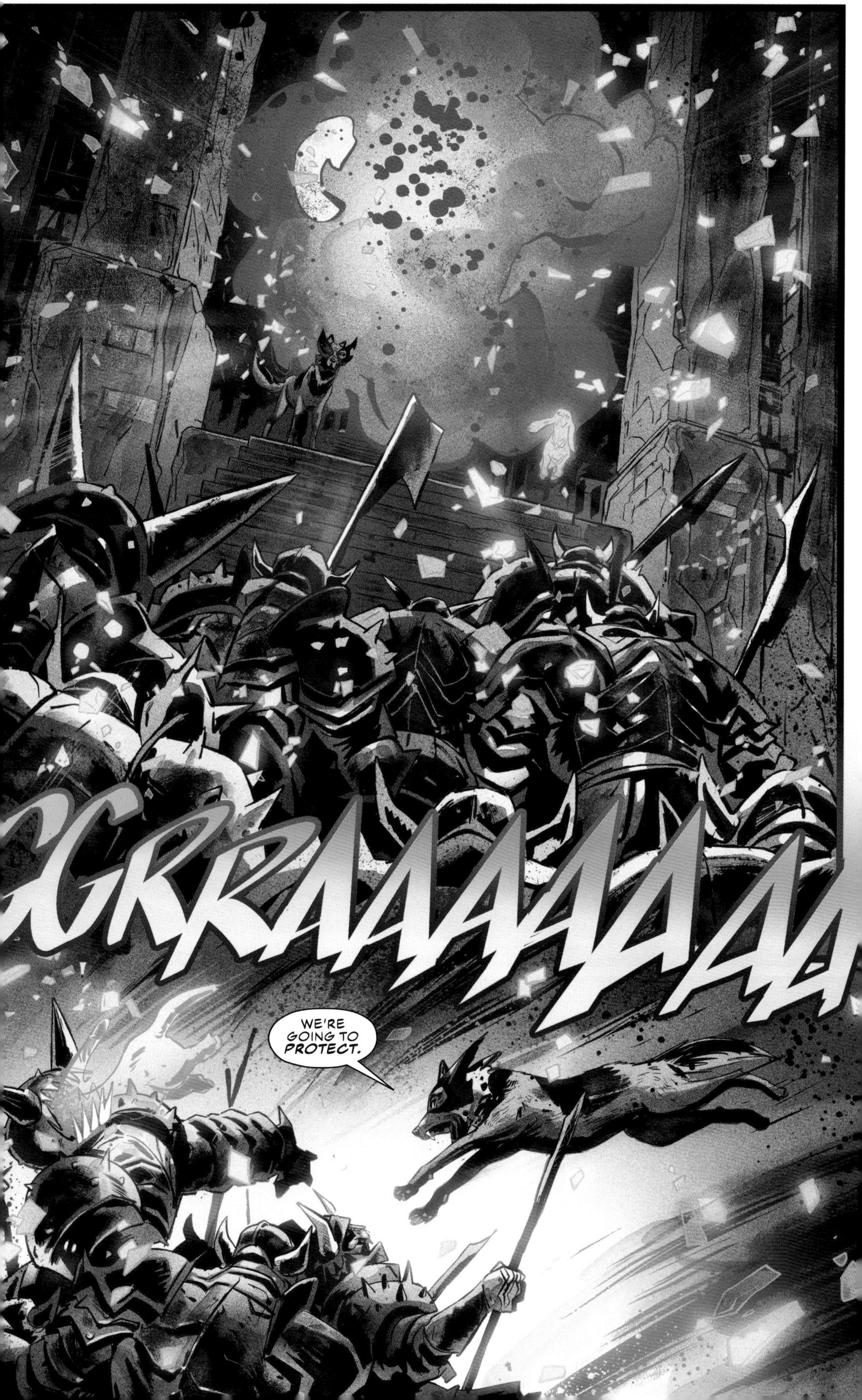
GRAAAAAAA
WE'RE GOING TO PROTECT.

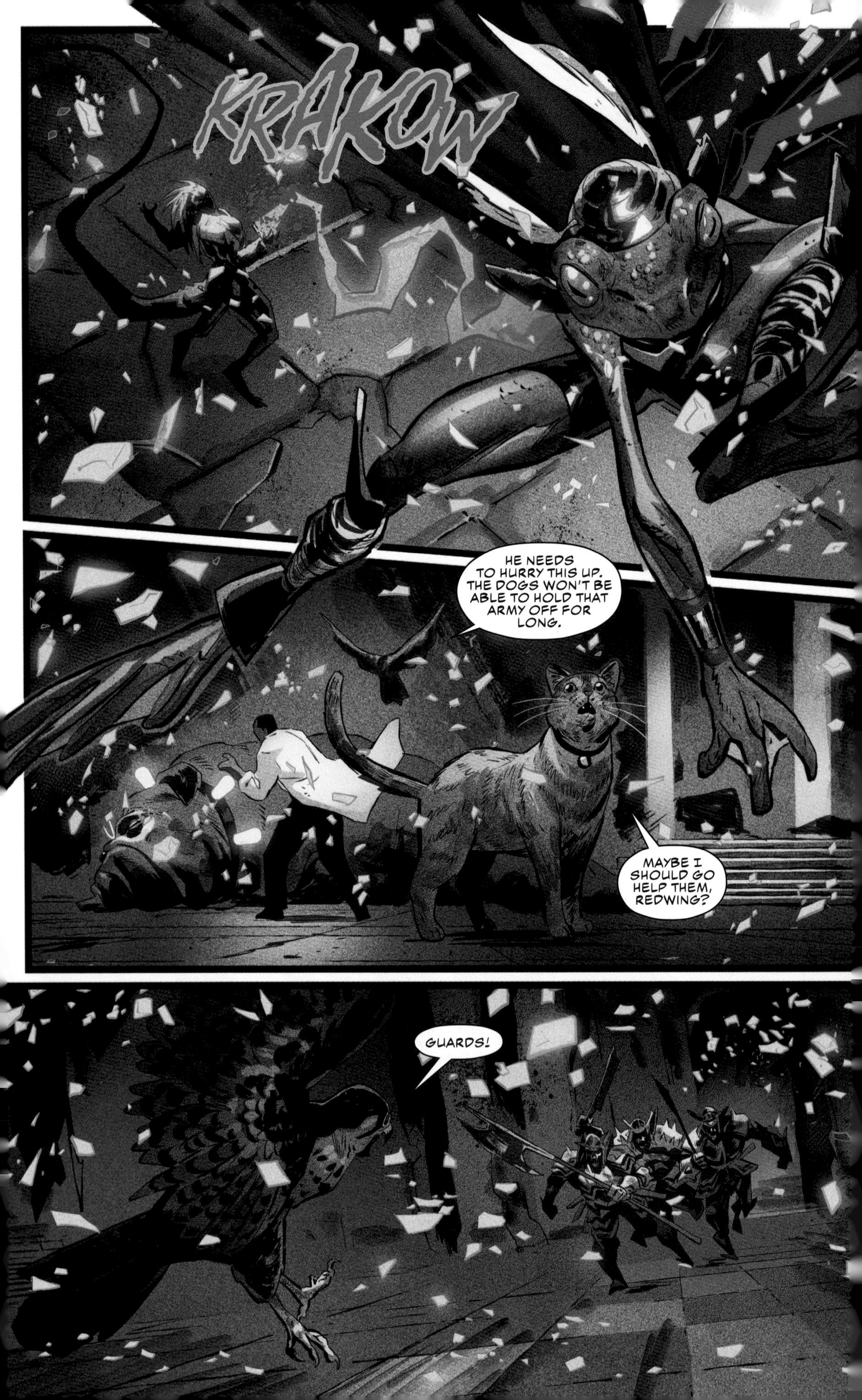
KRAKOW
HE NEEDS TO HURRY THIS UP. THE DOGS WON'T BE ABLE TO HOLD THAT ARMY OFF FOR LONG.
MAYBE I SHOULD GO HELP THEM, REDWING?
GUARDS!

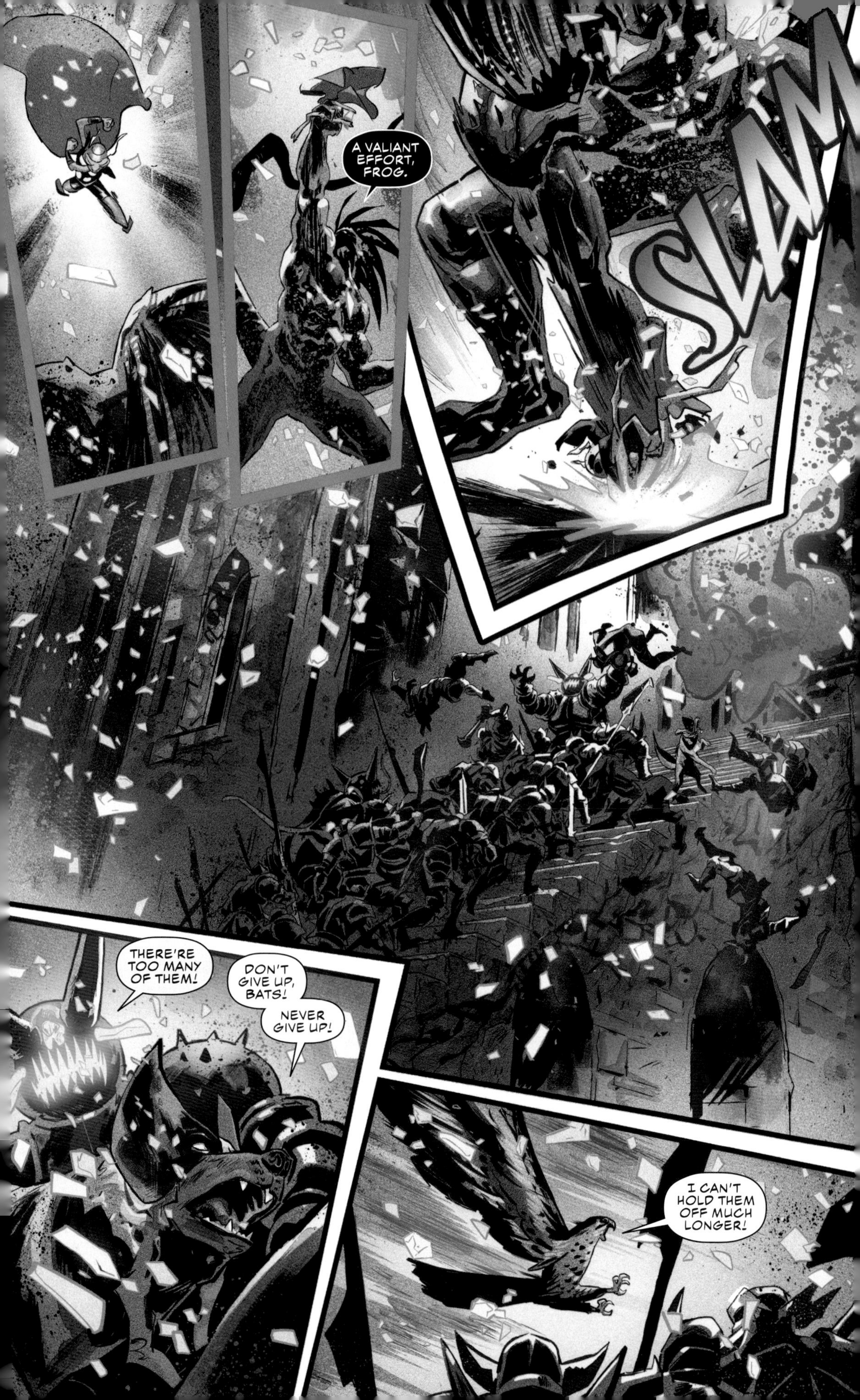
A VALIANT EFFORT, FROG.
SLAM
THERE'RE TOO MANY OF THEM!
DON'T GIVE UP, BATS!
NEVER GIVE UP!
I CAN'T HOLD THEM OFF MUCH LONGER!

BUT VALIANCE HAS NO CURRENCY IN THE TENTH CIRCLE.

GASP!

THE ONLY THINGS OF MERIT HERE ARE CRUELTY, TORTURE AND HATE.

AND I'M GOING TO SHOW YOU THEM ALL AS I SNATCH THE LIFE FROM YOUR TINY, DESPICABLE BODY--

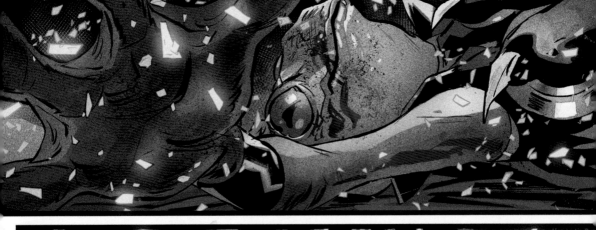

RUMBLE!

WHAT IS THAT NOISE?

SOMETHING LIKE...

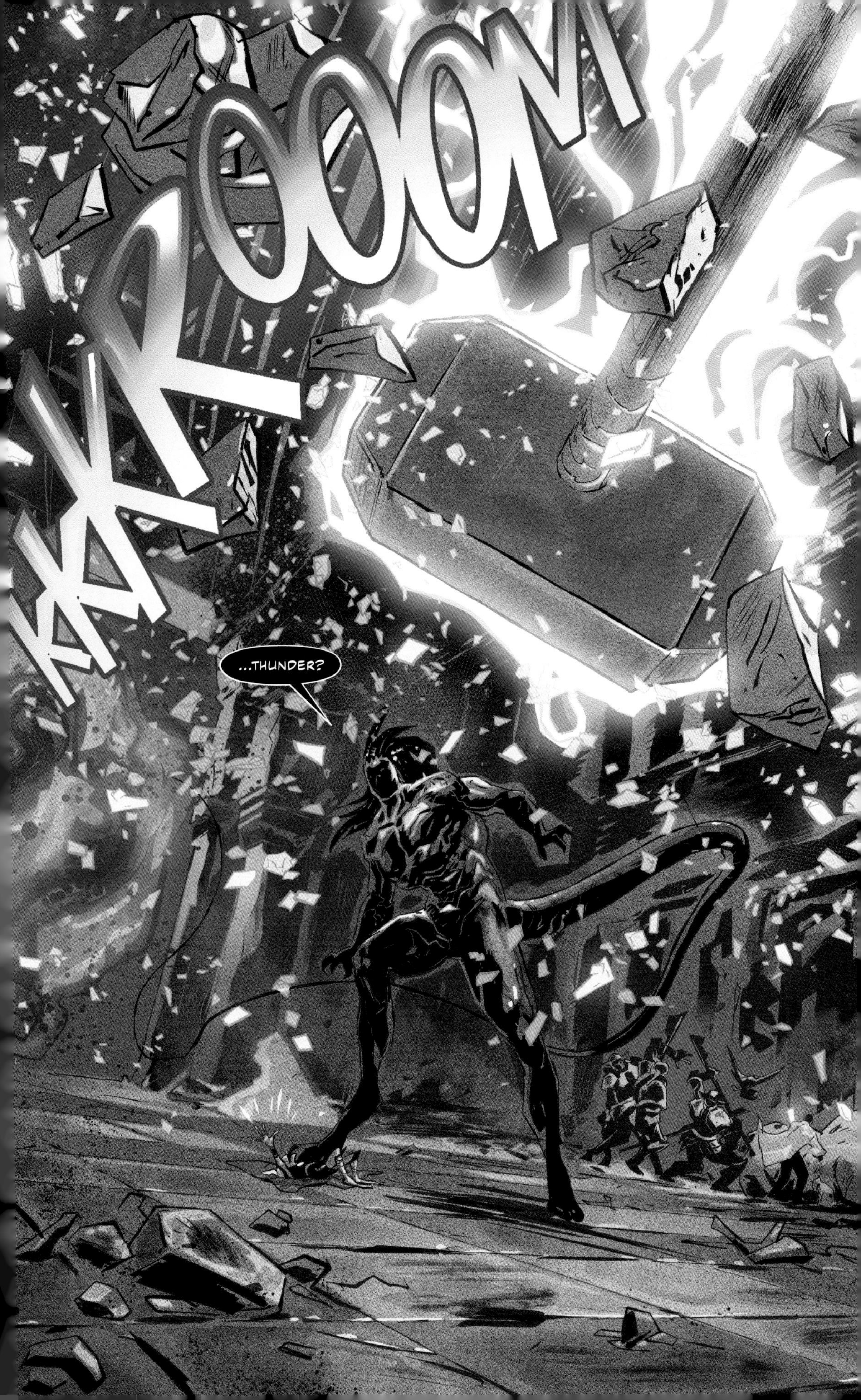
...THUNDER?

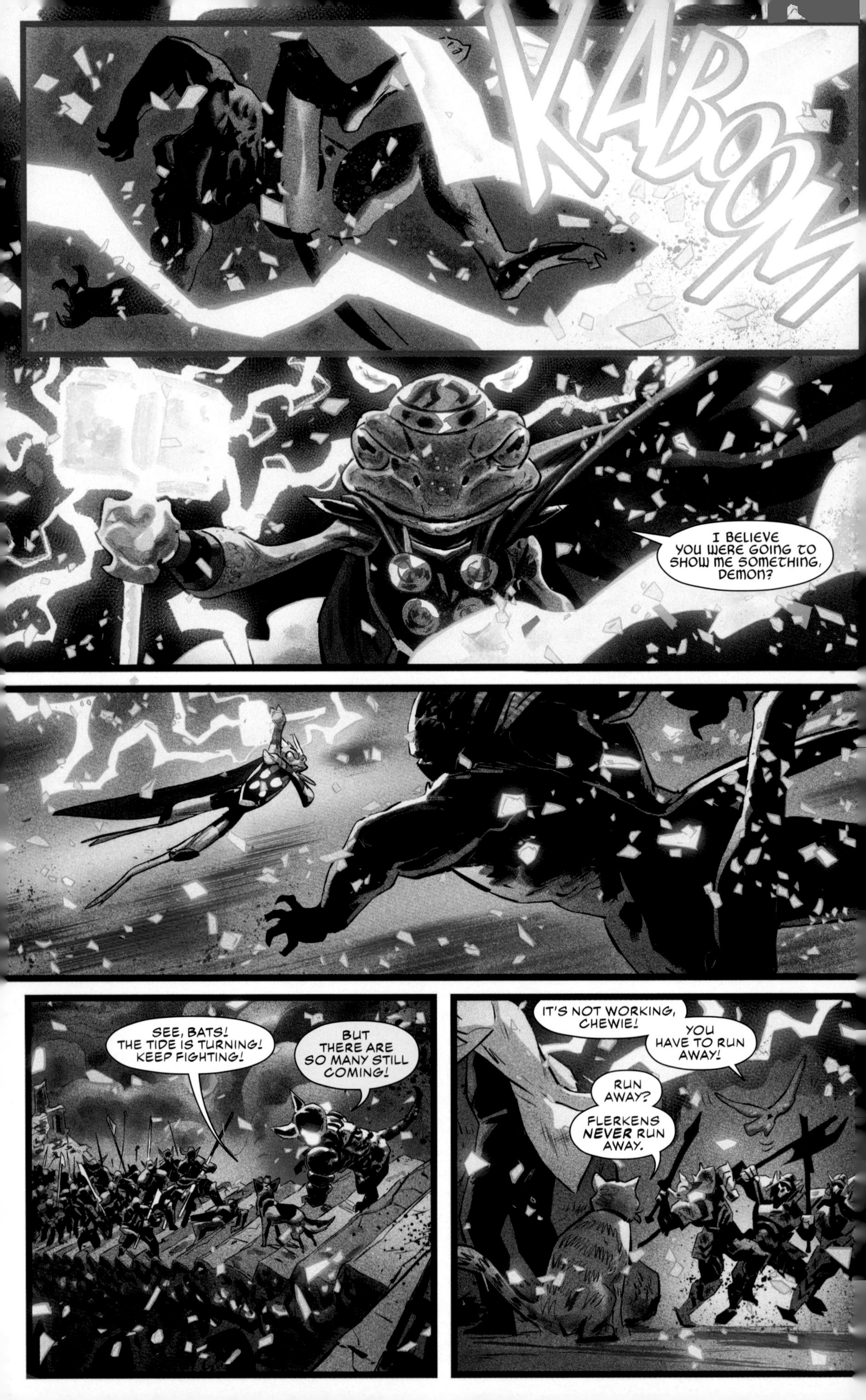

KA-BOOM
I BELIEVE YOU WERE GOING TO SHOW ME SOMETHING, DEMON?
SEE, BATS! THE TIDE IS TURNING! KEEP FIGHTING!
BUT THERE ARE SO MANY STILL COMING!
IT'S NOT WORKING, CHEWIE!
YOU HAVE TO RUN AWAY!
RUN AWAY?
FLERKENS NEVER RUN AWAY.

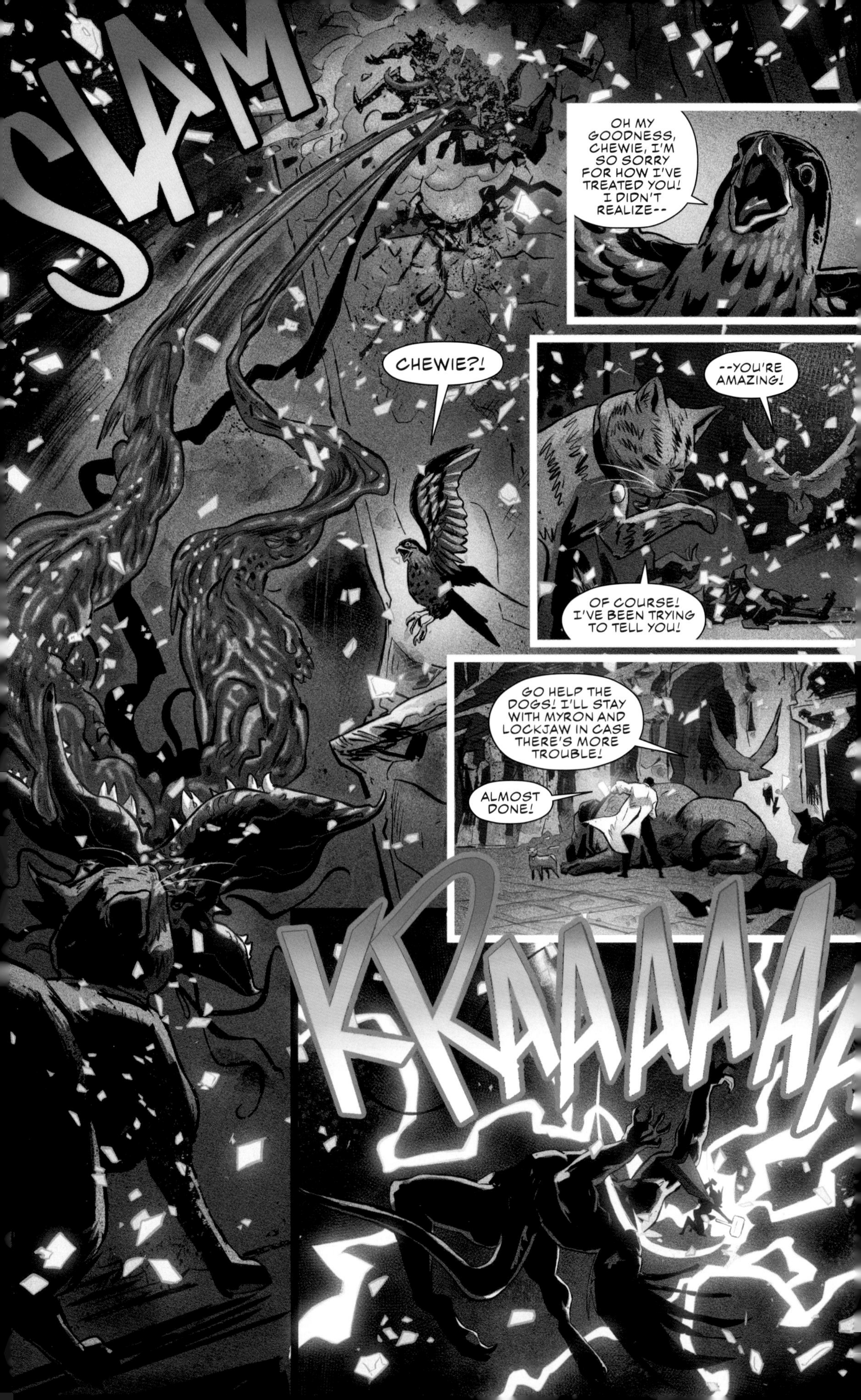
SLAM
OH MY GOODNESS, CHEWIE, I'M SO SORRY FOR HOW I'VE TREATED YOU! I DIDN'T REALIZE--
CHEWIE?!
--YOU'RE AMAZING!
OF COURSE! I'VE BEEN TRYING TO TELL YOU!
GO HELP THE DOGS! I'LL STAY WITH MYRON AND LOCKJAW IN CASE THERE'S MORE TROUBLE!
ALMOST DONE!
KRAAAAA

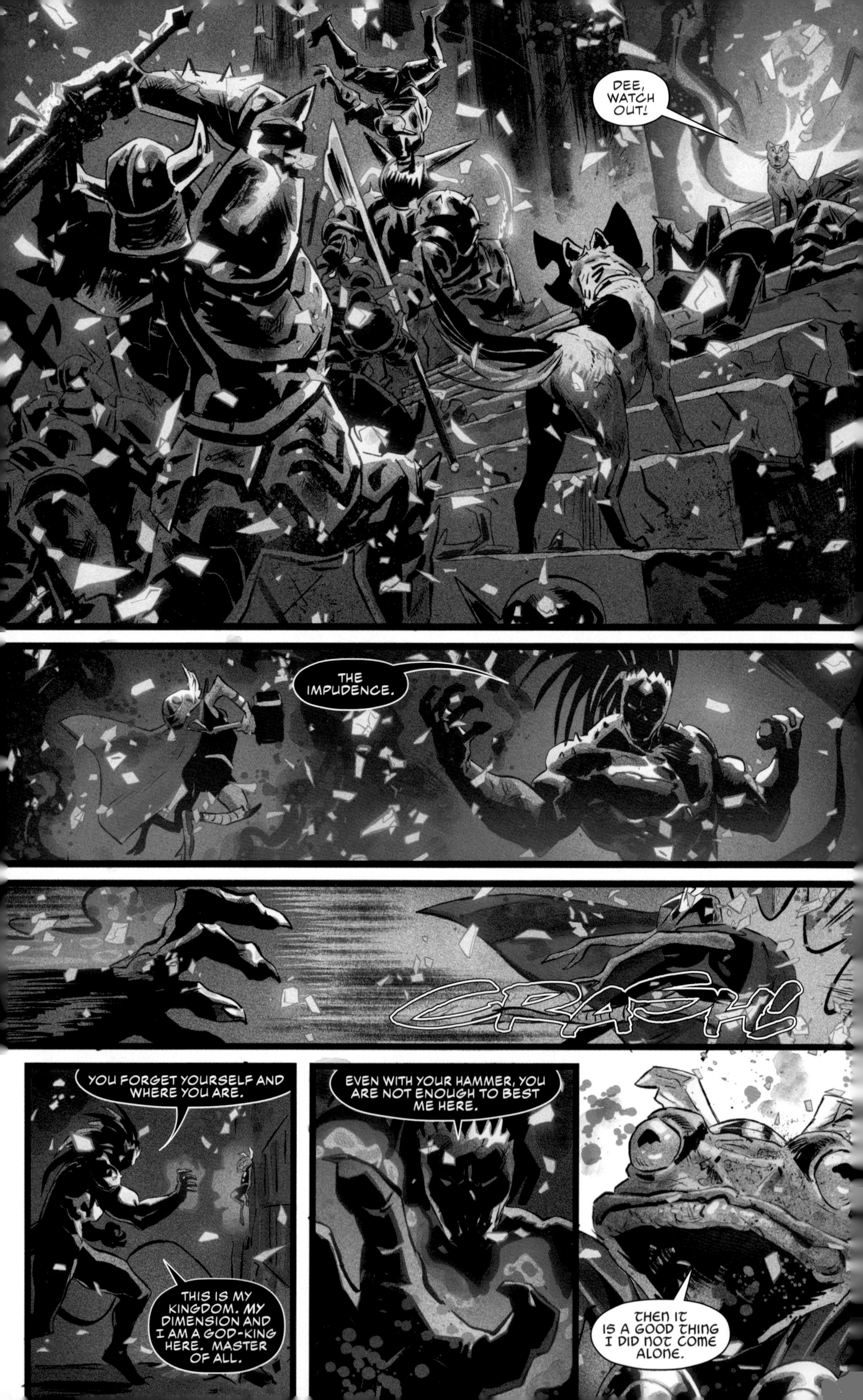
DEE, WATCH OUT!
THE IMPUDENCE.
CRASH!
YOU FORGET YOURSELF AND WHERE YOU ARE.
THIS IS MY KINGDOM. MY DIMENSION AND I AM A GOD-KING HERE. MASTER OF ALL.
EVEN WITH YOUR HAMMER, YOU ARE NOT ENOUGH TO BEST ME HERE.
THEN IT IS A GOOD THING I DID NOT COME ALONE.

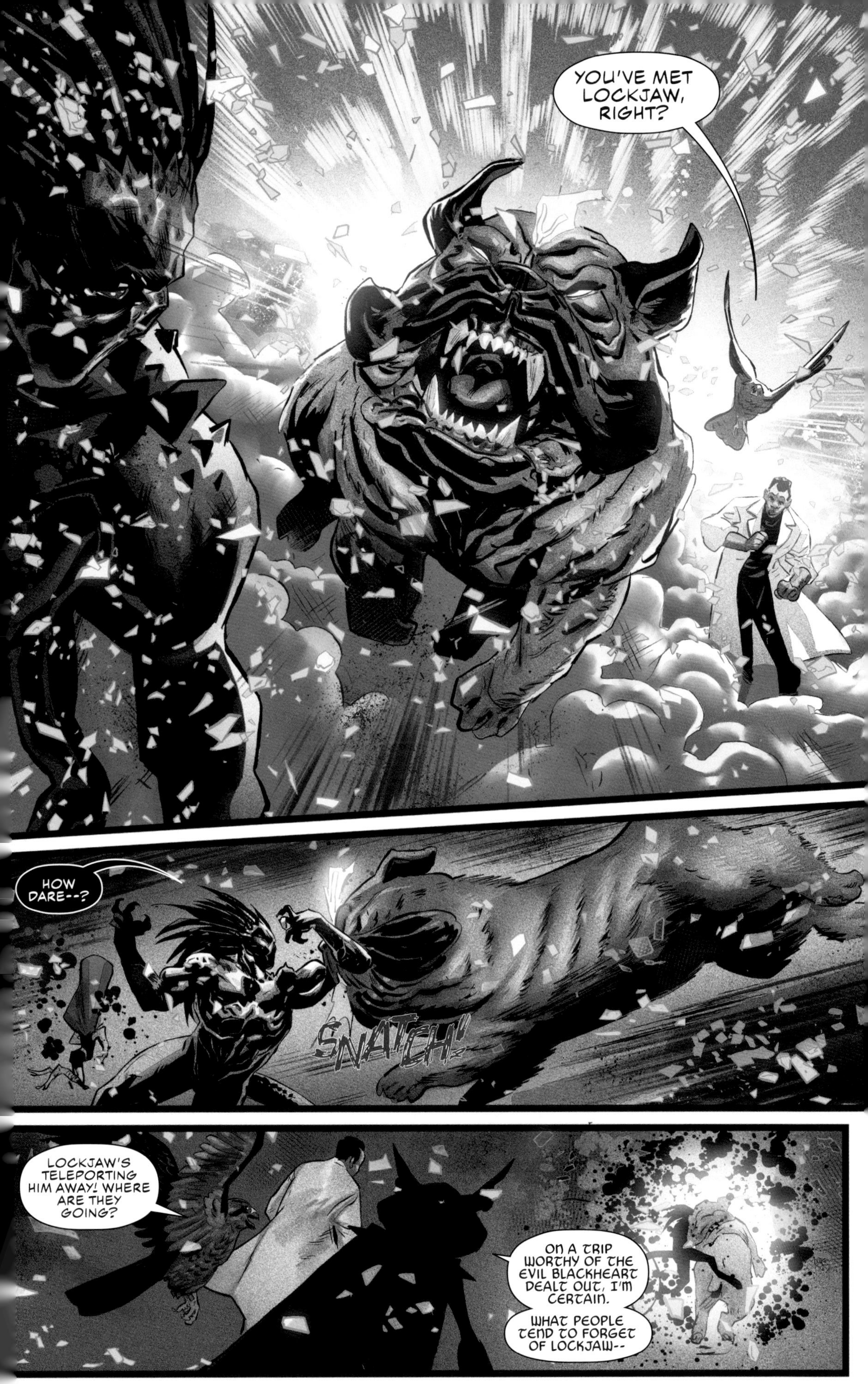
YOU'VE MET LOCKJAW, RIGHT?
HOW DARE--?
SNATCH!
LOCKJAW'S TELEPORTING HIM AWAY! WHERE ARE THEY GOING?
ON A TRIP WORTHY OF THE EVIL BLACKHEART DEALT OUT, I'M CERTAIN.
WHAT PEOPLE TEND TO FORGET OF LOCKJAW--

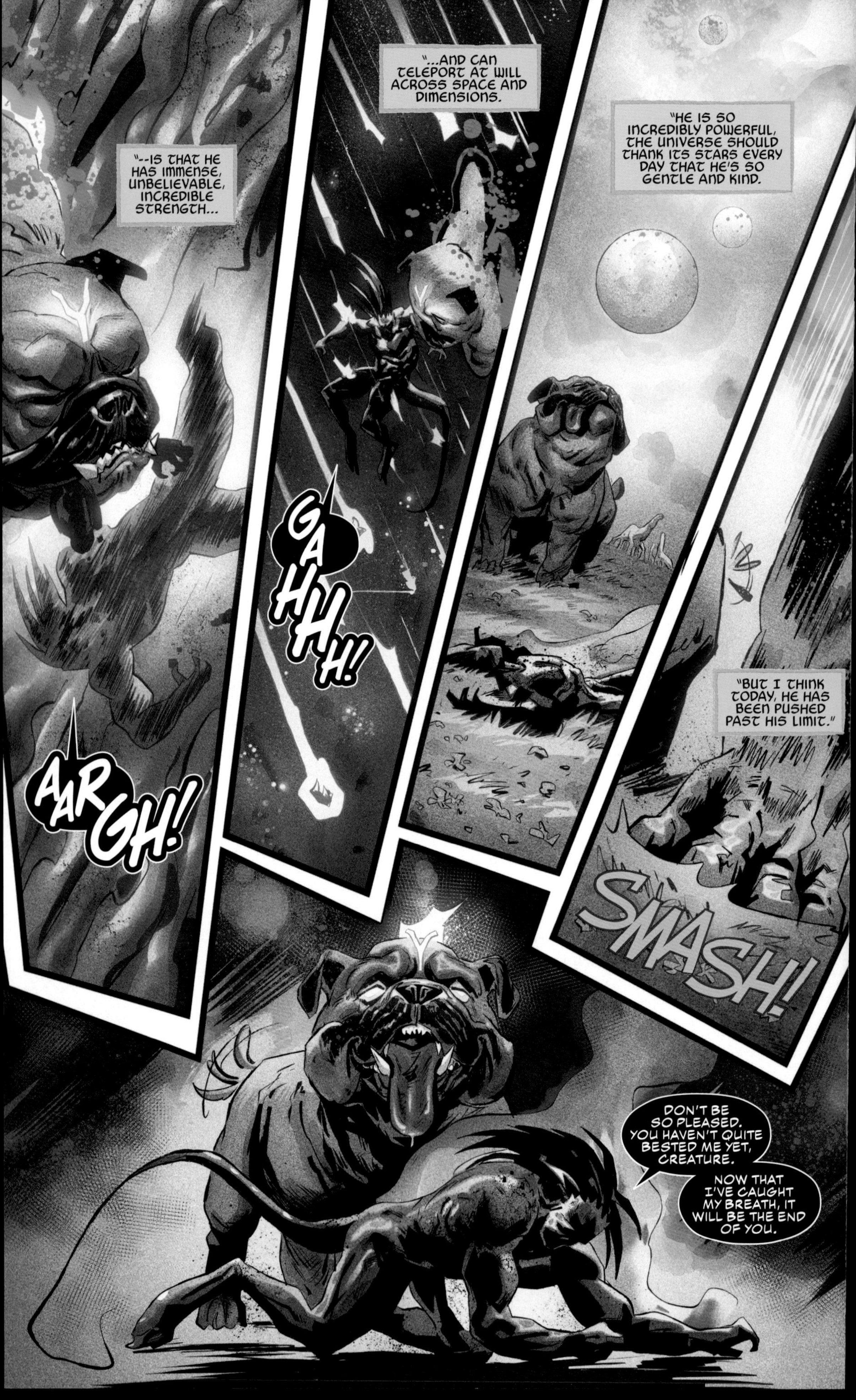
"--IS THAT HE HAS IMMENSE, UNBELIEVABLE, INCREDIBLE STRENGTH...
AARGH!
"...AND CAN TELEPORT AT WILL ACROSS SPACE AND DIMENSIONS.
GAHHHH!
"HE IS SO INCREDIBLY POWERFUL, THE UNIVERSE SHOULD THANK ITS STARS EVERY DAY THAT HE'S SO GENTLE AND KIND.
"BUT I THINK TODAY, HE HAS BEEN PUSHED PAST HIS LIMIT."
SMASH!
DON'T BE SO PLEASED. YOU HAVEN'T QUITE BESTED ME YET, CREATURE.
NOW THAT I'VE CAUGHT MY BREATH, IT WILL BE THE END OF YOU.

BLACK BOLT. KING OF THE INHUMANS. CAN DESTROY WORLDS WITH HIS VOICE.
LOCKJAW'S PERSON.
<DID YOU JUST THREATEN MY DOG?>*
*TRANSLATED FROM INHUMAN SIGN LANGUAGE.
NO!
NOOOOOOOOO!

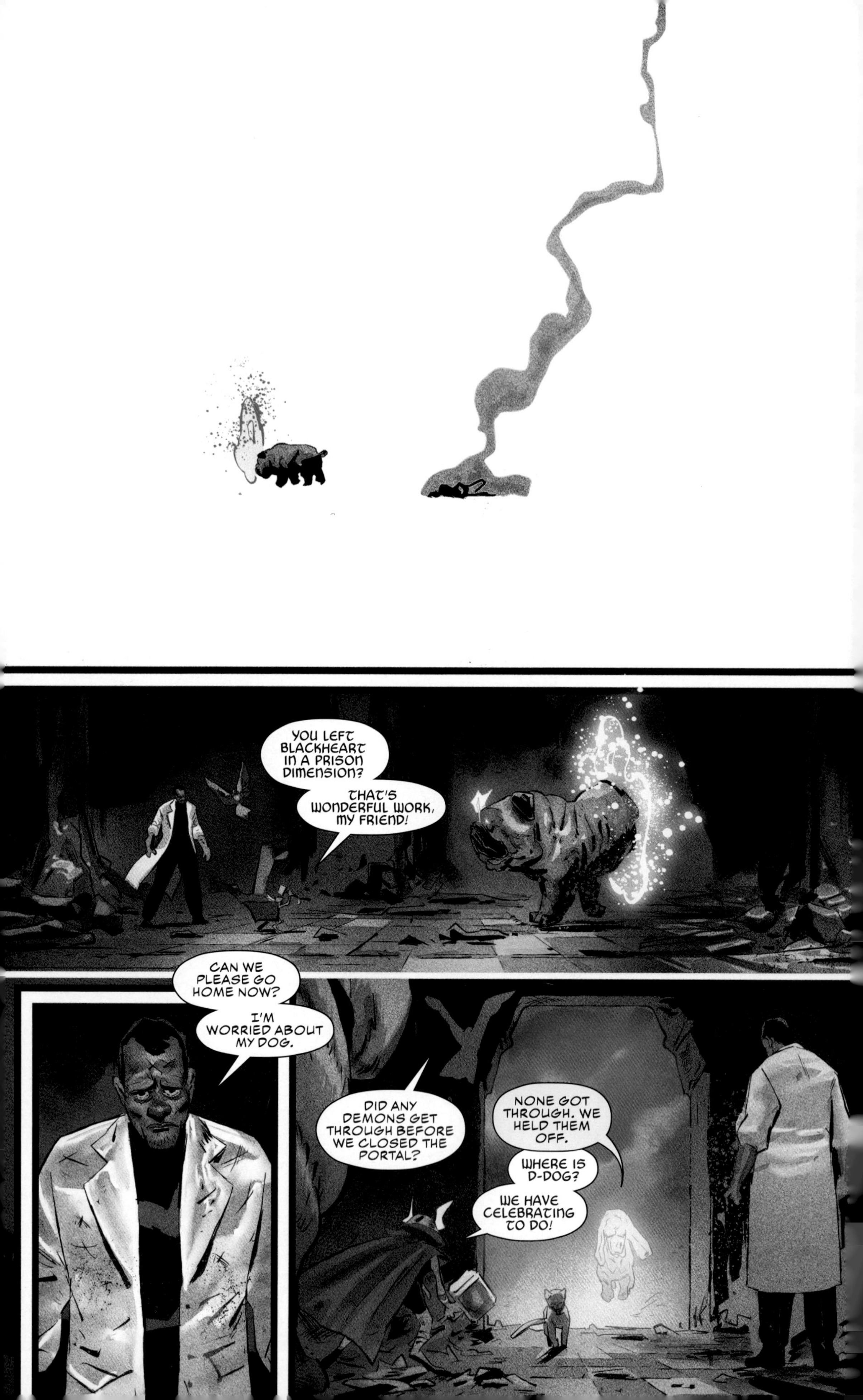
YOU LEFT BLACKHEART IN A PRISON DIMENSION?
THAT'S WONDERFUL WORK, MY FRIEND!
CAN WE PLEASE GO HOME NOW?
I'M WORRIED ABOUT MY DOG.
DID ANY DEMONS GET THROUGH BEFORE WE CLOSED THE PORTAL?
NONE GOT THROUGH. WE HELD THEM OFF.
WHERE IS D-DOG?
WE HAVE CELEBRATING TO DO!

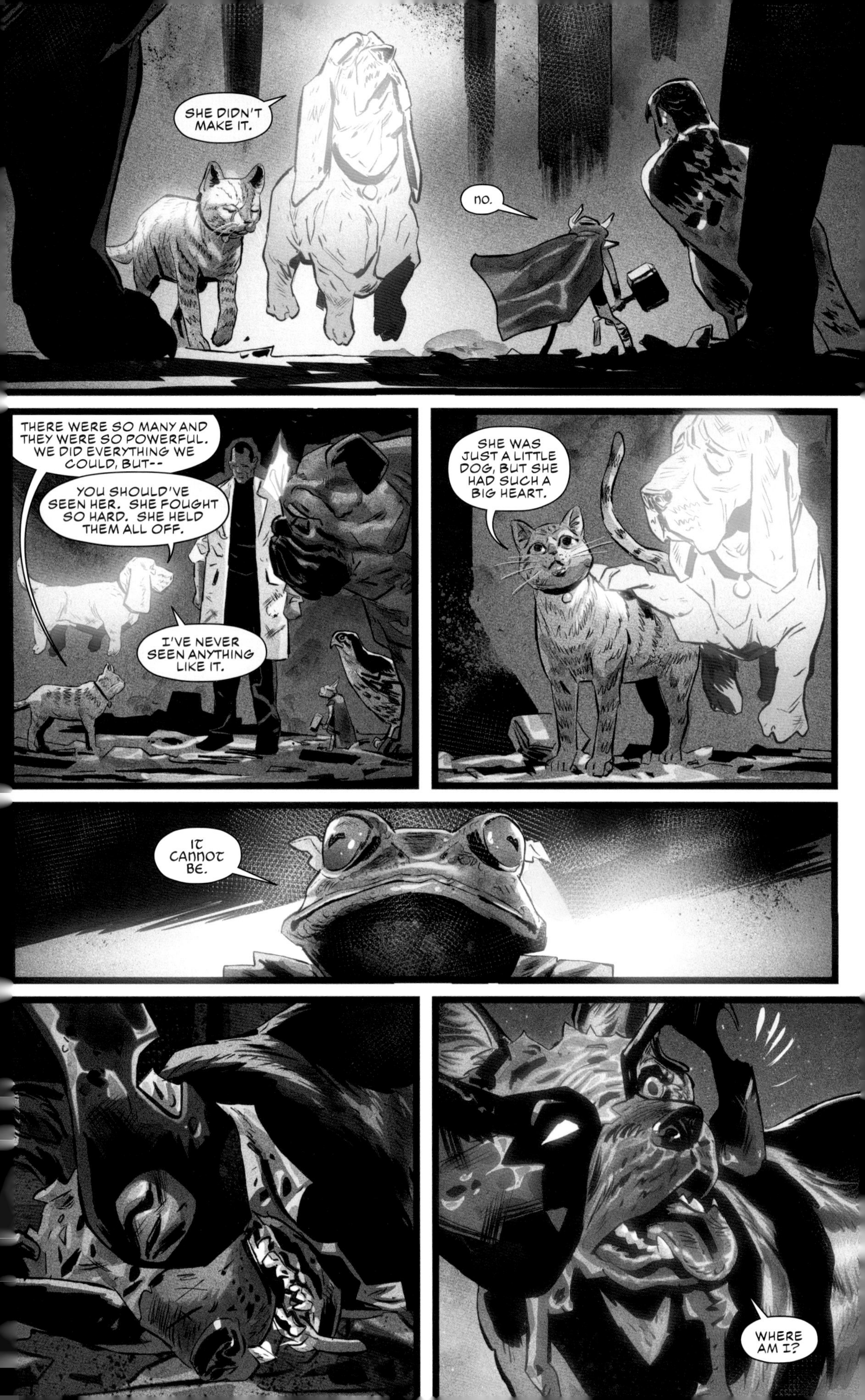
SHE DIDN'T MAKE IT.
no.
THERE WERE SO MANY AND THEY WERE SO POWERFUL. WE DID EVERYTHING WE COULD, BUT--
YOU SHOULD'VE SEEN HER. SHE FOUGHT SO HARD. SHE HELD THEM ALL OFF.
I'VE NEVER SEEN ANYTHING LIKE IT.
SHE WAS JUST A LITTLE DOG, BUT SHE HAD SUCH A BIG HEART.
IT CANNOT BE.
WHERE AM I?

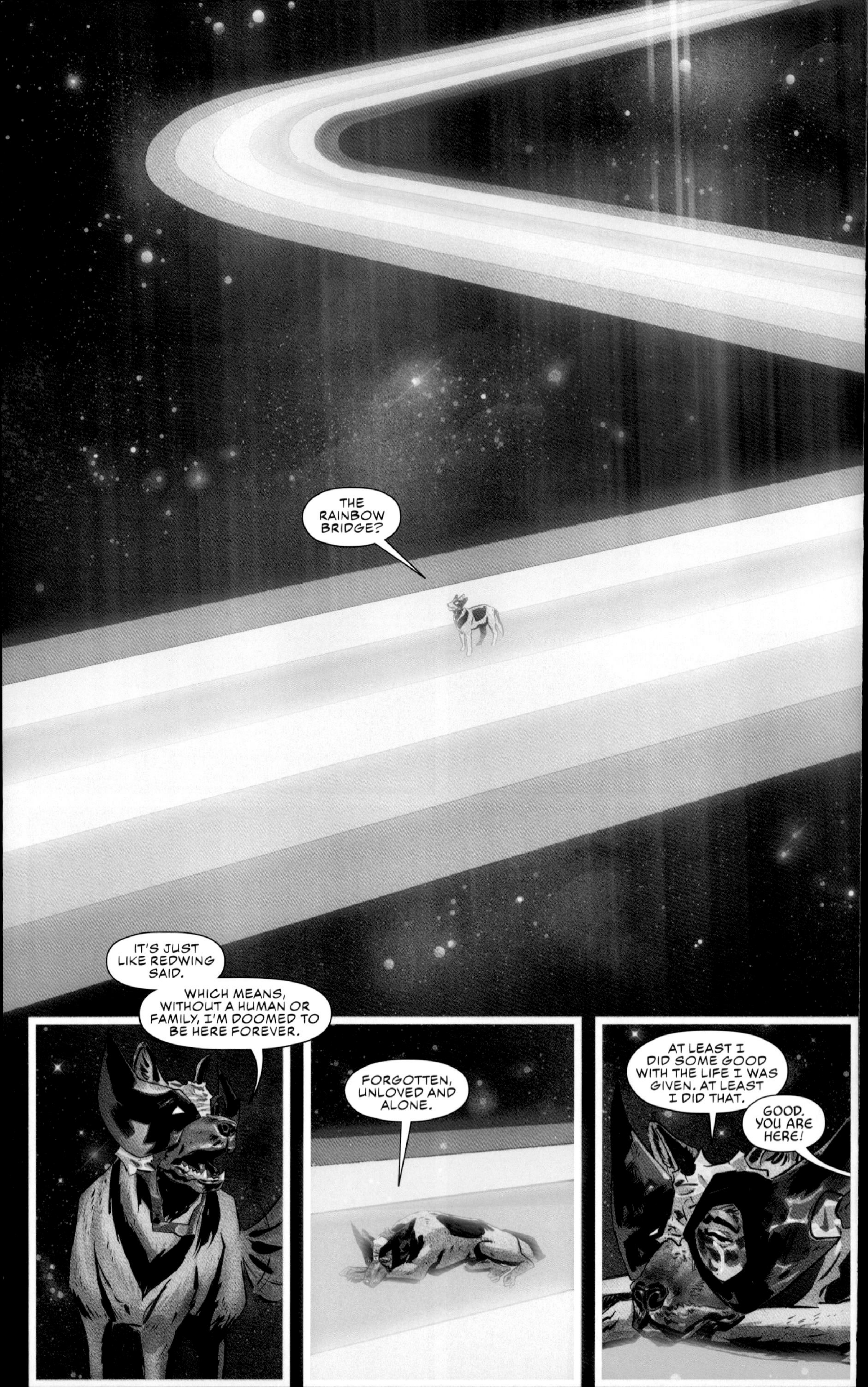
THE RAINBOW BRIDGE?
IT'S JUST LIKE REDWING SAID.
WHICH MEANS, WITHOUT A HUMAN OR FAMILY, I'M DOOMED TO BE HERE FOREVER.
FORGOTTEN, UNLOVED AND ALONE.
AT LEAST I DID SOME GOOD WITH THE LIFE I WAS GIVEN. AT LEAST I DID THAT.
GOOD. YOU ARE HERE!

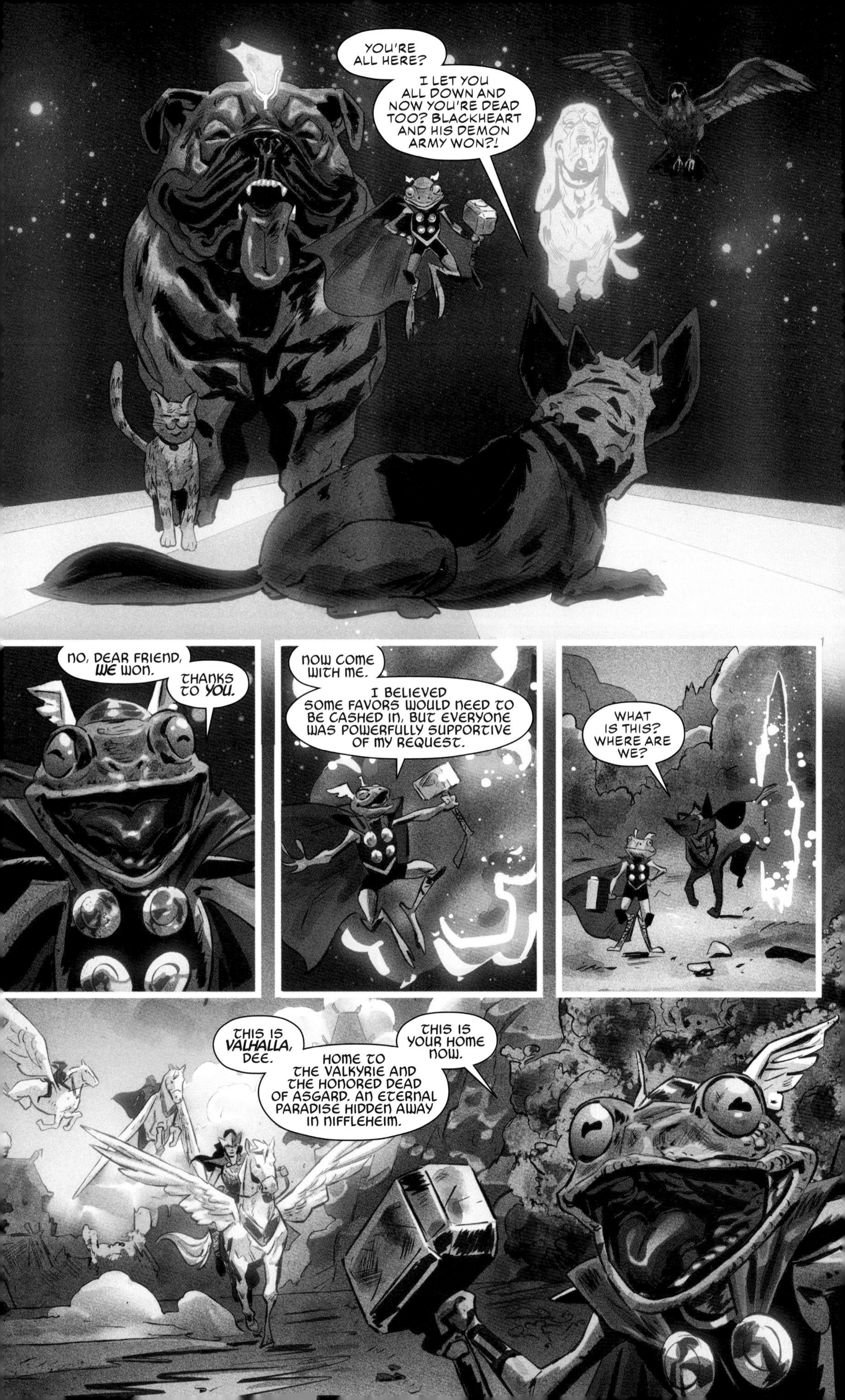
YOU'RE ALL HERE?
I LET YOU ALL DOWN AND NOW YOU'RE DEAD TOO? BLACKHEART AND HIS DEMON ARMY WON?!
NO, DEAR FRIEND, WE WON.
THANKS TO YOU.
NOW COME WITH ME.
I BELIEVED SOME FAVORS WOULD NEED TO BE CASHED IN, BUT EVERYONE WAS POWERFULLY SUPPORTIVE OF MY REQUEST.
WHAT IS THIS? WHERE ARE WE?
THIS IS VALHALLA, DEE.
HOME TO THE VALKYRIE AND THE HONORED DEAD OF ASGARD. AN ETERNAL PARADISE HIDDEN AWAY IN NIFFLEHEIM.
THIS IS YOUR HOME NOW.

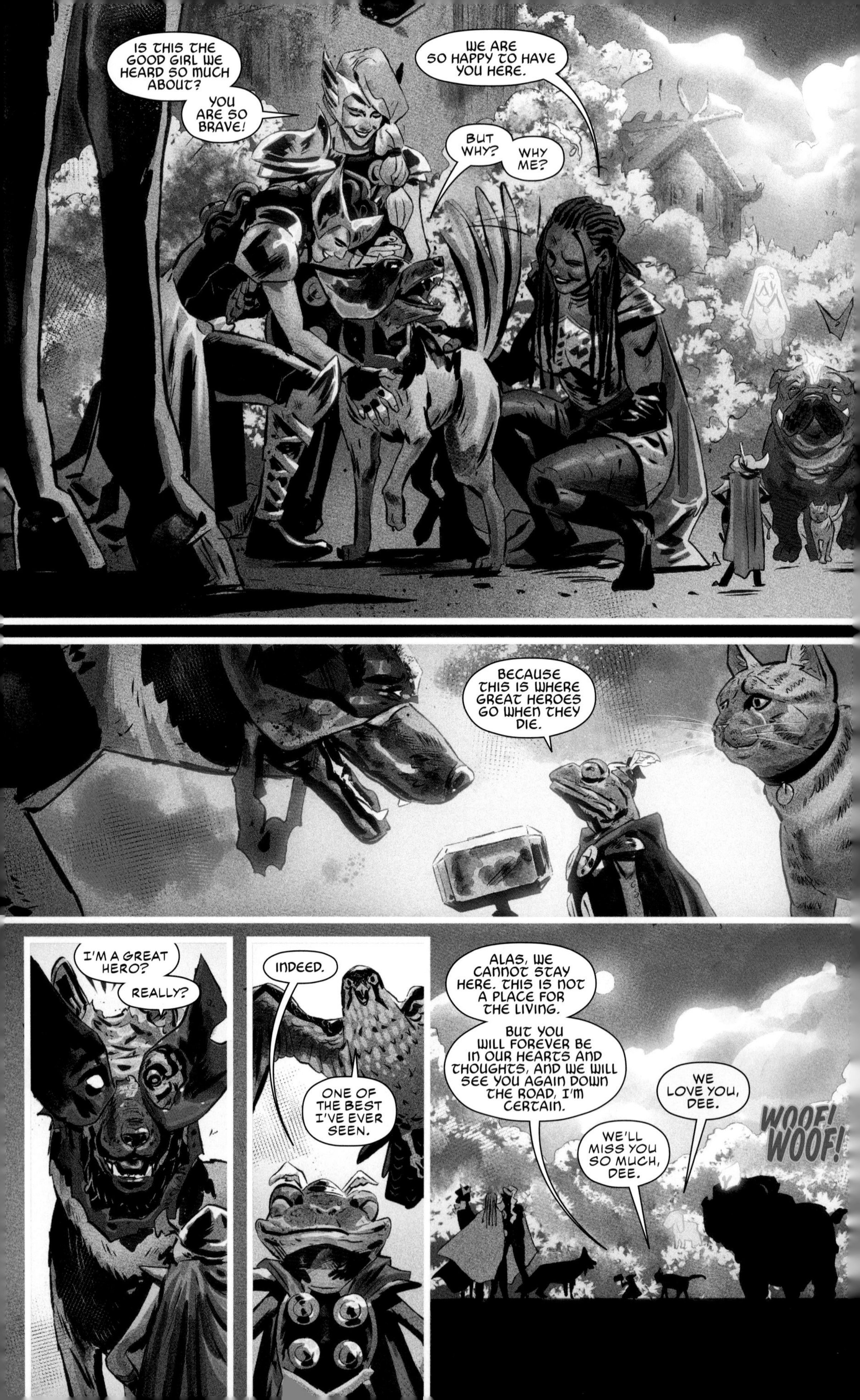
IS THIS THE GOOD GIRL WE HEARD SO MUCH ABOUT?
YOU ARE SO BRAVE!
WE ARE SO HAPPY TO HAVE YOU HERE.
BUT WHY?
WHY ME?
BECAUSE THIS IS WHERE GREAT HEROES GO WHEN THEY DIE.
I'M A GREAT HERO?
REALLY?
INDEED.
ONE OF THE BEST I'VE EVER SEEN.
ALAS, WE CANNOT STAY HERE. THIS IS NOT A PLACE FOR THE LIVING.
BUT YOU WILL FOREVER BE IN OUR HEARTS AND THOUGHTS, AND WE WILL SEE YOU AGAIN DOWN THE ROAD, I'M CERTAIN.
WE LOVE YOU, DEE.
WE'LL MISS YOU SO MUCH, DEE.
WOOF! WOOF!

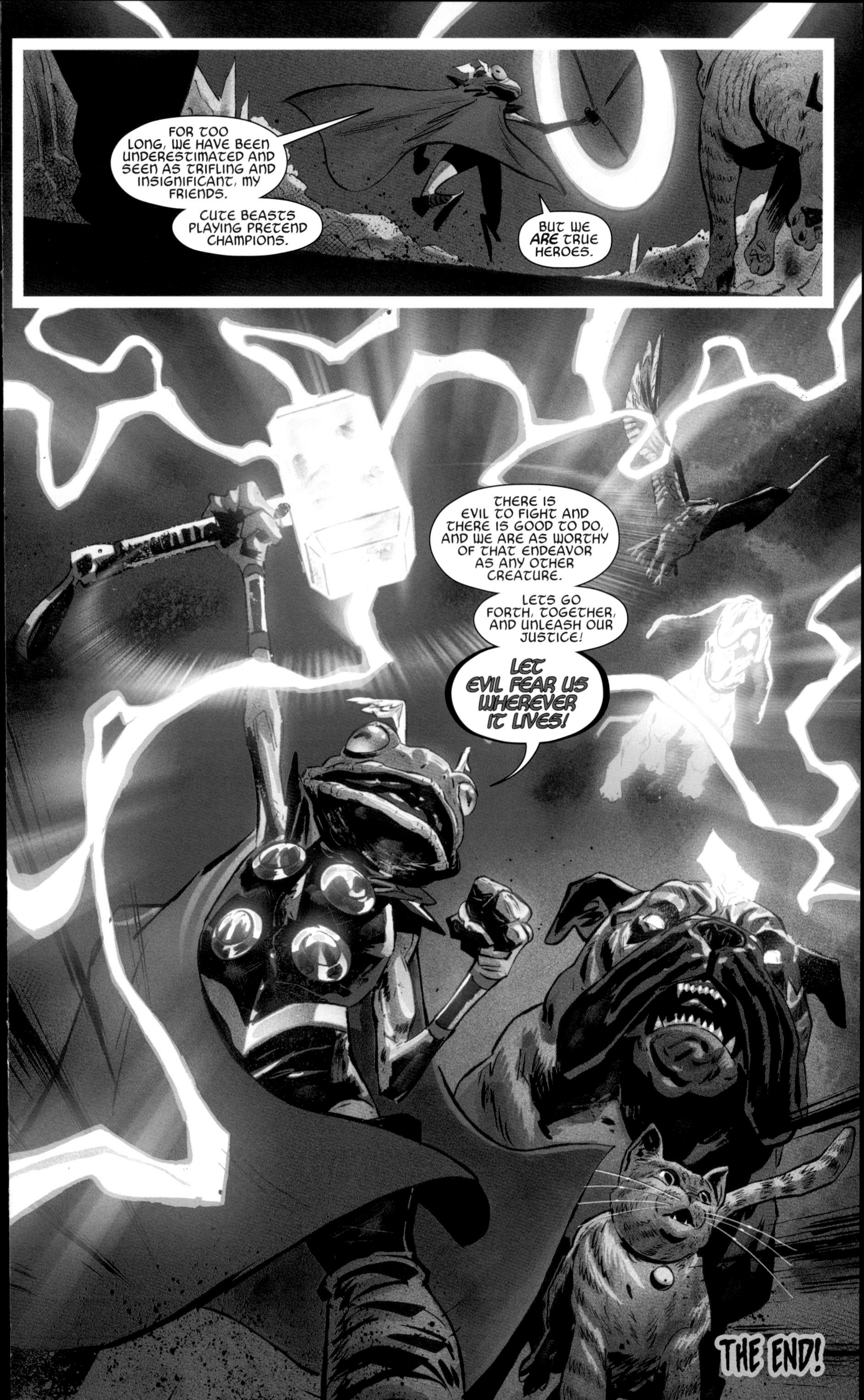
FOR TOO LONG, WE HAVE BEEN UNDERESTIMATED AND SEEN AS TRIFLING AND INSIGNIFICANT, MY FRIENDS.
CUTE BEASTS PLAYING PRETEND CHAMPIONS.
BUT WE ARE TRUE HEROES.
THERE IS EVIL TO FIGHT AND THERE IS GOOD TO DO, AND WE ARE AS WORTHY OF THAT ENDEAVOR AS ANY OTHER CREATURE.
LETS GO FORTH, TOGETHER, AND UNLEASH OUR JUSTICE!
LET EVIL FEAR US WHEREVER IT LIVES!
THE END!

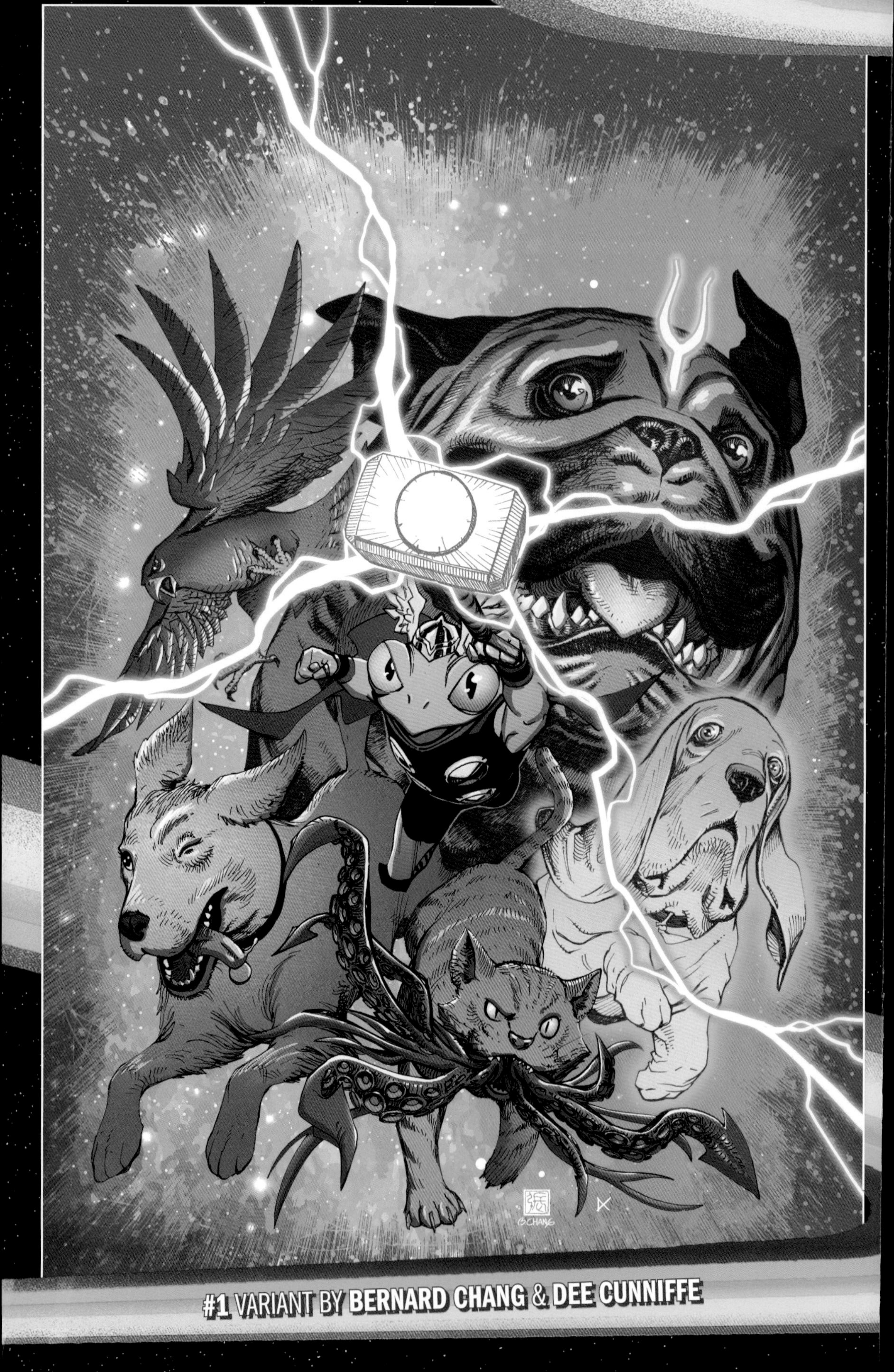

#1 VARIANT BY **BERNARD CHANG** & **DEE CUNNIFFE**

#1 VARIANT BY **ADAM KUBERT** & **ISRAEL SILVA**

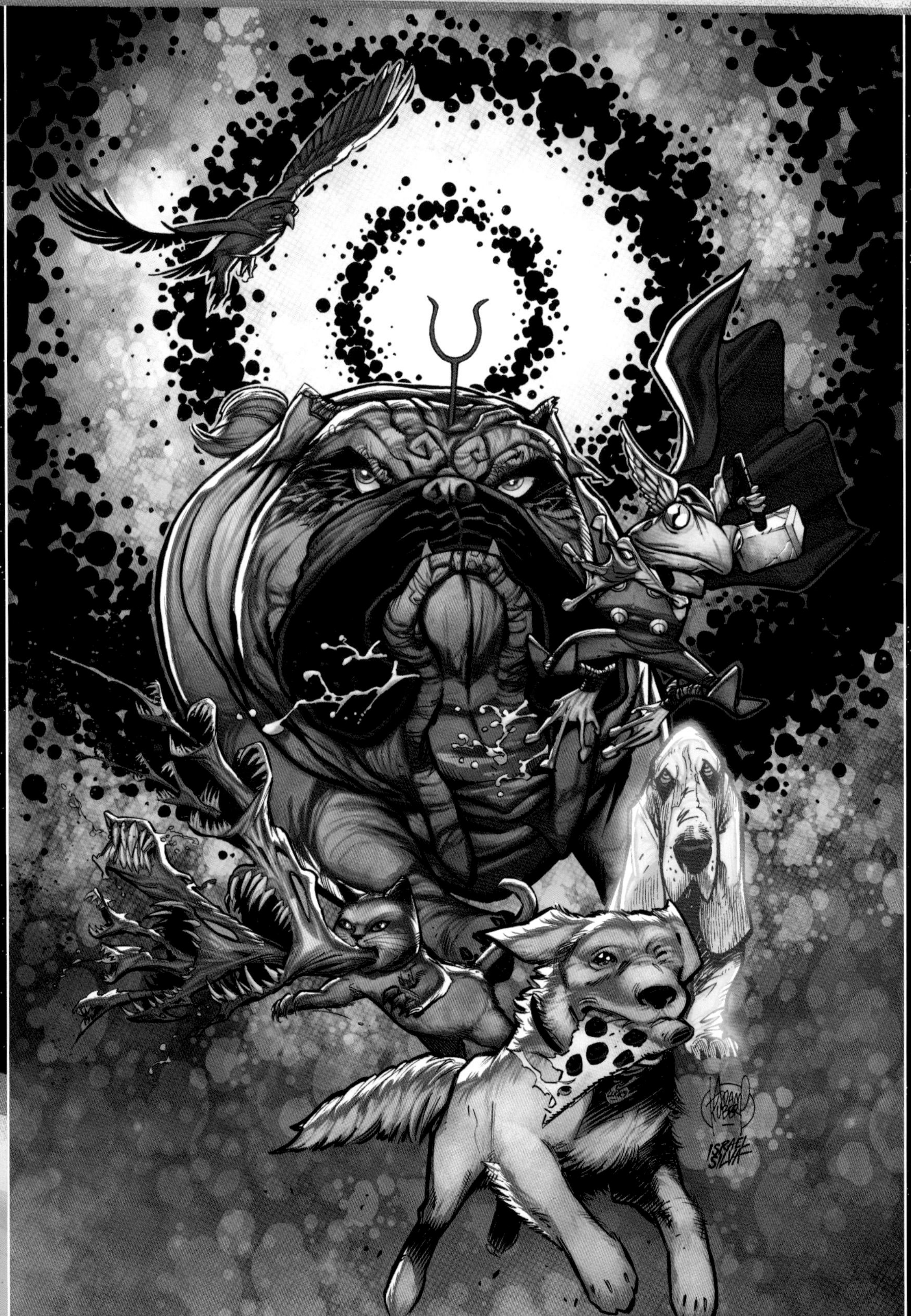

ADAM KUBERT
ISRAEL SILVA

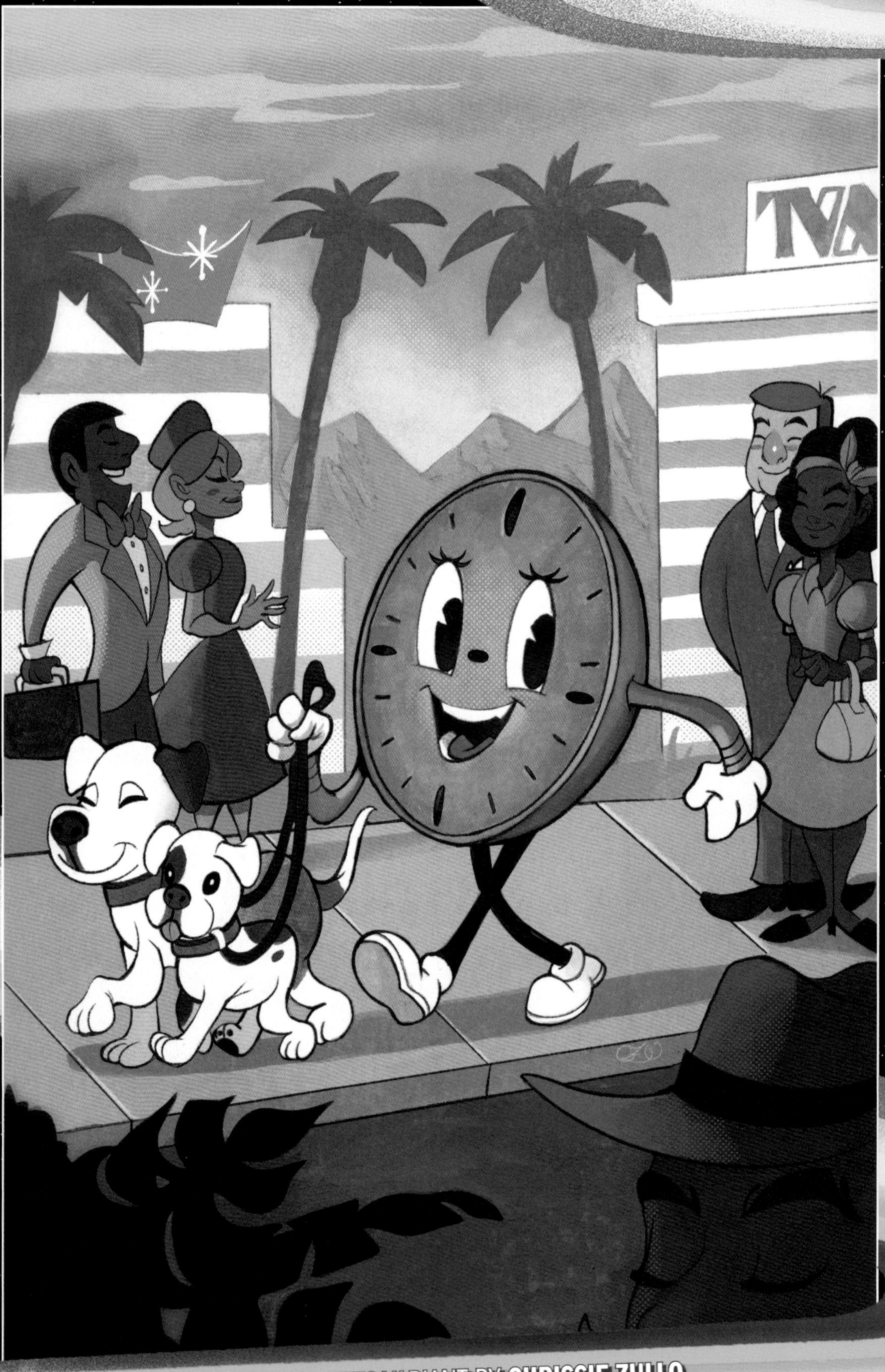
TVA

#1 MISS MINUTES VARIANT BY **CHRISSIE ZULLO**

#1 REDWING VARIANT BY RON LIM & ISRAEL SILVA

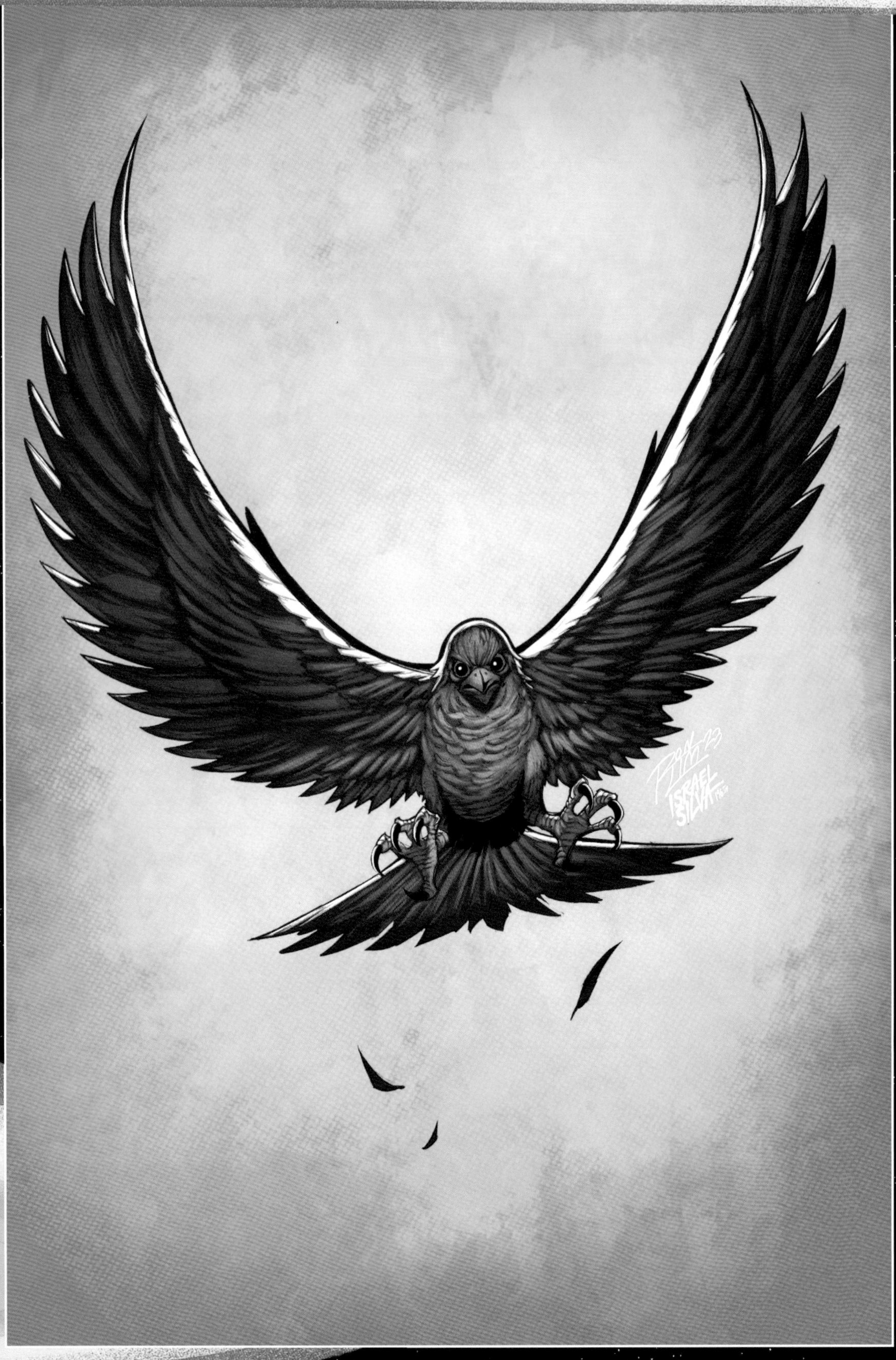

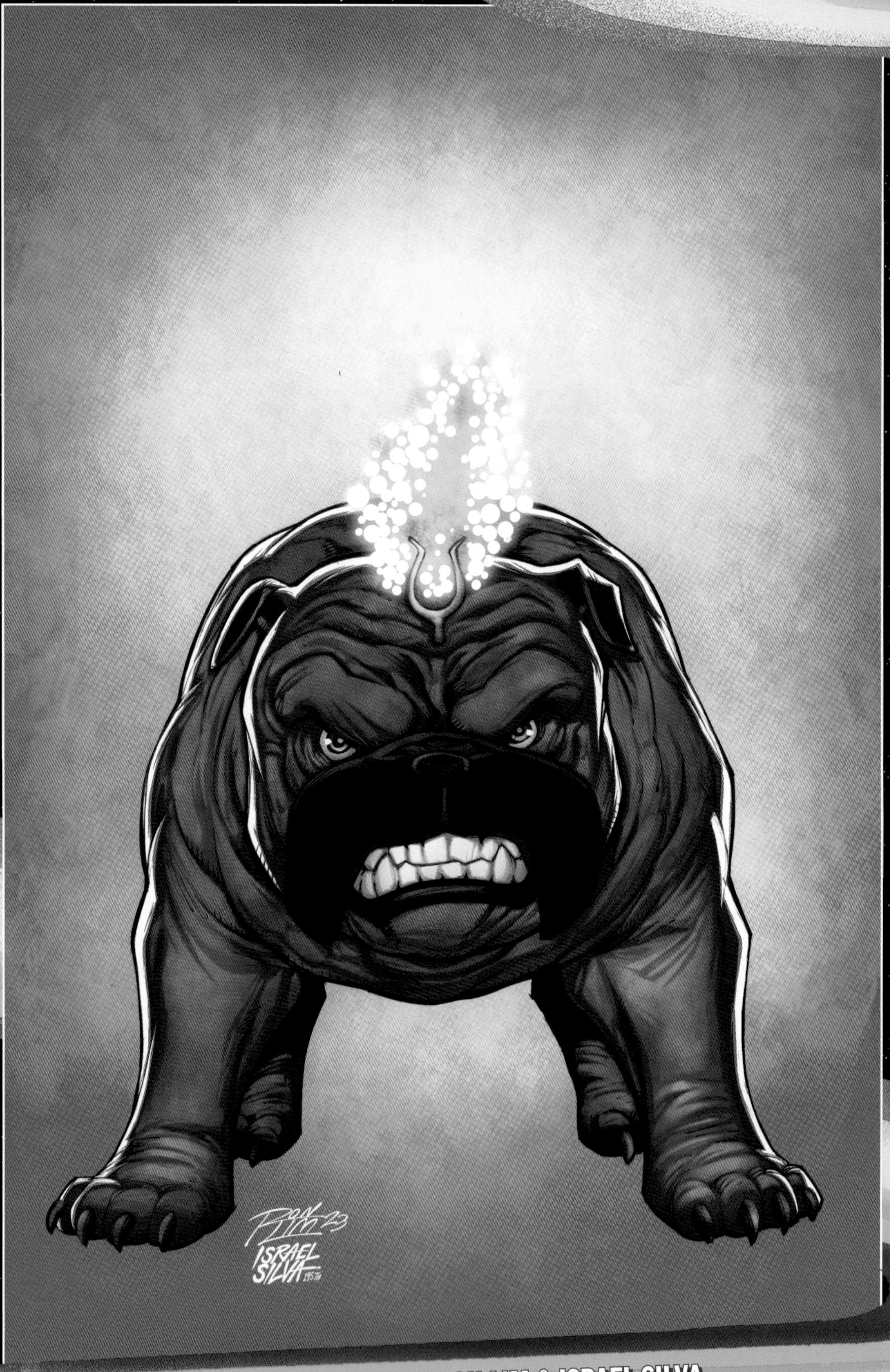
Ron Lim 23
ISRAEL SILVA

#1 LOCKJAW VARIANT BY RON LIM & ISRAEL SILVA

#2 LUCKY VARIANT BY **RON LIM** & **ISRAEL SILVA**

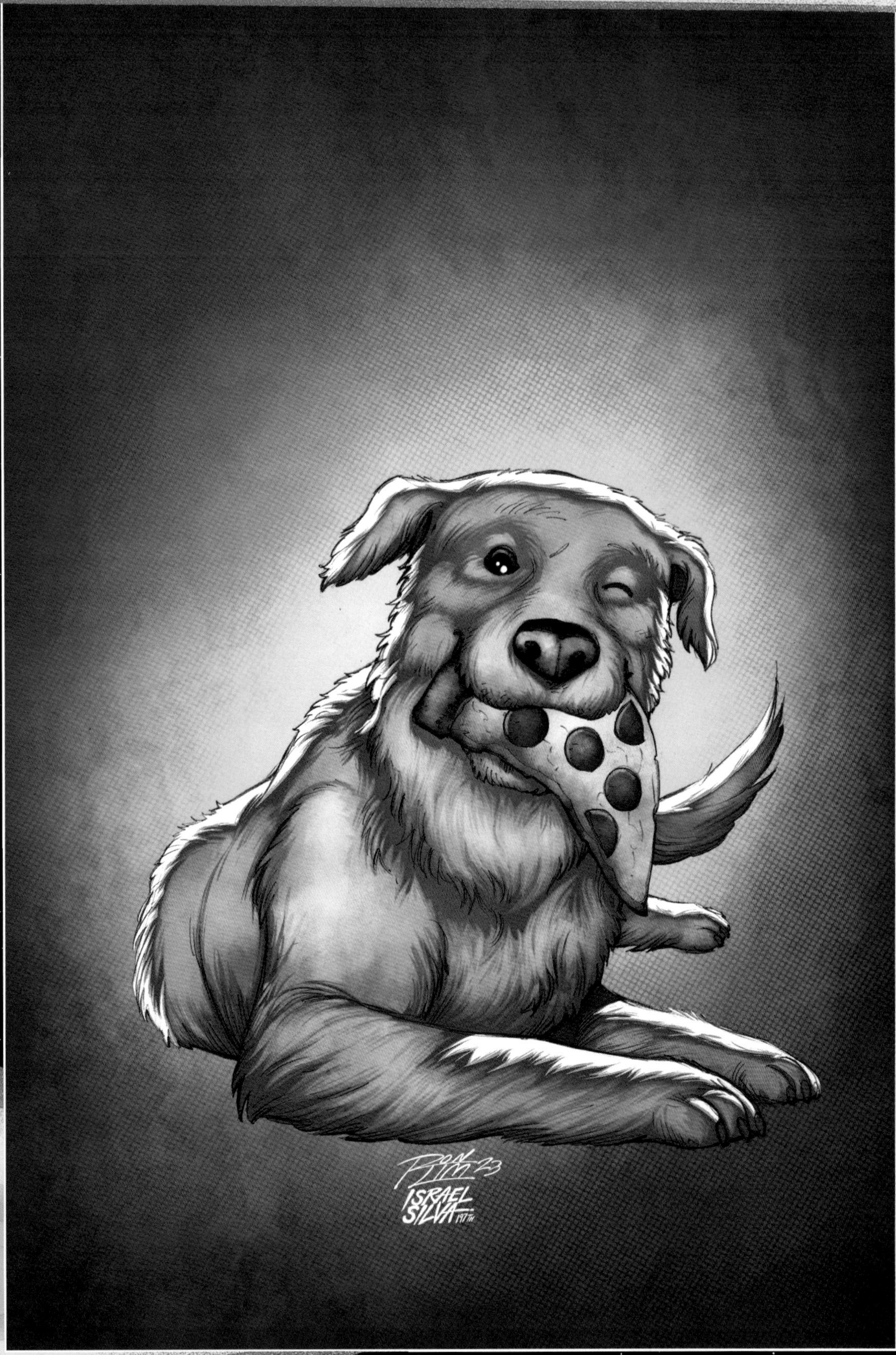
ISRAEL
SILVA

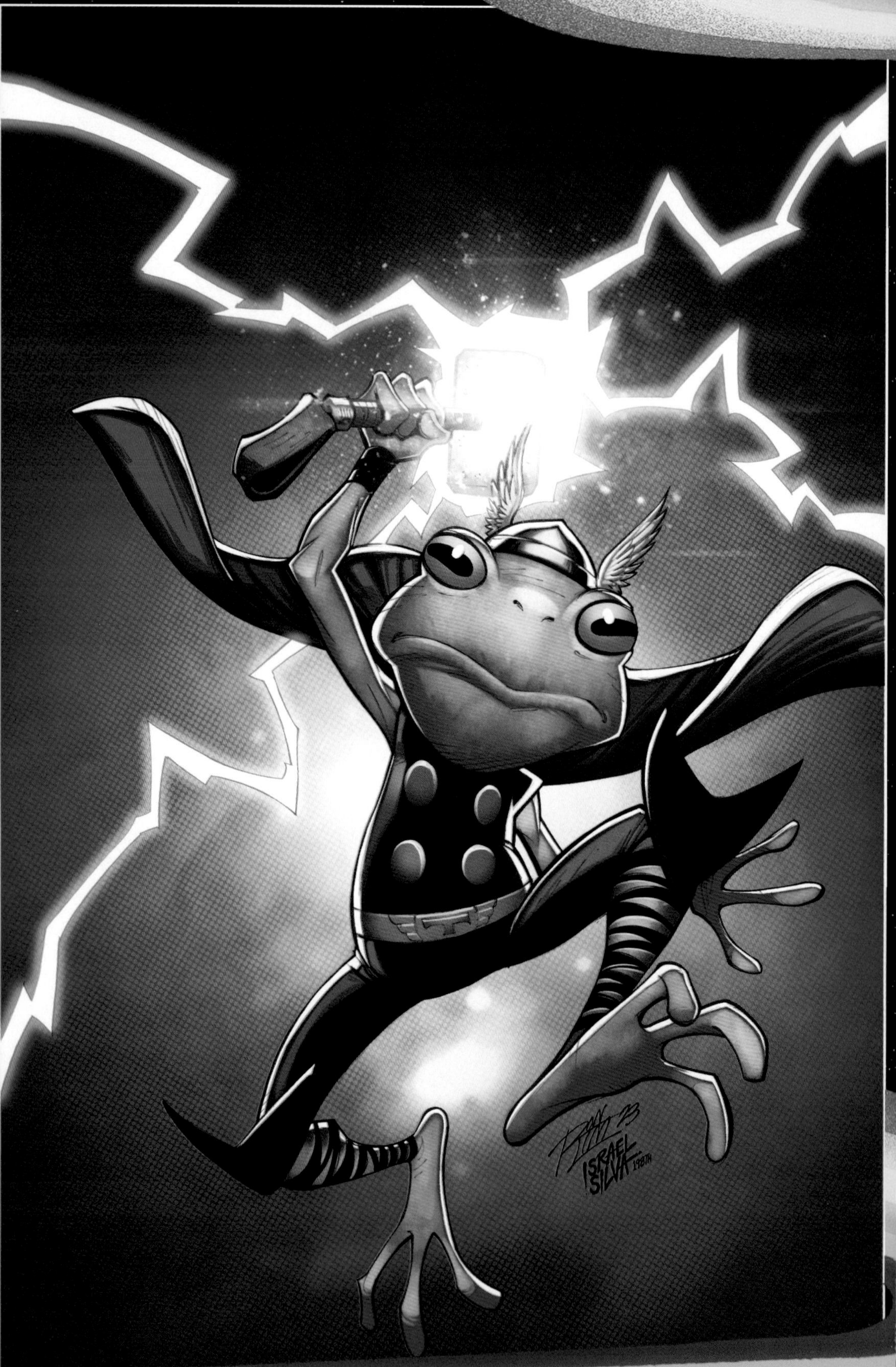

#2 THROG VARIANT BY **RON LIM** & **ISRAEL SILVA**

#3 CHEWIE VARIANT BY **RON LIM** & **ISRAEL SILVA**

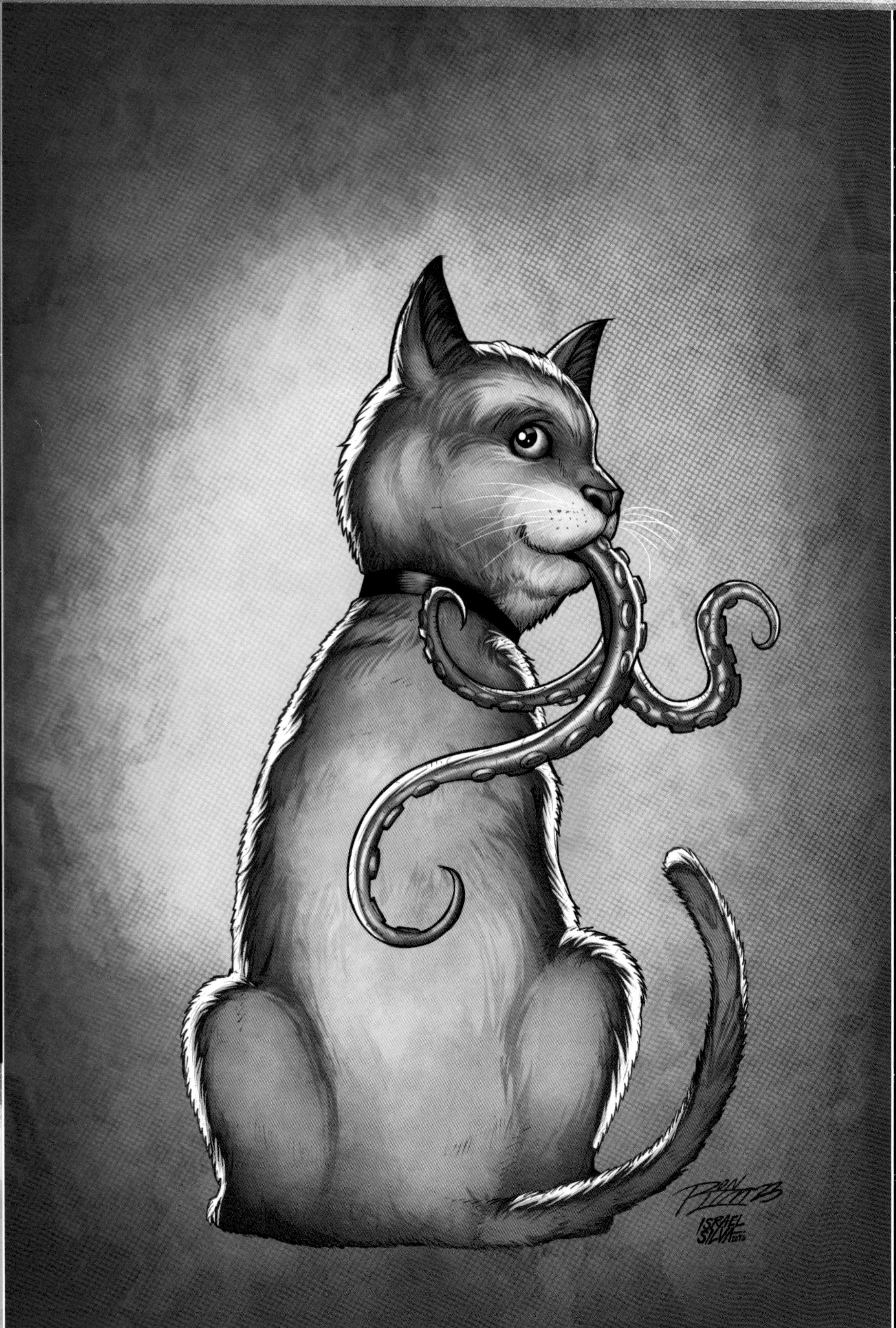

ISRAEL SILVA

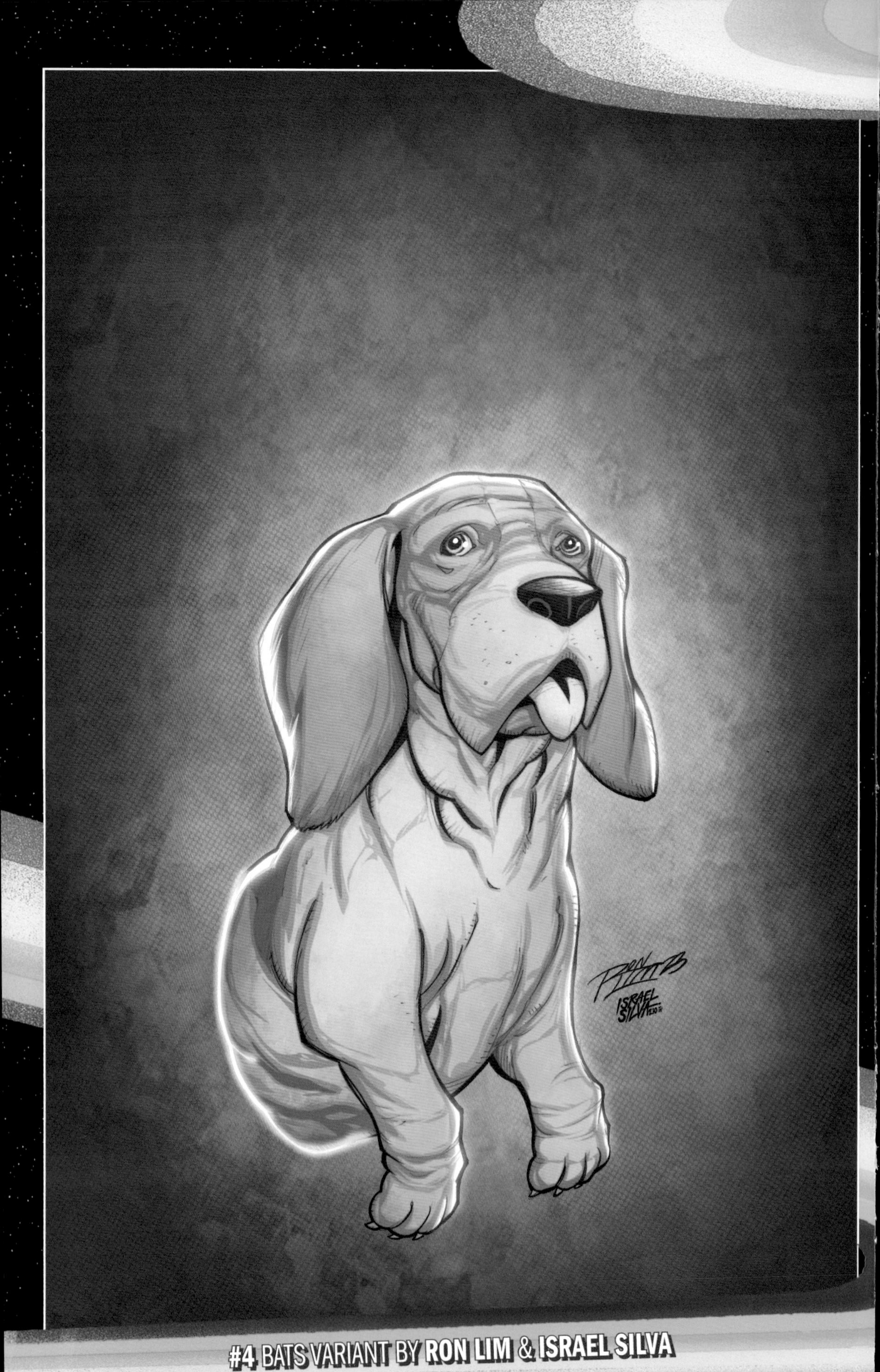
ISRAEL SILVA

#4 BATS VARIANT BY **RON LIM** & **ISRAEL SILVA**

BLACKHEART'S SOLDIER DESIGNS BY KYLE STARKS

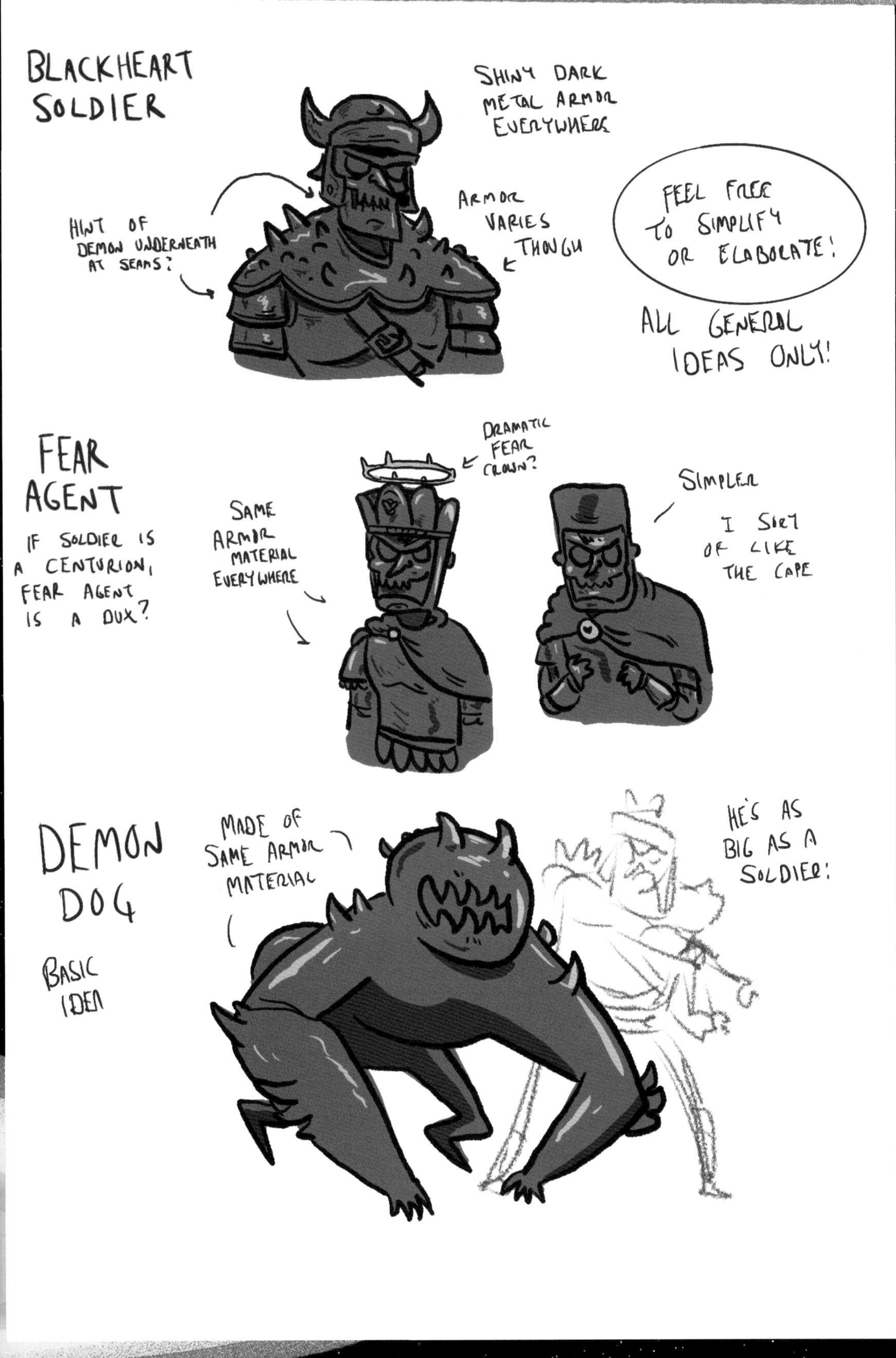
BLACKHEART SOLDIER
SHINY DARK METAL ARMOR EVERYWHERE
HINT OF DEMON UNDERNEATH AT SEAMS?
ARMOR VARIES THOUGH
FEEL FREE TO SIMPLIFY OR ELABORATE!
ALL GENERAL IDEAS ONLY!
FEAR AGENT
IF SOLDIER IS A CENTURION, FEAR AGENT IS A DUX?
DRAMATIC FEAR CROWN?
SAME ARMOR MATERIAL EVERYWHERE
SIMPLER
I SORT OF LIKE THE CAPE
DEMON DOG
BASIC IDEA
MADE OF SAME ARMOR MATERIAL
HE'S AS BIG AS A SOLDIER!

D-DOG

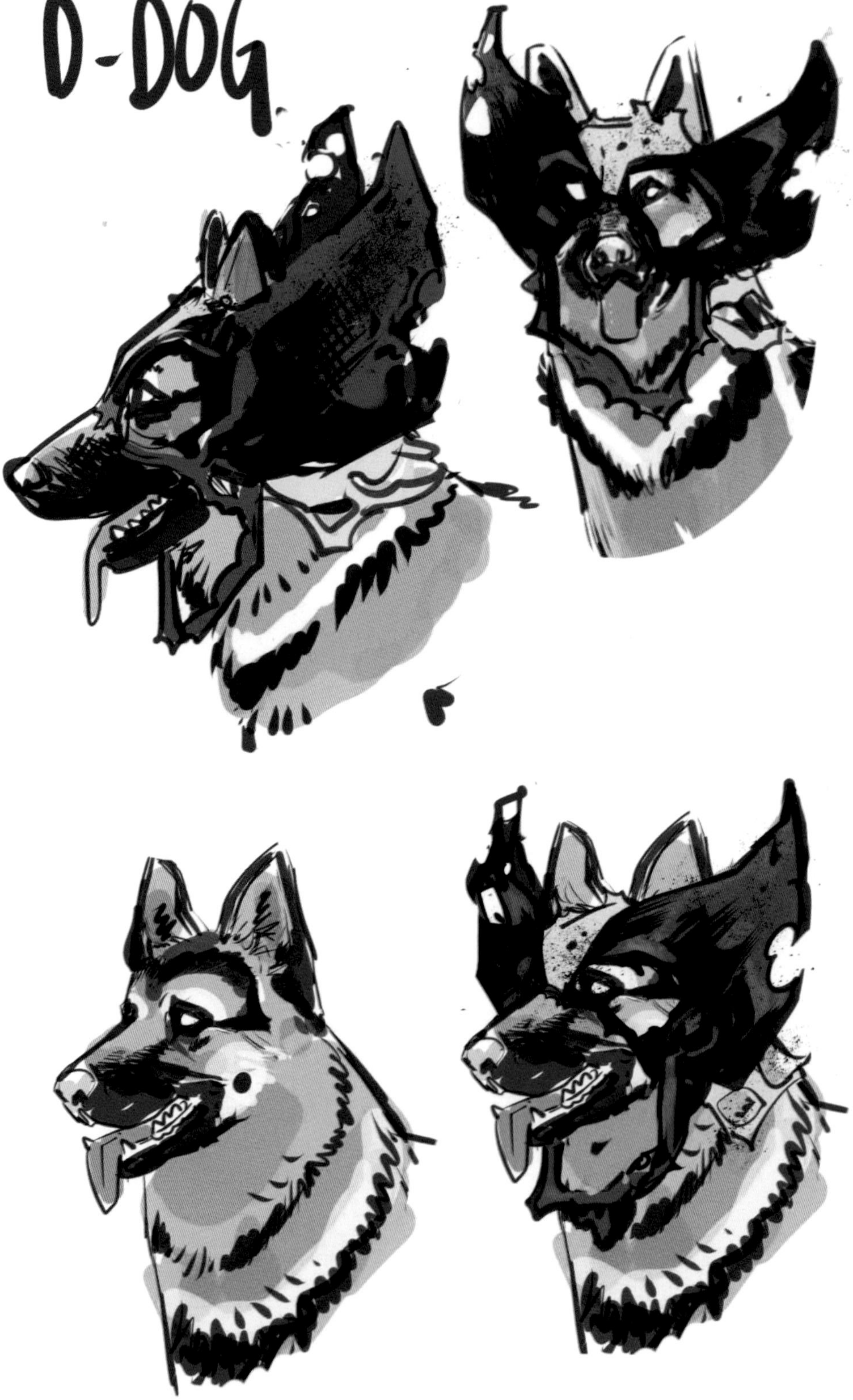

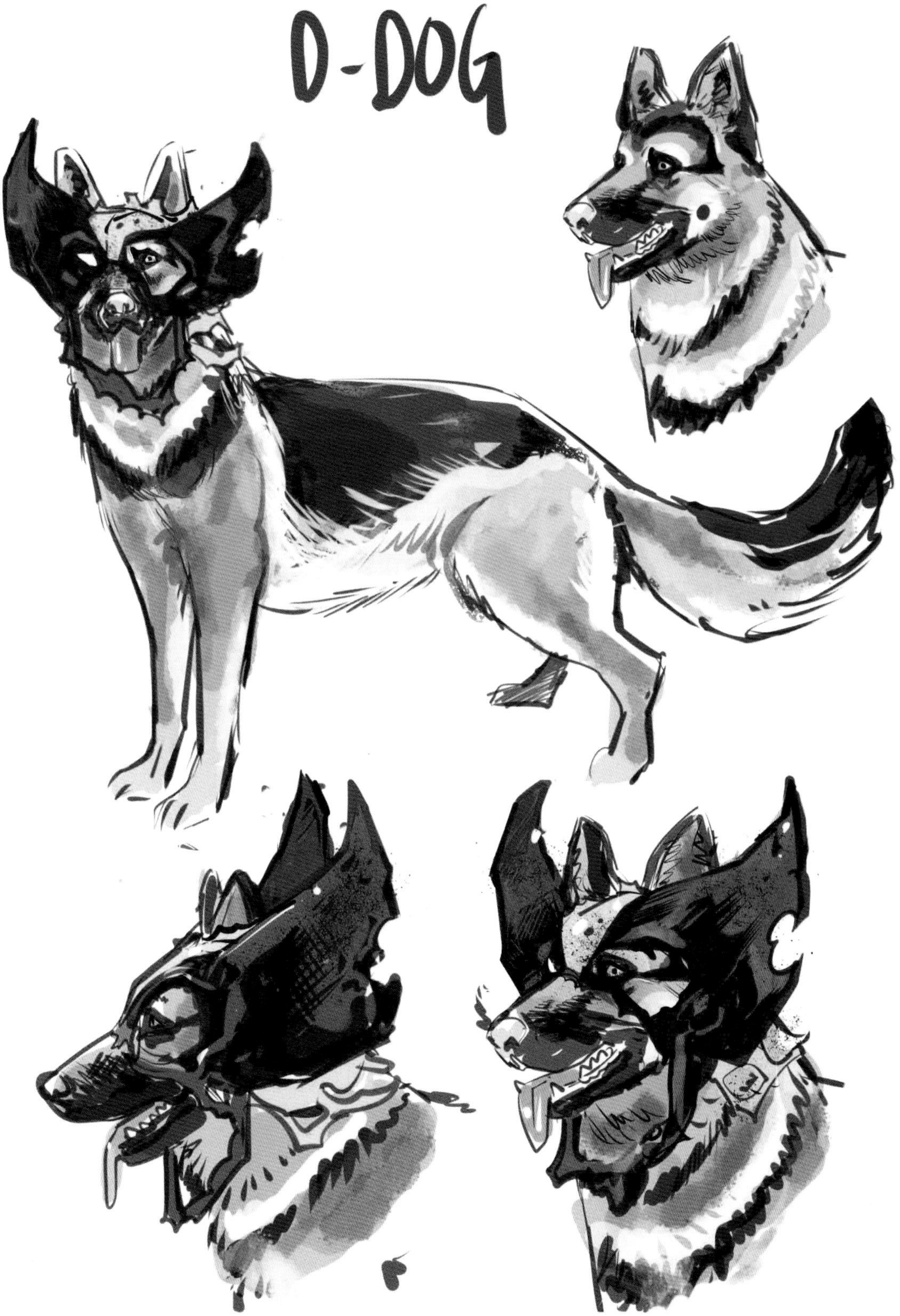
D-DOG

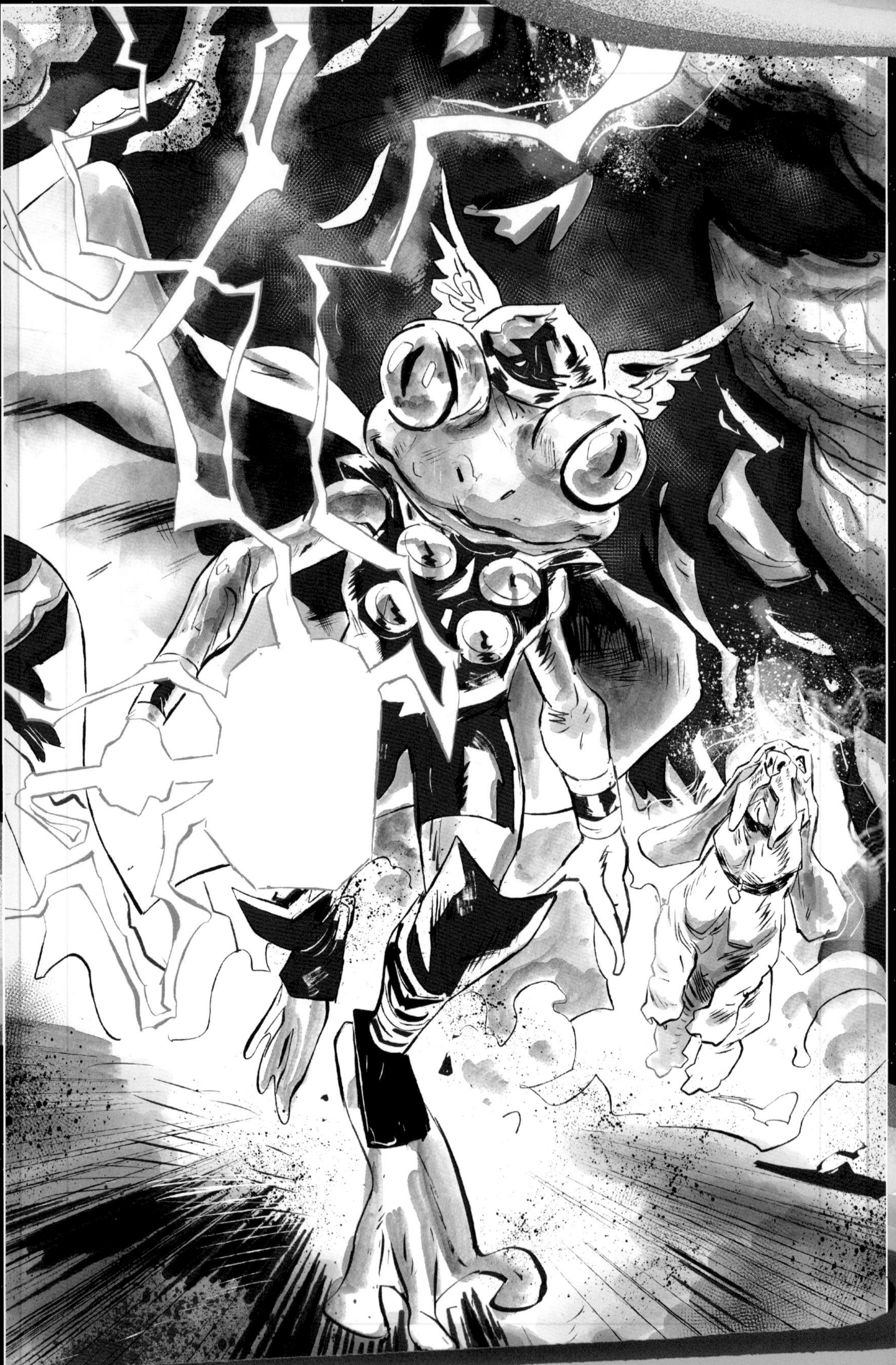

#2 PAGE 13 ART BY JESÚS HERVÁS

#3 PAGE 12 ART BY JUAN GEDEON

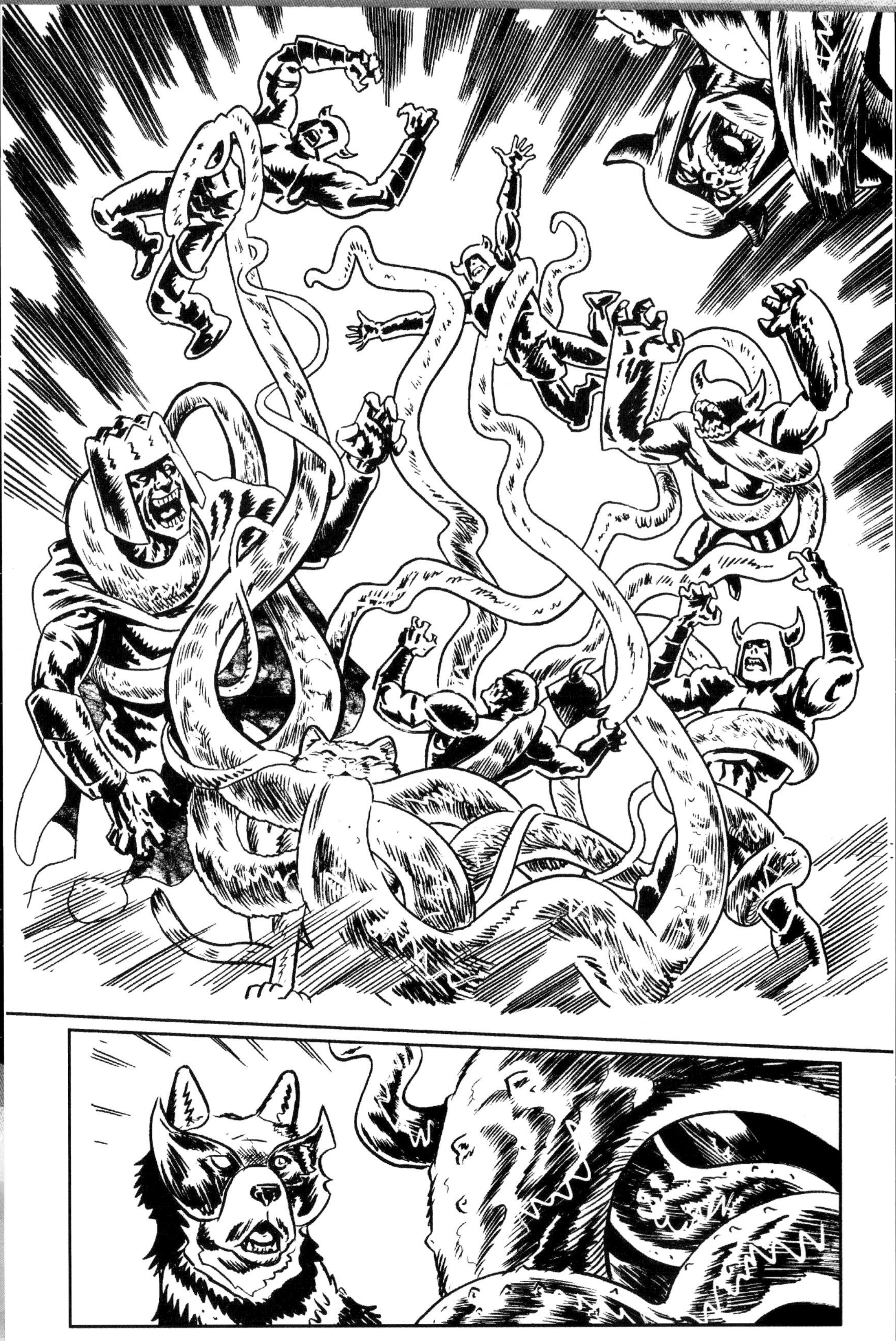

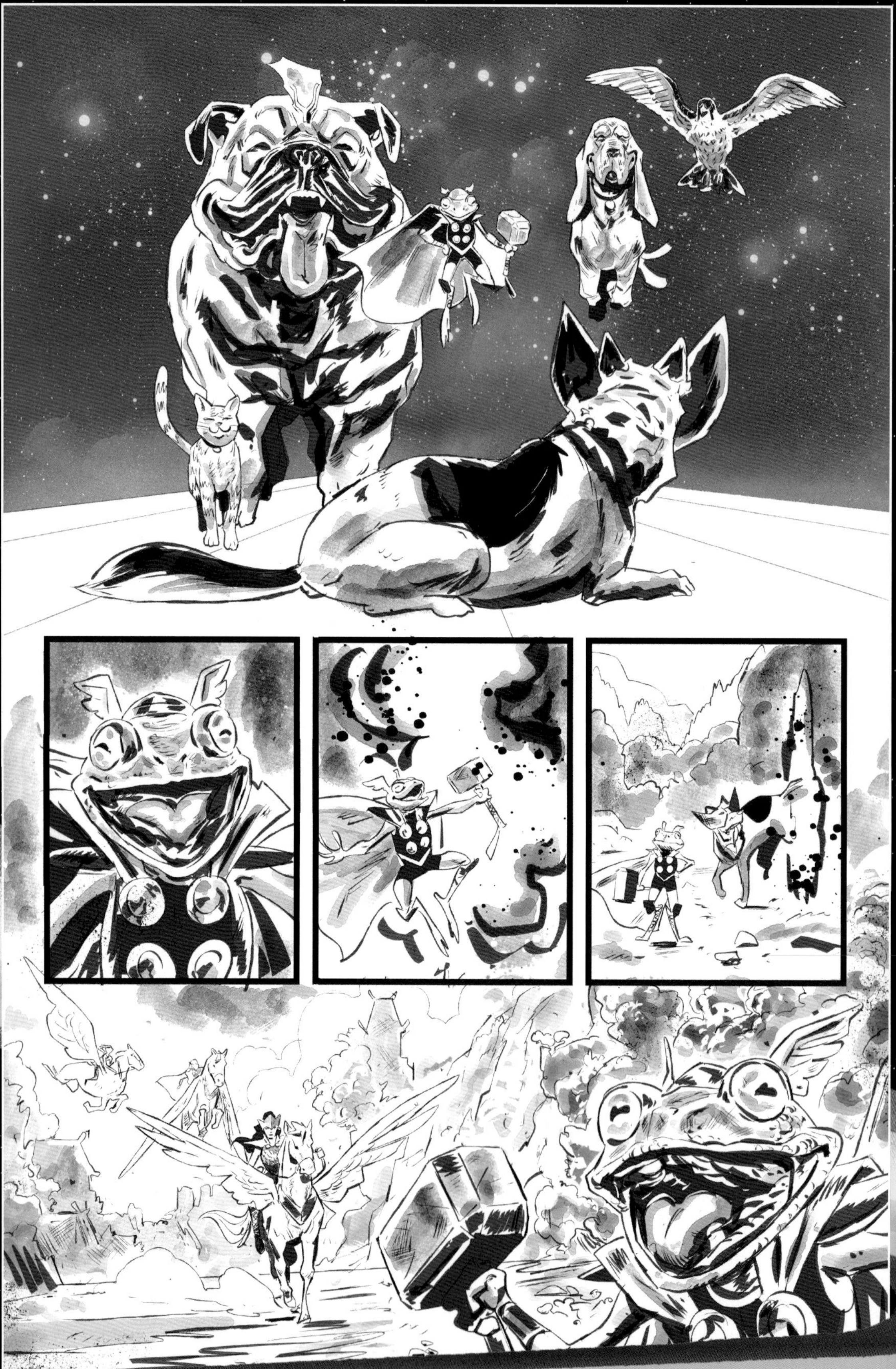

#4 PAGE 18 ART BY JESÚS HERVÁS